AMOS AND MICAH

Readings: A New Biblical Commentary

AMOS
AND
MICAH

Graham S. Ogden

SHEFFIELD PHOENIX PRESS
2024

Copyright © 2024 Sheffield Phoenix Press
Published by Sheffield Phoenix Press
University of Sheffield, S10 2TN

www.sheffieldphoenix.com

All rights reserved.
No part of this publication may be reproduced or transmitted in any form or by any means, electronic or mechanical, including photocopying, recording or any information storage or retrieval system, without the publisher's permission in writing.

A CIP catalogue record for this book
is available from the British Library

Typeset by the HK Scriptorium

ISBN: 978-1-914490-40-8 (HB)
ISBN: 978-1-914490-41-5 (PB)

Contents

Abbreviations	ix
Preface	xi

AMOS

Introduction	3
Authorship	4
Amos and his Background	4
Amos the Visionary	6
Why Did Amos Go North to Israel?	6
Historical Setting of Amos	8
A Reading Strategy	9
The Structure of Amos	10
Literary Features	11
Amos's Visions?	13
Amos's Theological View	14
The Root Word *nb'*, 'Prophesy'?	16
Foreign Nation Oracles	17
Transmission of the Text of Amos	18
Amos and the Scroll of the Twelve	18
Amos and Nahum	20
Amos and Wisdom	20
Outline	22
Exegesis	23
1.1-2 Editor's Introduction	23
1.3–2.5 Yahweh and the Nations	26
2.6-16 Yahweh and Israel	39
3.1–5.17 'Hear This Word ...'	45
3.1-15 'I Will Punish'	45

4.1-13 'You Did Not Return to Me'	55
5.1-17 'Seek the Lord and Live'	63
5.18–6.14 'Woe to Those Who . . .'	71
5.18-27 The Day of the Lord	71
6.1-14 'Woe to Those Who . . .'	74
7.1–9.10 Amos's 'Visions'	83
7.1-9 Three Visions	85
7.10-17 Amaziah Encounters Amos	89
8.1-3 Fourth 'Vision'	93
8.4-14 'Hear This . . .'—a Famine of Words	94
9.1-4 Fifth 'Vision'	98
9.5-6 Yahweh the Creator	100
9.7-10 Yahweh, the Lord of History, Shakes Israel	101
9.11-15 Judah's Fortunes Restored	105
Postscript	108
God, Israel and Humanity	108
Selected Bibliography	112

MICAH

Introduction	115
Who and What Was Micah?	117
Authorship	119
Date	120
Structure of Micah the Book	120
Outline of Micah the Book	122
Literary Features	123
Historical Setting	126
Micah's Relationship to Amos and Isaiah	127
A Reading Strategy	128
Micah's Theological Perspective	129
Micah 1	132
1.1 Superscript	132
1.2–2.13 Yahweh's Complaint against Samaria and Jerusalem	134
1.2-7 Yahweh Acts against Samaria and Jerusalem	134

1.8-9 Lament over Israel's Incurable 'Wounds'	138
1.10-16 Lament over Assyria's Threat to Judah	139
Micah 2	146
2.1-5 Leaders Abusing Power	146
Micah 3	158
3.1–5.14 The Sins of the Rulers	158
3.1-4 Rulers of Jacob and Israel Hate Justice	158
3.5-8. Prophets Who Lead Astray	160
3.9-12 Priests, Rulers and Injustice	163
Micah 4	167
4.1-5 In Days to Come …	167
4.6-7 Gathering the Lame	171
Micah 5	178
5.1-9 (Eng 5.2-10)	178
5.6-8(7-9) The Remnant of Jacob	182
5.9-14(10-15) The Day of the Cut Off	183
Micah 6	187
6.1–7.20 The Lord's Controversy	187
6.1-5 O my People!	188
6.6-8 What Does the Lord Require?	191
6.9-16 Treasures of Wickedness	192
Micah 7	197
7.1-7 Woe Is Me!	197
7.8-13 The Lord's Vindication	200
7.14-20 Who Is a God Like You?	203
Postscript	207
Micah, Amos, Isaiah and a Prophetic Crisis.	207
On the Verbs *nb'* and *ntp*, and 'Prophecy'	208
On Translating the Phrase *dᵉbār-yhwh hāyâ 'el PN*	209
'Bread' as a Codeword	211
Selected Bibliography	212

Abbreviations

ANE	ancient Near East
AYB	Anchor Yale Bible
BDB	F. Brown, S.R. Driver and C. Briggs. *A Hebrew and English Lexicon of the Old Testament* (Oxford: Clarendon Press, 1907, repr. 1957)
BHS	*Biblia Hebraica Stuttgartensia,* Ed. K. Elliger and W. Rudolph (Stuttgart: Deutsche Bibelstiftung, 1968-1977)
BT	*Bible Translator*
DH	Deuteronomistic History
JPS	Jewish Publication Society (Bible version)
LXX	Septuagint
MS	Manuscript
MT	Masoretic Text
NRSV	New Revised Standard Version
NT	New Testament
PN	personal name
VT	Vetus Testamentum
WBC	Word Biblical Commentary

Preface

Perhaps one advantage of old(er) age is having more time to consider the wealth of experiences enjoyed over a lifetime, and their contribution to how I should understand my own self alongside that of 'the other'. My teachers and mentors over the years, colleagues from diverse backgrounds and traditions, students and their questions, experiences of varying 'value' in and with the church, thirty-five years of living and working in Asia, all have played their part in reshaping the worldview with which my life journey began.

The most significant realization has been that *I had so much more to learn from 'the other' than I could ever have hoped to teach*! A deep sense of respect in the presence of another person's rich cultural heritage can truly change the way one relates to one's own past. The cross-cultural experiences that have proven the most challenging, yet most fruitful, have been those that forced a reconsideration of early ideas and beliefs formed within and bound by a Western and so-called Christian, cultural world. No matter at which point along the Christian spectrum a person stands, the primacy of that position and its supporting tenets have minimal meaning and relevance when in a foreign cultural context; so much of one's past education and life experience has to be revisited and viewed anew by attempting to see it from the perspective of 'the other'. Defining what it means to be truly human, understanding the numinous, acknowledging one's tribal identity and the emotions that are enshrined in one's heart-language and its cultural resources, its art and song, its historical celebrations—these are just some of the issues raised when one encounters at depth 'the other'. The same human and social issues are as crucial to the other person's self-understanding as they are to my own, and they have to be so honoured and respected, even while acknowledging that as a foreigner I can barely begin to comprehend how profound is that other cultural world, its language, worldview and fundamental ways of thinking and speaking. That was my experience, especially while living in East Asia with its rich cultures whose roots go back beyond that represented in the Hebrew Bible. While there is so much in the cultures of Japan and China that is different from the world of my upbringing, some of it for me unrelatable and unfathomable, yet there is also much that resonates as similar, even if clothed in a different vocabulary. In particular, as a foreigner one does not have the deep emotional response that another's culture and language offer its own community. I may come to have a good 'head' knowledge of that culture, its history and language, but never does it reach into the deeper recesses of the heart. What also prevents a deeper level of understanding and meaningful communication between two different cultural communities is the claim by one party to owning a superior and exclusive insight into those issues that matter; humility and openness in face of one's limited understanding of 'the other' is demanded.

In a fascinating way these many rich cultural experiences have impacted my view of the Hebrew Scriptures—how could it be otherwise? Those texts are reports of the valued traditions and insights of an ancient people whose culture and language, no matter how well learned, is not my own. Its texts do not resonate emotionally, despite the 'head' knowledge. My cultural heritage shaped the perspective from which I was taught to read these texts and their religious content. How should I read them now that I have been exposed to other worldviews? For example, a traditional Christian view of the human condition as 'sinful'—perhaps even 'totally depraved' for some—when confronted by a different view that sees humanity as 'good', challenges my reading of Genesis 3. It forces questions about the nature of sin, casting doubt on the thesis that the Christian Bible offers the full (and only?) story of God redeeming one from an inherent sinful state. Does the Hebrew Bible really portray humanity in the manner basic to so much of the Christian tradition? Does Genesis 3 really begin the story of all humanity that finds its climax only in the life and death of Jesus? Ancient Israel, the guardians of this Scripture, did not read it thus. Fundamental questions have to be asked with sensitivity and respect from the perspective of 'the other', especially when that text being read has been 'borrowed' from another time and another culture.

Referring to the Hebrew Scriptures as the 'Old Testament' immediately exposes one's reading strategy as rooted in a Christian theological worldview; it identifies as Christian jargon with its implications clear. What those Scriptures actually represent are the voices of, and invaluable witnesses to, a past community, its range of theologies and its up-and-down romance with its God, and as such it has its own integrity. That witness, in all its diversity, has a validity and must be honoured for what it is to the extent that such is now recoverable, without an imposed and alien reading agenda, especially one that regards those texts as having been superseded by 'the New'. Such a value judgment, grounded in yet another cultural and linguistic world, the Graeco-Roman, prejudices the search for a contextual meaning of those Hebrew Scriptures, pre-determining one's reading perspective and thus one's conclusions drawn therefrom.

Preface

The commentary here is offered as one way to read the Hebrew text of the books of Amos and Micah sympathetically while questioning some of the 'myths' still perpetuated in academic circles about both men. As a result, minimal input from or reference to other scholars will be evident to the reader of what follows. These two books are read from the perspective that the text belongs to 'the other', despite having been adopted or co-opted by my own tribe.

Graham S. Ogden
Ballarat, Vic., Australia
2023

I wish to acknowledge the huge contribution that the late David Clines made to the study of the Hebrew language and of the biblical text. Though we had met briefly only once before he left for the United Kingdom, David was later a real encouragement to me in my more modest endeavours. There must have been something in Sydney's water supply in 1938 that led to us both spending our lives in this unlikely field of Hebrew studies. May his contributions live on!

AMOS

A Commentary

Introduction

The starting point for a study of Amos must be 7.14-15, the brief autobiographical note in which Amos emphatically denies being a prophet, a *nābî'*, and denies ever having any part in the prophetic movement. He explains that he was a simple southern country boy, a goatherd and a pruner of trees as occasion required. This note sheds light on the opening words of the book (1.1), identified simply as *'the words of Amos ... that he saw'*—not that he saw words, but rather his words relate to what he saw. What Amos saw and spoke about was what troubled him, namely the social, political and religious conditions he encountered, especially those in northern Israel. Amos was a visionary, never a prophet, and in this he was very similar to Nahum, another visionary (Nah. 1.1).

Because the text throughout refuses to identify Amos as a prophet, prophetic stereotypes should never be applied to Amos, although such an office, title and role continue to be attributed to him by virtually all commentators, inevitably determining the manner in which they read and discuss the text. Amos did speak out on issues he saw needed exposing, but Israelite society was never so simply structured that one who spoke about social and religious issues and expressed ideas about a community's direction must automatically be deemed a prophet. Sages also taught and advocated for traditional values, as did priests based on conformity to Torah. Insight and vision such as are attributed to Amos, however, derive from an individual's own perception and reflection, thus the text specifies the collected material as representing Amos's words (Heb. *dibrê 'āmôs*), his own thoughts and projections.

Identifying Amos as a visionary and accepting his own denial that he was a prophet is our starting point, but it then raises questions about the use of some standard 'prophetic' literary forms found in the editor's report. It is especially relevant when noting the reference in 7.15 to his claim that he was called by God to *'go ... to my people Israel'* for a specific purpose. That 'call' is expressed as 'go, *hinnābê* ...' to Israel, usually rendered in English as 'go, *prophesy* ...'. Such a rendering of the Hebrew verb *nb'* has become standard, but is clearly problematic and in conflict with Amos's reputed rejection of the prophetic label. Defining the semantic value of the Hebrew root *nb'* is what requires settling, along with Amos's conformity, or lack thereof, with the common stereotype of the Hebrew prophet that centres about (1) a divine source revealing secrets, and (2) prognostications with regard to the future.

Authorship

Assuming that, like most rural people of the time, Amos was non-literate, his message/words were orally delivered, remembered and kept alive by his audiences. Amos was the author of those words/ideas that were shared with the community, words especially critical of the regime in the northern kingdom, words that eventually led to his difficult encounter with Amaziah the priest at Bethel, the royal sanctuary (7.10-15).

It is the literate editor, however, who, as the second 'author', took Amos's words, retaining their spirit and setting them in fixed written form. He it was who devised the structure and applied the chosen literary forms throughout. Presumably the editor was sympathetic with Amos's point of view and so has presented Amos's orally delivered words in a lively and more literary manner. Subsequent additions, such as 9.11-15, have been made, presumably by other now-unidentifiable entities at a much later date, but contributed from a perspective thought to be representative of Amos himself.

Amos and his Background

Who was this upstart with the southern accent telling Israel how to order its life? Amos the book contains the one and only biographical reference to the man who, for a time, apparently caused a great deal of angst in priestly and even royal circles in northern Israel in the mid-eighth century BCE. If he was such a remarkable and troublesome figure, as appears the case, one wonders why there is no reference to him in the southern kingdom's Deuteronomic record, nor in any other known biblical source. Without this one surviving report we would know nothing of the man or of his mission. Whether other material relating to Amos's mission was lost or suppressed we shall never know.

According to the editorial Introduction in Amos 1.1, Amos was from Tekoa, a rural district 15 km or so southeast of Jerusalem. This region of Judah was a very marginal area bordering the wilderness, geographically isolated and remote, deficient in rainfall, with poor soils and sparse vegetation; and though it has been customary to speak of Amos caring for sheep, it would more likely have been goats, given the region's geographical and climatic situation. The comment that 'the Lord took him *from behind* the herd' further strengthens the possibility he was a goatherd since herders generally led sheep but followed their goats—the more intelligent animal! Additionally, looking after the family's herd of animals usually fell to the least gifted or youngest member of a family—it was no glamour job despite its importance!

Pruning what may have been sycamore or fig trees, another element on Amos's *curriculum vitae*, was only ever a seasonal task, not a full-time one. However, there is a serious question here as to whether fig trees could or were ever grown in the Tekoa environs given that they require good soil and much water, both in short supply in that marginal area. Perhaps he went down occasionally to Jericho or over to the Shephelah foothills where there were ideal conditions for fig trees to prune there? We are not told whether the flock and trees belonged to him, to his family or to others for whom he worked. Suggestions by some that Amos was a consultant with a large agribusiness in the region, and an arborist to boot, show a complete lack of attention to or awareness of the general climatic and soil conditions pertaining in the Tekoa region of Judaea; their suggestion has more the appearance of an unwarranted desire to elevate Amos's social status.

Amos, though presumably non-literate—literacy rates began to improve somewhat from the sixth century BCE—was nevertheless extremely intelligent, as the text evidences. He was a keen observer of life around him, and his reaction to the problems he saw in northern Israel was deep—he was a *passionate* man, as seen in his description of the women of Bashan in 4.1-3, and in his sarcastic call for all to come to Bethel to sin (4.4-5). As a visionary he wanted to see problems he identified dealt with and so used challenging language and a wide range of rhetorical features to express his views and critique (see, e.g., 6.4-6).

Although Amos is traditionally viewed as 'working' only(?) in the north, that conclusion has to be questioned in light of the generalized language used throughout the report. While there are specific issues identified as of the north—and, after all, it was in his time by far the largest and most important part of the Israelite kingdom—others are more general and embrace the south as well. See below under **Literary Features**

The closing section of the book, 9.11-15, suggests that there was an interest in his work among those in Judah as well. Whether those words were added much later by the final editor is unclear, but the sudden addition of that note of Judah's future and that of the Davidic family suggest it belongs to a date at the end of the sixth century when there was renewed but very short-lived hope of restoration following the Judaeans' return from exile in 538 BCE. From this point of view it can reasonably be assumed that it is an insert from a much later hand.

Amos the Visionary

Like Nahum, Amos is described as 'seeing' things, as having a vision about matters relating to life in Israel. The Hebrew verb used in this context is *ḥāzâ*, and the noun form *ḥôzeh* is the form used by Amaziah to describe Amos in 7.12. It is vital that the root be understood, for it is applied to several individuals, such as Isaiah (1.1), Nahum (1.1), Obadiah (1.1) and Habakkuk (1.1). In the case of the latter three, it is very clear that they are not prophets in any traditional sense; they too were visionaries, perceptive and understanding of what was happening around them and of what they believed needed to change. The root word also has close links to the Wisdom context in that Prov. 29.18 uses *ḥāzôn* of one *being aware of* a vitally important life principle, namely restraint. (It is most unfortunate that many English translations of that Proverbs text prefer to render *ḥāzôn* as 'prophecy' when in fact it points to a principle so much broader, a person's vision for the future based on a personal assessment of the present.)

Why Did Amos Go North to Israel?

What needs to be remembered is that when the Israelite kingdom divided following Solomon's 'turning away from the Lord', ten of the twelve tribes sided with Jeroboam, who then became the north's first ruler (1 Kgs 11.1-40). The result was that more than 80 percent of the kingdom's territory and population separated from Judah (with Benjamin). The old Israel was so reduced in size that Judah in the south was left as a small, isolated and rump community. Despite that blow, Judah continued to see itself as the more 'valid' party because of the 'eternal covenant' with the Davidic family (2 Sam. 7). For Judahites, Yahweh was ever 'resident' in Jerusalem and its Temple, never in the north; and the Deuteronomistic History, the work of Judah's main theological cohort, poured condemnation on Jeroboam and the vast majority, their fellow Israelites in the north, for seeking to establish their own religious and cultural programme independent of Jerusalem. That was what defined 'sin' in Judah's view. Since so much of the Hebrew Bible's record reflects that southern viewpoint, it is sometimes easy to overlook that it is in fact a very biased minority report.

What could have led Amos to go to the more significant and prosperous north, given that there were the same or similar problems in Uzziah's Judah that needed addressing? See the charge against Judah in 2.4-5! Had he already shown some deep personal interest in social conditions in Judaea that he was an obvious choice to be sent north? Was he just running away?

Unfortunately, we have no background information pointing to why Amos was the one allegedly 'chosen'.

Attributing his travel to the north to a divine call conforms with the 'call' component found in most edited reports of a prophet's commission, so from the literary point of view it has relevance. But readers might consider another likely possibility. It is not difficult to imagine that Amos, and many others, would be personally drawn to see and experience what life in the much larger and significant north might offer. Migratory activity or travel within and between the kingdoms surely took place regularly, and folk knew what was going on in both north and south. While one cannot be certain as to why Amos moved north, nor how long he remained, that he would want to see and experience a different and flourishing life there is perfectly understandable. Once there, he 'saw' many aspects of the northern lifestyle and social conditions, and could not refrain from criticizing its more negative side because of his passionate belief in the requirement for justice, compassion, and especially the demand for religious faithfulness. The criteria by which he evaluated life and that drove his mission were those espoused by his 'theologians' and priests in the much smaller, isolated and religiously arrogant Davidic/Deuteronomic south.

Explaining his mission as a divine 'take-up' (7.15) was the formulaic way Amos is said to have explained his presence in Bethel. The notion of divine initiative in 'being called' was and is a widespread trope in faith communities when explaining one's own chosen field of service. However, the text is also clear that Amos's words were not only directed at those in the north.

The traditional view that Amos's primary audience was in the northern kingdom of Israel has to be questioned in light of the generalized language used throughout the report. While there are specific issues identified as of the north—and, after all, it was in his time by far the largest and most important part of the Israelite kingdom—others are more general and embrace the south as well. The fact that he was told to 'go ... to my people Israel' acknowledges that the north was by far the larger community, the one retaining the 'Israel' identity—ten of the twelve tribes formed that entity. Yet so much of what Amos criticized was true also of the south—see, for example, 2.4-5; 6.1. There are many comments in the editor's report that show that what Amos had to say applied equally to the nation as a whole, to 'Israel' in its original united sense—see, for example, 3.1-2; 4.6-13; 8.11-12; 9.7. Amos obviously saw both kingdoms as inheritors of the one 'promise', sharing one fundamental identity; hence what he had to say was not exclusive to Samaria and its people but was spoken to the whole nation—see, for example, exegetical notes on 7.14-15.

Historical Setting of Amos

As the opening verse states, Amos spoke his 'words' during the period in which Uzziah was ruling tiny and isolated Judah and Jeroboam II was on the throne in Samaria—this locates Amos's mission around the mid-eighth century BCE. More specifically, an earthquake is said to have occurred somewhere in the region two years after Amos first 'saw' what he spoke about, that is, what he saw of conditions in Israel at a moment in time. There is still a vagueness about the statement here as we cannot be certain whether the date refers to the written report or to Amos's mission more generally, but the note assumes readers were aware of such an event.

The rule of Jeroboam II (c. 785–745 BCE) was one in which conditions in the northern kingdom were prosperous and peaceful, with the king's armies expanding into territory farther north as well as south to the Dead Sea. The international situation was such that both Egypt and Assyria were relatively weak, and with the major international trade route passing through the kingdom, Israel's economy grew and grew and the north's character began to reflect more of its international connections. Amos's words, along with those of Hosea, speak to that increase in wealth and leisure. Literacy, bureaucracy, specialized economic production, a professional army were all signs of the affluence noted during the period, and authenticated by archaeology. However, much of this then collapsed when Jeroboam II died in 747 BCE. Dynastic rivalries shook the northern kingdom; there was a succession of kings leading to increased foreign intervention until the kingdom finally fell to the Assyrians in 721 and became absorbed, Samaria remaining as its only enclave.

Amos witnessed life in Israel that would have been in stark contrast with his home experience in rural and remote Tekoa. In terms of the religious policy of the northern king, little is known since the report found in 2 Kgs 14.24 is cast in a purely narrow and negative light in line with the Deuteronomist's bias against the north.

The fact that there is strong evidence of Deuteronomic language and concepts in parts of the book reflects Amos's and the editor's southern origins. It suggests to some commentators, however, that even if Amos's mission is dated toward the end of the eighth century BCE, there is the possibility that what we are now reading comes from the exilic or even postexilic period. While it is true that the compilation of Deuteronomic traditions can be located in the exilic and postexilic periods, that is, mid-to-late sixth century BCE, it should not be forgotten that that tradition and its sectarian language have roots that go back far into the earlier oral period. Finding what is later defined as Deuteronomic language and ideas in Amos is to be expected, and so one needs to identify much more concrete evidence before concluding that this or that element in Amos is so late. What one can say is that the fact that the book was stitched into the Scroll of the Twelve between Joel and Obadiah, with textual links to both books added, indicates that this written form has to be dated c. 538 BCE. The book's compilation from Amos's oral materials has involved a long process that cannot now be traced (see **Amos and the Scroll of the Twelve**).

A Reading Strategy

While many past commentators have sought to identify sections of the book as deriving from different hands and different historical periods, this reading recognizes that from original oral presentation(s), Amos's message has been recalled, passed on, modified, been added to, and some words perhaps even omitted, leaving us with the text as it now remains. Whether the complexities of this oral-to-written journey can be adequately told is quite another issue, and personal preferences play a major role in one's confidence about whether it is plausible or even helpful to try. The reading being offered here is one that takes the text as we now have it and relies on investigating its literary and rhetorical features as primary evidence of what the report says about the nature and concerns of Amos's mission.

The opening statement (1.1-2) makes clear that the report being made is of *Amos's words*, his message. Its intent was to challenge Israel with regard to issues critical to its social and religious world. That challenge was predicated totally on Amos's Judaean point of view, based on values set forth by the Deuteronomic cohort, later found in fuller form in Deuteronomy and the Deuteronomistic History. Many of the social values on which Amos insisted were, of course, timeless and universally commendable, but in judging Israel harshly for what was considered its failure in religious terms we see that his perspective or theological basis was entirely that of a southern or Judaean cast and, as such, a minority perspective.

This reading will focus on literary and rhetorical components of the book, along with cultural and geographical/climatic issues that inform the text. Asking the 'why?' question, or the 'how?' question, to probe the perspectives of Amos and his reporter is a requirement if one hopes to 'get inside' what a surface reading of the text may not immediately reveal. It will also be a reading that aims to keep the world of Amos intact, a reading that intentionally does not impose on the text a Christian overlay that looks constantly to a NT connection or goal. Amos the book must remain an integral component of the Hebrew Bible within which it has been preserved.

A keen reader of Amos would surely notice that so much of the content of the book is oriented to the past, to events or matters that have featured in the nation's past, that offer an explanation for its present circumstances. Amos is walking backward into the future! Correspondingly, the references to any potential or future action are minimal. One example will suffice: 4.6-13 refers to actions attributed to God that should have had a particular response from the people, but they failed, and so each of the five examples concludes with the depressing note that *'you did not return to me'*. This litany of failure is followed by the single, future-oriented *'therefore, I will do to you ...'* (4.12), along with a justification (4.13). It is difficult therefore to think of Amos as primarily future oriented, for the text is mainly focused on his assessment of what has led to the current circumstances in Israel, both north and south, and on the potential threat that that now raises.

This reader's understanding is that, in light of his own reported denial, Amos is never to be identified as a prophet but as a spokesperson, a subtle but vitally important difference. For this reason the verbal forms used throughout will be carefully assessed, hopefully demonstrating that the imperfective verbs are best read as challenges or threats, as what Amos and/or God would wish to see happen, or what could happen. Each use of the imperfective and its equivalent form throughout has to be considered in its context as volitional, unless there is clear evidence to the contrary, such as the use of imperfects as frequentatives in 4.6-11. So-called 'prophetic perfects' are absent from this kind of text. The use of hyperbole in many of Amos's words is another obvious example of a rhetorical form that, while sounding future oriented and certain, was never a realizable fate for a nation or entity.

The Structure of Amos

This reading takes the view that the book is largely structured about discrete blocks of material that have a common theme or shared direction, interspersed with other generally short, related speeches. The book is thus a compilation of Amos's oral speeches, his 'words' as remembered set within a literary style:

1.3–2.16 consist of a series of seven similarly structured statements about the nations surrounding Israel and their potential demise (1.3–2.5), followed by an extended eighth statement that targets Israel (2.6-16), itemizing its failures and the punishment due.
3.1–5.17 present three sections, each introduced by the call to *'Hear this word ...!'* in which a variety of accusations are made against the people, especially in their failure to *'turn to me'* (4.6-11).
5.18–6.7 contains three sub-sections, each beginning with the lament form *'Woe to you who ...'*

7.1–9.6 report on Amos's five so-called visions (musings?), interspersed with an autobiographical section (7.10-17), another call to *'Hear this ...'* (8.4-8), and a section relating to *'that day'* (8.9-13).
9.11-15 refer to a hoped-for return of the Davidic rule to Judah.

This structure as identified here does not mimic an original oral presentation; rather, it is a planned rearrangement of Amos's words as recalled, now reset within the requirements of written language.

While other commentators have uncovered a possible 'ring structure' centred on 5.1-17, that reading is not without its inconsistencies and requires a very close reading in order to be appreciated, if at all. Additionally, the ring structure alleged to be involved in chaps. 3–6 moves the material further from an oral form to a more sophisticated written form—certainly not the form in which the contents were originally offered. This reader finds the 'block' approach a more helpful way of outlining the themes and content of the book's many individual speeches.

Literary Features

A number of literary forms or rhetorical devices mark Amos the book. There are forms associated with prophetic material, together with those linked more closely with wisdom literature, as well as narrative and dialogue. While the text is mostly in poetic style, prose elements are visible—for example, 3.7. Each contributes to form a rich tapestry of literary forms that heighten the message of the book as a whole. Modern readers, however, must never forget that one is dealing with a document deriving from a foreign language and culture, and ever be aware that many linguistic and cultural subtleties may be misread or not even noticed by non-native speakers/readers.

A. I have noted above that there is so much in the text as it now stands that embraces both north and south. Apart from the statements in 2.9-16, 3.1-2 and 9.7 that apply to the entire community of Israel, the most obvious linguistic feature of the book as a whole is the use of *generalized language*. A section such as 4.6-12 or 8.11-12 illustrates that they speak of and to the historic community, north and south, in a completely generalized manner—the 'you' (pl.) addressed is comprehensive. The use of the term 'Israel' is throughout ambiguous (deliberately?), referring to both the unified nation as well as to the northern kingdom in particular. At the same time, the phrase 'house of Jacob' in 3.13 and 9.8 most often refers to the whole nation—see, for example, Isa. 2.5; 14.1; 46.3; 48.1;

Obad. 1.17-18. This implies that while Amos's mission was largely to northern Israel, his concerns also included the south.

B. The use of repeated structures or frames is one marked feature of Amos the book. From the initial eight oracles in 1.3–2.16 with their fixed pattern and vocabulary, or the repeated form *'I ... , I ... , I ... , but you did not return to me'* in 4.6-11, to the fixed forms of the so-called visions reported in chaps. 7–8, repetition is a major rhetorical feature of the book.

C. Amos's denial of any prophetic connection (7.14) means then that the more traditional 'prophetic' forms such as *'Thus says the Lord ... , ... says the Lord'* and *'Hear this word that the Lord has spoken ...'* are all *pro forma* expressions provided by the editor that add authority to what Amos had to say in his criticism of life in Israel. Readers of the report need to bear in mind that the written form is not the same as the spoken form. In written language, complex syntax patterns, unusual vocabulary, and grammatical consistency are generally preferred over the easily remembered pithy sayings, plays on words and simple grammar that typify oral speech. The report of the fourth 'vision' in 8.2 is a perfect example of an oral presentation now enclosed in a more formal edited report.

D. Amos's words express what he would wish to see happen, or what could or might happen, and thus they are akin to exhortations, challenges and/or threats. For example, in the opening section 1.3–2.16 what are usually seen as prophetic 'promises' to send fire, fire that will devour, and to break the gates etc., are all pronouncements about what God *would* or *could* do, rather than iron-clad promises that this is what God certainly *will* do. In other words, the verbs are essentially volitional.

E. The entire first section is a cleverly constructed piece of writing intended to lull northern Israel into feeling smug about God's claimed readiness to destroy all potential enemies; it uses hyperbole that exaggerates the demise of every surrounding enemy. Hyperbole is a prominent rhetorical form throughout the book. Failure to recognize the rhetoric and its function, to seek to historicize the content, leads to significant misreadings of editorial intent.

F. In addition, the text exhibits a number of rhetorical features throughout such as taunts, satire (4.4-5), a play on words (8.2), numerous rhetorical questions (3.3-6; 9.7), a series of nine first-person statements (4.6-12) that include five criticisms of Israel's failure to *'turn to me'*, and much use of *'therefore ...'* to indicate the hoped-for divine response to charges made against the people (3.2, 11; 4.12; 5.11, 13, 16, 27; 6.7; 7.16, 17).

G. An unusual feature of the book is that when referring to God, various compound phrases are used, ranging from the basic form *yhwh*, to the more complex, *'ᵃdonay yhwh, yhwh 'ᵉlōhê-ṣᵉbā'ôt 'ᵃdonay,* and *'ᵃdonay yhwh haṣṣᵉbā'ôt.* What might be the purpose of such variety and complexity is unclear. My translation will use 'Yahweh' when rendering the tetragrammaton and 'my lord' for *'ᵃdonay,* in order to preserve this unique feature.

H. I consider 1.2 and 3.2 to be two important Introductory theological statements deliberately and carefully placed, whose literary function is to indicate to the hearer/reader how the material in the sections that follow, 1.3–2.16 and 3.3–5.17, should be approached. They are guides to interpreting the collected sayings thus introduced that must be understood against the background of those two profound statements.

Amos's Visions?

One of the more prominent components of the report of Amos's 'words' are what have been called his five 'visions' in 7.1-3, 4-6, 7-8; 8.1-3; 9.1-4. These are not to be thought of as ocular visions, things seen in some concrete or hallucinatory form; rather, they were things he 'saw' in his head, though perhaps that in 8.1-3 is an exception.

The language used in the editor's report presents the 'visions' as something that the Lord *'caused me to see/understand'*. The verb 'see' here is figurative. This form of expression is consistent with Amos's overriding notion of God as the one who causes everything—good, bad, indifferent—to happen. So, what we are dealing with in each of these cases is Amos coming to see/understand (Heb. *rā'â*) something as a result of his own reflection or musing, expressed in terms of his theological understanding. He did not catch a glimpse of the invisible Yahweh creating locusts in the first example in 7.1-3, or standing by a wall in 7.7, or by the altar in 9.1. Nor was the object he 'saw' in 7.7-9 a physical object. The verb 'see' in each of these texts is figurative, referring to gaining an understanding. His 'dialogues' were not with some unseen speaker; they were with himself, in his own head, along with the conclusions he drew from his reflective processes. To historicize these in any manner is contrary to the language used and the reality faced.

In the case of the first two matters on which he claimed to have some insight, he concluded that by appealing that 'Jacob' was so small he could persuade God to change his mind and not inflict the punishment said to be due. The editor has reported both cases as after the manner of Moses's bargaining with God (Exod. 32). The reference to being small may reflect the status of Judah vis-à-vis Israel, or of Israel's status vis-à-vis the surrounding powers. The remaining three 'visions', in which God simply says that destruction will take place, run contrary to his relenting in the first two, setting up conflict between them. It is a conflict that remains unresolved in the report, though some commentators suggest that there is 'theological development' in this process, aiming to dispel the possibility of conflict.

Amos's Theological View

The editor's Introduction to his report of Amos's mission in 1.2 is vital to a proper understanding of Amos; it is intended to shape how one reads and understands the report. Yahweh, in Amos's thinking, is an awesome, terrifyingly powerful God, whose 'voice' is capable of untold destruction. This is the basic theological notion that lies behind all that Amos represents.

Perhaps the briefest summary of Amos's perspective on his God is then the note in 3.2-8 and especially v. 6b—*'Does disaster befall a city unless the Lord has done it?'* For Amos, Yahweh works out his plan and purpose in a clear and decisive manner; every event has its God-driven purpose, especially when the community involved, Israel, stands within that special covenant relationship with Yahweh (3.2). No matter what happens, good or ill, some divine initiative lies behind each occasion (8.4b), to be revealed 'in that day'. This kind of worldview, this theocratic regime in which YHWH controls all natural and world events (9.5-10), underpins Amos's vision, his understanding of Yahweh, and any modern reader will be troubled by its implications. The most problematic passage is 4.6-12, in which God is said to have deliberately caused a variety of natural disasters in order to achieve his purpose for Israel—see also Hag. 1.2-11. Regardless of the failure of that strategy, it points to a concept of God consistent with that of the Deuteronomic tradition, but one that many readers will find difficult to reconcile with their Christian faith and probably with their experience as well.

Much in the initial chapters has to do with Yahweh, the God of hosts, resident in Zion/Jerusalem (1.2) punishing Israel for its social injustice and its empty religious activity by (a) causing crop failures as God withholds the rain, (b) sending pestilences, and eventually (c) sending the nation into exile as punishment. Amos sees no escape from this divine punishment when the 'day of the Lord' appears. In this, one can see so clearly the basic attitude of the Deuteronomic cohort's underpinning theology and cosmology—see especially the fifth vision (9.1-4).

Amos seems to present two contrasting, even conflicting, views about Israel and its claimed relationship to YHWH such that the thesis that Israel was 'chosen' may be questioned, or at least modified. In 3.2 the primacy of that unique relationship is noted, and the verb 'know' adds power to the statement given its related focus on intimacy. It is this notion of their having been chosen that makes the Israelites more culpable should they fail to live by the covenant conditions. The exodus-from-Egypt tradition was fundamental to Israel's belief that it was God's 'chosen' people. However, in 9.7-8 it would appear that there was nothing special about Israel's relationship with Yahweh, since that same Yahweh is credited with having led other nations in their 'exodus' as he did Israel. In 6.2-3 that similarity in the divine interaction with the nations is also emphasized, and Israel as a whole faces the very same punishment as those other nations if it should fail to live by God's laws. This seems to highlight a view that no nation is 'better' than another, nor more special or 'chosen'. Did Amos have a universalist view of his national God Yahweh? How did he live with that exclusivist tension?

So much of what Amos is reported to have said focuses on the past–present situation. Amos's evaluation of Israel's communal life as he saw it was mostly negative. He announced that because of the nation's past failures, disaster that could be brought upon the entire community by its God was about to strike (3.11-15; 5.2-3 etc.). The past divine actions bringing crop failure and natural disasters had not been effective in leading the people to 'turn back' (Heb. *šwb*) to God (4.6-12). But, how did the local farmers misunderstand these disasters? Did they not see these as God acting for a purpose? The local Deuteronomic theologian could have explained it readily in those terms. The verb *šwb* is often seen by commentators as a call to repentance from sin, but its use elsewhere indicates that that interpretation is far too facile and restricted—see Joel 2.12-14 and Mal 3.7; rather, the 'turn' is a mutual turning, so was Amos using the verb in the same way, God and people both needing to turn to one another, to become reconciled?

Amos does not speak about love or compassion as characterizing his God; rather, his view of God is of an awesome, stern and demanding judge who inflicts hardship on his people in order to achieve an end. The 'day' will reveal what God is like—see 5.18-20; 9.1-6.

One dominant theme is that of the relative unimportance of religious activity of any kind when compared with the need for justice and righteousness—see especially 5.21-24. It can be seen also in the sarcastic invitation for all to come to Bethel, the sanctuary that rivalled Jerusalem, but come to sin (4.4-5)! That was a religio-political call, given that Amos viewed worship at Bethel, or anywhere in the north, as illegitimate. No matter what the Law demanded in terms of daily religious activity, it was irrelevant in face of God's valuing of society-wide justice and honest dealing.

Amos in its final form, however, closes with a more positive note, namely that Judah would be restored and its fortunes returned 'on that day' (9.11-15). The 'day' concept, as already noted, points to some undefined moment in the future, but that future is always imminent, about to break in, or even now in process; it is not some time in the far distant future, and certainly not a reference to the NT.

In reversing what 'the day' envisages for Israel, these closing verses reflect the values and theology surrounding Jerusalem and the Temple as the divine dwelling place. This hope or longing for a Davidic restoration has to be considered a much later addition that contrasts with the more negative tone of Amos's own critique of Israel. If one regards it as a 'prophetic' note, one must acknowledge that it is a hyperbolic longing that was never realised—Judah met the same fate in 587 BCE as did the north in 721 BCE—and even the restoration to Jerusalem in 538 was not a Davidic restoration as Judaea became a Persian satellite and Judaean kingship was never restored. Amos 9.11-15 was almost certainly a statement that came from a source other than from Amos himself.

The Root Word *nb'*, 'Prophesy'?

The Hebrew noun *nb'* is rendered in the LXX as *prophētēs*, from which the English noun 'prophet' is derived. The problem begins there, for the cultural and linguistic sense of the Hebrew are thereby subverted. The basic idea denoted by the Hebrew root seems to be that of making public statements, be they one's own or made on behalf of another, to announce or inform. As a verb, however, it is recognized as 'denominative', relating it to the overall activity of the *nābî'*, 'prophet' (?), meaning that whatever such individuals were, said, wore and how they behaved, contributes to its semantic value, that is, it describes a particular manner of being or demeanour, as in 1 Sam. 10.11. It could describe an individual's temporary state rather than any permanent 'professional' assignment. Isaiah described his role as like one having hot coals put to his mouth (Isa. 6.7), while Jeremiah is recorded as likening it to his bones being on fire (Jer. 20.9). It describes a person's state of mind, a state of being and feeling. In the absence of a better or more appropriate term for these individuals, this commentary will continue to render *nābî'* as 'prophet' while recognizing its gross imperfection.

The more problematic issue is the *hinnābê'* forms used in Amos 7.12-16. The nuance in these niphal imperative forms is far from clear as the verb appears to assume an active voice rather than its normal passive or reflexive sense; it has no identifiable object that fills out its content. So, when Amos is said to have received a divine command to 'go, *hinnābê' 'al-yiśrā'ēl'* (7.15), it is difficult to determine quite what was intended, or how Amos might have understood the command—did Amos understand it as an order to assume a certain kind of identity, dress or pose like some of the earlier 'ecstatic' prophets? There is no definable content in the imperative, but it does attempt to convey the sense that Amos was driven by the impulse to speak out, even if given a reflexive sense of 'appear as a prophet'.

What remains a mystery is Amos's denial of any prophetic connection if in fact he was responding to the command to 'go, *hinnābê'* ...' Whatever he did in response to that command apparently did not equate to his being, or becoming, a 'prophet' in any traditional sense; he retained his non-prophet herdsman identity. If the common understanding and rendering of *hinnābê'* as a command to 'prophesy' is retained, then it would imply that Amos denied his commission, a conclusion that seems totally inappropriate. All we have available as a guide to how Amos understood the concept within his cultural context is the edited speech material in the book itself.

If Amos was a visionary rather than a prophet, as the text makes clear, then Amos's insights and concerns were expressed as his own hopes and longings for change, for a return to justice and compassion, for religious devotion that expressed real commitment to God and neighbour. His starting point was the reality of daily life as observed. The imperative *hinnābê'*, as a jussive form, called for Amos to evaluate, challenge and speak out. The primary element is the speaking, announcing, challenging, not any alleged divine source of the vision or command, nor any potential outcome or result.

Foreign Nation Oracles

Amos the book opens with a series of eight brief oracles that, on the surface, address seven of Israel's opponents before turning to the northern kingdom itself. Addresses to foreign nations within the context of the Hebrew Bible are relatively common—see the collections in Isaiah 13–23, Ezekiel 25–32—but these statements are not intended to be heard by those nations, for they are fundamentally addressed to Israel and Judah, the prophets' home audiences, carrying messages of comfort and offering 'hope' as they hear of the demise of their enemies and of their own divine rescue.

The oracles created in Amos 1–2 are distinctive as adapted forms of what are generally known as 'numerical proverbs' in which consecutive numerals such as 2 and 3, 3 and 4, even 6 and 7 (i.e. x, x+1), are used to highlight certain traits that may then be specifically itemized according to the final x+1 number (see Prov 30). In the context of Amos the book, they serve as accusations that characterize those various opponents of 'Israel', using common perceptions of each nation. Amos 'stands back' from the scene so that his accusations can embrace the failures of his own community as well as those of the nations. It is therefore pointless to seek to identify an occasion or a specific event that is being referred to in each charge; all are generalizations about the character of each enemy as seen from the overall Israelite viewpoint, with the possible exception of 1.11 and the charge against Edom. They also offer generalizations with regard to their vision of a possible future, for none of the so-called promises was realistic, none was so realized. For this reason the rendering of the verbal forms in this reading treats them as threatened possibilities rather than as divinely promised inescapable outcomes.

Transmission of the Text of Amos

Given the limited literacy of the period in question, copies of the written text of Amos and access to it were severely limited. Where an 'original' MS might have been kept, and who had access to it, cannot be ascertained, but as a hand-written document it would never have been available to more than a very select and literate few. Oral transmission of the words of Amos would have been the only way in which the majority of Israelites would have come to know of Amos's mission and responded to it or against it. The completed MS that is now available is the result of those many individual words and speeches, remembered and handed on orally, that were gradually collected and finally brought together in this one written form. How many hands played a part in that operation is unknown, so we can only speak of an editor, knowing that it probably was a collective. That process itself was one that took time and effort, but it is not a journey that can be traced in specific detail. Wider dispersion of and awareness of a written record took time as hand-made copies began to circulate perhaps many years after the 'final' document was completed, then incorporated into the Scroll of the Twelve in the late-sixth century or early-fifth century BCE.

Amos and the Scroll of the Twelve

The Scroll of the Twelve, known also as the Minor Prophets, includes shorter books and documents, not all of which are 'prophetic'. They range from the mid-eighth century BCE to at least some time after 520 BCE, that is, they cover a period of some two hundred years. Hosea, Amos and Micah are among the earliest books, with most of the others of uncertain date apart from Zephaniah, Haggai and Zechariah, the latter two fixed at 520 BCE and dated according to the reign of Darius of Persia.

Amos's words, and even a written version of them, as here, obviously predate the full scroll by some length of time, so they must have had an independent existence before eventually being copied onto a developing scroll at the no. 3 position. Copied by whom and when are questions without answers, but with Hosea and Joel preceding Amos, and given the generally accepted dates for Joel and Obadiah, the book of Amos's words has been copied into the scroll in the postexilic period. What additions and omissions might have taken place throughout that transmission period are questions without clear answers, except for the more obvious late addition of 9.11-15.

While Amos may well be the earliest of the men whose words are assembled to form this library of so-called 'minor prophets', the book has not been placed chronologically at the head of the collection; primacy of place is given to Hosea. Why Amos should be placed third is unclear, but there is no question that Amos is deliberately set between Joel, a later post-538 BCE work, and Obadiah a post-587 BCE leaflet. This is evidenced by the 'literary knitting' of books, with Amos 1.2 tied to Joel 3.16, and Amos 9.12 linked to Obad. 1-2. It is a feature of the scroll that is most tantalizing, pointing as it does to further and late editing, well after Amos's presumed eighth-century BCE mission. While the fact that Deuteronomic language and concepts are now enshrined within the book suggests to some that it derives from a later date, one should not overlook the reality that what became the so-called Deuteronomistic material had much earlier pre-exilic roots in Israel's life.

Amos's place in the Scroll of the Twelve is the primary—I would say the only—reason the book has been and continues to be read incorrectly by so many as 'prophetic', despite Amos's reported denial that that was what he was (7.14). How to read Amos against its traditional context is the challenge. As for other books and documents in the Scroll, the book of Jonah presents a parable about a grumpy man (another never identified as a prophet!) whose theological understanding was 'correct' (Jon. 4.2-3) but personally discomforting, whose nationalist priorities over-rode his compassion, and whose 'sermon' consisted of only a few words (Jon. 3.4b). Habakkuk registers a serious complaint, expressing deep distress at God's failure to respond adequately to justice concerns, while the three *maśśā'* books, Nahum, Habakkuk and Malachi, all show close connection to proverbial wisdom literature. In other words, the scroll contains material of such diverse content, form and background that the single descriptor 'prophetic' cannot do justice to every entry, Amos being an important case in point. Either one must revise and expand the definition of 'prophet(ic)' or dismiss the prophetic ascription altogether for several of the 'books' included in the scroll; each must be read on its own terms. This reader, as has been said, regards Amos as a visionary, and the book as evidence of the emergence of a form of literature that may have some future concerns, but that is not 'prophetic' in any narrow sense; rather, it reflects the trend toward a new genre that incorporated important wisdom elements, especially ideas and advice that derived from individual and group reflection on life, not from what was claimed to be divine revelation.

Amos and Nahum

The possible relationship or editorial connection between Amos and Nahum is something worthy of reflection. In Amos's first 'vision' (7.1-3) the rare Hebrew noun *gobay* is used to speak of a locust plague; it appears only elsewhere in Nah. 3.17. Then in that same vision and repeated in the second 'vision' (7.5), Amos asks the rhetorical question *mî yāqûm*, *'who can stand/rise?'* This same question form is used in Nah. 1.6, in each case making the point that none can stand before or in the presence of the awesome God. A further link may be in the use of the two Hebrew terms in 'vision' no. 4, when *qēṣ* and *qāyiṣ* are inter-related rhetorically; and in Nah. 2.9 and 3.3 we see both nouns also being used, though the context differs. One further evidence is the unusual phrase *'pride of Jacob'* (Heb. *gᵉ'ôn yā'ᵃqob*) in 8.7, found also in Neh. 2.3. Perhaps the greatest link between the two comes in their Introductory verses: both speak of Yahweh in terms of powerful destructive violence and vengeance.

While the date of Amos's mission is generally defined as late-eighth century BCE, Nahum's report seems to be closer to the end of the seventh century, so they were not exactly contemporary. However, the oral traditions to which they gave rise continued to circulate within the community until they were each fixed in written form, so it is conceivable that there was some editorial connection that accounts for their sharing of unusual linguistic elements.

Amos and Wisdom

On the assumption that Amos the book is a work that accurately records or reflects what Amos's words were about, even that Amos himself wrote the book, it has been traditional among some commentators to ask about Amos's qualifications as a sage, especially in light of the literary structure of 1.3–2.16.

Amos, an intelligent but non-literate man, clearly had an earthy or practical wisdom. It was his innate ability to 'see' what, from his perspective, was deficient and what needed to be set right in Israel, something he shared with the editor, who must have had some knowledge of wisdom's literary forms. This would help explain the opening to this report built upon wisdom forms, and specifically the x, x+1 form as found in 1.3, 6, 9, 11, 13; 2.1, 4, 6. In other words, it is the editor who had whatever more technical wisdom connection is manifested in the book, but one should not rule out an awareness of the tradition by Amos himself, given his reflective approach to life and work.

In this connection, it is vital to appreciate the fundamentally different agendas of the prophet and the sage in Israel, the former dependent on (in general terms) divine revelation, and the latter dependent on keen observation of, and reflection on, the world as experienced. Each came to their view of Yahweh the national God and of the world around them from a different but valid starting point. There is evidence that prophets often looked down on the wise as a class, those whose 'counsel' they regarded as fake—Isa. 29.13-16; 31.1-3; 44.25; Jer. 49.7; Obad. 1.8—resulting in tension between them. At the 'professional' level they each had their own distinct functions (Jer. 18.18), but at the literary level there was a degree of overlap as both had concerns about the impact that their work would or could have into the immediate future. Thus it was that there came a point when the peculiar features of each began to merge in the *maśśā'* form, seen in Nahum, Habakkuk and Malachi.

The question about the contribution of the adapted wisdom form used in 1.3–2.16 remains, as it seems not to offer any particular advantage as a form of reporting other than brevity or conciseness. The lack of itemized issues in each paragraph suggests that the numerals 'three' and 'four' are not specific, but general. It is therefore difficult to see any very close link between Amos and the more formal Wisdom movement, apart from the editor's awareness of the number-based form that he has adapted and effectively used. Amos was neither sage nor prophet, in that formal sense, but his inclination as a visionary was to observe, reflect and comment on life as he encountered it.

Outline

1.1-2	Editor's Introduction
1.3–2.16	Yahweh and the Nations
2.6-16	Yahweh and Israel
3.1–5.17	*'Hear this word ...'*
	3.1-15 *'I will punish'*
	4.1-13 *'You did not return to me'*
	5.1-17 *'Seek the Lord and live'*
5.18–6.14	*'Woe to you who ...'*
	5.18-27 The Day of Yahweh
	6.1-14 *'Woe to those who ...'*
7.1–9.10	Amos's Visions
	7.1-9 Three Visions
	7.10-17 Amaziah Encounters Amos
	8.1-3 Fourth Vision
	8.4-14 *'Hear this ...'*—a Famine of Words
	9.1-4 Fifth Vision
	9.5-6 Yahweh the Creator
	9.7-10 Yahweh, the Lord of History, Shakes Israel
9.11-15	Judah's Fortunes Restored

EXEGESIS

1.1-2 Editor's Introduction

1 *The words of Amos, a herder from Tekoa, (words) about what he saw regarding Israel during the reigns of Uzziah king of Judah and of Jeroboam, son of Joash, king of Israel, two years before the earthquake. He said:*
  2 *Yahweh from Zion roars, and from Jerusalem gives voice;*
    the pastures of the herders mourn, and the top of Carmel dries up.

These two verses, the first in prose and the second in poetry, constitute the Introduction to the report as a whole. They introduce the person called Amos, briefly noting his place of origin in rural Judah, and the regnal period during which he spoke to audiences in Israel, whether north or south. There is no external evidence that can support the details in this editorial statement. A vague temporal reference tied to an earthquake in a region where such were frequent is added, also without any further information with respect to fixing a specific date. However, the tradition has been to locate Amos in the mid-to-late eighth century BCE.

The opening phrase states its function as a report of what Amos said; they are his 'words' as reported by the editor, in summary or occasionally as direct quote, but as becomes obvious from its more literary forms, these 'words' can only reflect the actual content of Amos's oral presentations. The noun 'words' is essentially code for his message.

Notably missing from the introductory material is the use of the traditional phrase *'the word of Yahweh was (came) to …'*, commonly used in prophetic books to suggest that the words derive from a divine source. This is a significant, and, I would argue, a deliberate omission because it points directly to the fact that the words now reported originated with Amos himself. Such a view appears to conflict with the use of those *pro forma* bracketing devices provided by the editor and found throughout the book, the purpose or function of which needs to be appreciated; they are added to emphasize the importance of the words, not their source.

The form of Introduction provided thus sets Amos apart, like Nahum, as a visionary; he was clearly not to be identified as a prophet because all the necessary markers are omitted.

Who was this man called *Amos*? See more detail in the Introduction, but here it is worth noting again that this book is the only place in the Hebrew Bible where his name appears. Apart from the autobiographical record in 7.14-15, we know nothing about the man other than what can be gleaned indirectly from the report's content. How is it that such a significant person is never mentioned, or even alluded to, in any source apart from this report? Was it 'accidental' that no other editor knew of Amos's exploits, hence the silence surrounding him and his service? Or is it more a case of lost evidence? The fact that there is appended in 9.11-15 a note about restoring the Davidic dynasty in Judah does suggest that someone or some group in the south did remember Amos, unless attaching that section at the end of the report was purely serendipitous. Nevertheless, it does appear odd that he is not remembered in any other source.

The words of Amos are then qualified as a report of what he 'saw' (Heb. *ḥāzâ*), namely (1) the social and religious conditions in Israel during the reign of Jeroboam II (c. 785–745 BCE), and (2) what he envisioned of its future if there was no change of heart. The figurative use of the verb 'saw' should not be read literally; it speaks of his insight and understanding—see also Qoh. 2.13, 24; 3.19, 16; 4.1 etc.

The period of time Amos spent in the north is not further specified other than to connect his presence to an *earthquake*. In a region where earthquakes and tremors are frequent, there is little certainty about identifying one specific quake, and the figure of 'two years' is sufficiently vague that it would not be possible to fix the words to other than a general period of time. It is not clear, however, whether the 'two years' referred to is the time of Amos's original speeches or of the report itself as the syntax of the verse is complex. If the former, then the time during which Amos spoke could have been relatively short; if the latter, then it would suggest Amos's address to the northerners was probably of a longer duration. When and if he returned to his home in Tekoa also is unknowable.

Amos is reported to have come from *Tekoa*. For a discussion of its location and its climatic and geographical conditions, see Introduction. He is said to have been a *nōqēd*, a term found elsewhere only in 2 Kgs 3.4. It has been generally rendered as 'shepherd', but the root itself has a basic meaning of 'speckled', as referring to small animals, including sheep and goats. In 7.14 the word *bôqēr*, 'herder', is used, though some wish to emend that to *nōqēd*, as here, because the letters in Hebrew are similar and could be misread. There is no evidence that this has actually happened, nor is it justified. The text of 7.14 also refers to *ṣ'ôn*, 'flock', again often assumed to be 'sheep', but this reader is arguing that in such a marginal area as was Tekoa, Amos herded goats, not sheep, though flocks were sometimes mixed.

1.1-2 Editor's Introduction 25

1.2 Looming over this report is the editor's summary of Amos's view of Yahweh as a truly frightening, awesome figure whose thundering 'voice' is capable of devastating the nation. Brief yet terrorizing, the imagery is intended to shape how one reads the report; it reveals Amos's understanding of the nature of his God, and thus of what drives his mission.

The statement is focused on Yahweh's destructive and awesome power, suggesting that it is this devastating power that for Amos was fundamental to his theology. Using the metaphor of a roaring lion, Yahweh's soundless 'voice' is said to thunder across the land. There are echoes of this figurative language used of Yahweh throughout, such that it can be said to be a common image of perceived divine power and awesomeness that generates fear (3.4, 8, 12). The imperfect verb forms express a constant or on-going state of being—this is how Amos perceived Yahweh to be (see also Nah. 1.2-8).

Additionally, that 'voice' proceeds from his dwelling place in Zion/Jerusalem, reflective of the Deuteronomic tradition in which Jerusalem is Yahweh's chosen dwelling place from which his laws and commands proceed. Yahweh's figurative 'roar' is so overwhelming that it impacts the physical landscape, causing grass and trees to wither and die. No wonder that the herders mourn for the loss of pasture. The statement, representing Amos's belief in the awesome nature of his God, provides a further connection with Nahum, whose opening words adopt a very similar theme and vocabulary. Both authors perceive Yahweh as fearsome and threatening, a God of intense wrath, and here to be exemplified in the charges against each of the nations.

The *'top of Carmel'* is a multivalent phrase, for the noun *karmel* describes a plantation or well-watered garden, as well as being a place name referring to the mountain that lies on the southern side of the Jezreel valley. Its trees will lack water and die if Yahweh's voice so orders, causing angst for herders of the flock. We can also note that the phrase *'top/head of Carmel'* recurs in 9.3, though the distance between these two references is probably too great for the phrase to qualify as a kind of inclusion for the whole report.

Verse 2a repeats Joel 3.16, a verse that provides a link between the two books on the scroll, as does Amos 9.12 provide links to the following Obad. 1-2. This linkage is an editorial contribution that impacts the scroll more generally as one book is tied to another to establish a sequence, though that sequence is not chronological, given that Amos, the earliest record in the scroll, is placed at no. 3.

1.3–2.5 Yahweh and the Nations

This cleverly constructed unit has its own independent identity. As a literary unit it also has its own shape and form, as well as directing attention to the general setting within which Israel and Judah, the divided nations, existed. It builds to a climax with the comments on Israel's largest component, the northern kingdom.

For the first time readers of Amos are met with the rhetorical device *'Thus says Yahweh ..., says Yahweh',* the phrases that bracket many sections of text, and these eight sub-sections in particular. These bracketing devices are typical of reported prophetic speech, but as *pro forma* elements, readers need to consider how to understand them, especially if one is tempted to read the contents literally as divine 'promises', for the fact is that they were never realized as stated. Given that this reading views the bracketing forms as 'imported' into the text by the editor, the verbal elements are read not as promised actions but as what Amos would wish to see happen, or as what God, in Amos's world, threatened to do—see v. 2. These literary devices set Amos's words in a frame that was intended to strengthen the challenge to the hearers. See Introduction.

Eight times in this introductory section the 'mathematical' x, x+1 form, well known in the wisdom literature, is adapted and used to introduce the monologue concerning northern Israel and the nations surrounding it. The initial series of seven short oracles are directed at the northern kingdom's 'enemies', including Judah as no. 7, before highlighting the issues in northern Israel itself in an extended version of the form. Whether presented orally or in written form, by focusing initially on the sins of the enemy, the intended target audience, Israel, is lulled into a false sense of security and hope that the enemy will be defeated. This makes the condemnation of Israel, the unexpected climax of the section, all the more powerful.

The general pattern in each oracle is:

1. *for three transgressions of (PN) and for four, I will not ...*
2. *because they have ...*
3. *So I will send a fire on ... and it shall devour ...*
4. *I would (also) ...* (not found in the case of Tyre, Edom or Judah)

1.3–2.5 Yahweh and the Nations

Specific actions are threatened in each case, but not necessarily enumerated as four discrete punishments.

The search for a consistent pattern or application in the presentation of these eight oracles directed against the nations generally fails, but it is interesting to note that while the condemnation of most is based on an alleged physical attack on a neighbour, Judah is condemned entirely on religious grounds, and in the final case, that against Israel, it is based on its social and economic oppression.

The form '*for <u>three</u> transgressions of (PN) and for <u>four</u>, I will not revoke? the ? ...*' (NRSV) demonstrates how terse is the form. It generally does not itemize the four issues as does the form when it appears in the pure wisdom context (see, e.g., Prov. 30). The formula raises several questions such as the purpose or intention of the adapted form. Is it an oath that serves to emphasizes an outcome? Why choose a wisdom form for such purpose? Does it have an advantage over the use of some other form? Are the numbers specific, or are they more general? Apart from the probability that the editor had some wisdom connection and was familiar with its literary forms, there is little other evidence for answers.

Since there is no clear listing of four discrete examples of the 'transgression' apart from that related to Edom (1.11), I read the numerals as general, giving a sense of multiple cases that could be rendered as, '*no matter how much they transgress ..., I would not ...*'. However, translators should retain the Hebrew x, x+1 form as it is integral to the rhetorical presentation.

1.3-5

3 *Thus has Yahweh spoken:*

> *For three transgressions of Damascus, and for four, I will not resile from punishment for their threshing Gilead with iron sledges.*
>
> 4 *I would set fire to the house of Hazael and it will devour the fortresses of Ben-Hadad.*
>
> 5 *I would smash the bars of Damascus's gate and cut down one who inhabits the Valley of the Strong, along with one from the house of Eden who holds the sceptre; then the Arameans will go into exile in Kir.*

Yahweh has spoken.

1.3 The preface to this first address involving Israel's enemies—and to each of the eight elements—is a standard introductory form, '*Thus says Yahweh*': It is found throughout the prophetic literature, often with a closing '*... says Yahweh*'. The form itself indicates that the material within the bracketing device is a report or retelling of a message received. It is a form that is generally taken literally to mean that these words derive from a divine source, and the function of the form is to give greater authority to the speaker and the message. The form is so widespread in biblical literature that it clearly has become a *pro forma* inclusion in an editor's report—see its non-standard use throughout Haggai as an emphatic. In that sense it differs from the pure oral form such as is used in Amos 3.1; 4.1; 5.1, where Amos himself is said to speak directly to his audience.

The *transgressions of Damascus* are not itemized, indicating that the numerals in the form are not specific but figurative. The Hebrew noun *pešaʿ* usually denotes having rebelled or deliberately contravened an order.

Damascus, the Syrian/Aramean capital representing the neighbouring enemy further north, is here threatened with punishment, charged with having figuratively 'threshed' the region of Gilead with an iron threshing sled. The 'sledge' was a heavy weighted device with metal pieces inserted into the wooden undercarriage that, when drawn across the drying grain stalks, threshed or separated out the grain, leaving the chaff behind to be separated further by winnowing (cf. Isa. 41.15). The threshing motif speaks of cruel treatment. No specific event is identified as relating to this charge, though considering that during the mid-eighth century BCE Israel enjoyed relative peace from attack, the reference here presumably relates to an earlier and perhaps constant threat from Syria. Some seek to link it with Hazael's attack on Gilead mentioned in 2 Kgs 10.32-33, but there is no supporting evidence.

Gilead refers to the community of people after whom a mountainous Transjordanian region near the Jabbok River and to the south of Bashan is named. OT tradition has it as being associated with the tribe of Manasseh, of whom Gilead was the strongest clan. It remained an Israelite stronghold through the mid-ninth century BCE.

The issue that is difficult to determine is the sense carried by the verb phrase *lōʾ ʾăšîbennû*, here rendered as *I will not resile from,* a first-person singular causative/hiphil of *šwb* plus a masculine pronominal suffix 'it'. The verb itself is notoriously flexible: from a basic sense of 'return, go back', it has many different applications depending on the verbal form and its context, among them 'reverse, withdraw, take back, give back, come back, turn toward, hinder, turn aside' and, in some special cases, 'repent'. Its causative nuance here is unclear—see Job 9.12; 11.10; 23.13; Prov. 29.8 for some examples. Translations generally regard the phrase as meaning 'I will not take back/revoke ...', and this reader has chosen to render it as an emphatic *I will not resile from ...'* portraying determination or stubbornness. The larger problem is the suffix 'it', which is undefined, the meaning of which is more uncertain. Most assume that 'it' is some form of punishment, a view consistent with the use of the form as an oath in which Yahweh claims never to revoke his action plan. The *šwb* root is also used in 5.8-11 when the people are accused of 'not turning back' to Yahweh despite encountering issues that were intended to bring about a 'return' (see also Hag. 2.17); repentance may be involved here, but not necessarily so, as it may simply mean a reconciliation, a restoring of a relationship in which both parties 'turn' to one another.

Interestingly, in Prov. 30.30, another 'three–four' wisdom form, *šwb* is used of the lion who 'does not turn back' when challenged; it speaks there of firm and fearless resolve. Having argued that Amos was a visionary, not a prophet, and that the report expressed his hopes and longings rather than predictions of divine action, I render *lō' 'ᵃšîbennû* in Amos 1 as '*I will not resile from it!*', expressing determination not to yield for any reason.

1.4 The threat facing Aram was: '*I would send fire ... on the house of Hazael*'. This is the first example of the volitional nuance of the imperfect verb—it does not promise to set fire to Hazael but states what should or could happen. The imagery of fire that consumes is a relatively common one, found in each of the first seven oracles, here directed at '*Hazael's house*' and '*Ben-Hadad's strongholds*', that is, the strongholds that Ben-Hadad had built. Both Hazael, a usurper who took the throne (c. 842–800 BCE), and Ben-Hadad his son (c. 806) were former northern rulers. (There were several Ben-Hadads, as it was a throne name, literally 'son of Hadad', the West Semitic storm god). The threat as issued implies that the 'house of Hazael' and the 'strongholds of Ben-Hadad' are current entities. If Amos's work in the north coincided with the reign of Jeroboam II (785–745 BCE) then the Ben-Hadad referred to must have been Ben-Hadad III who took the throne in c. 806, unless the throne name is applied generally as a reference to the ruling house.

Each of the first seven oracles refers to the 'strongholds' in each of the locations, metaphors for defence and local protection, so it is this that could be destroyed. It is more than possible that the use of the imagery in each of the oracles means that its use is figurative rather than concrete. The parallelism in the verse suggests that 'house' may refer to a physical building, but it is also conceivable that 'house' is figurative for the family, and thus the successor(s) of Hazael who usurped the northern throne. If both the references were to concrete buildings, however, then the threat would imply that representative royal buildings in Damascus should be destroyed. We shall probably never be certain as to what was intended here. The wording of 1.4b appears also later in Jer. 49.27 with regard to Damascus.

1.5 The *bars of Damascus's gate* refer to the wood or metal bars that were fitted into the inside of the gates to Damascus preventing the doors from being opened from the outside. Most ancient cities were walled, with several openings or gateways for access. These were closed when an enemy was attacking, or at some hour in the evening when farmers returned from their fields guaranteeing overnight security for those inside. If the bars were broken for any reason, the city and its inhabitants were vulnerable. A second meaning of the noun *'gate'* is a reference to the open public spaces or rooms built into the city wall just inside the gate, the place where all affairs of the city were conducted.

A second line speaks of one who lives in the Valley of *Awen* (NRSV) being 'cut down'. The Hebrew singular participle *yōšēb* may be collective, meaning 'all those who live' in a place, but some have suggested it means 'one who rules', based on the parallel in v. 5b, 'one who holds the sceptre'. The toponym *'Valley of Awen'* is now of uncertain location, made more complicated by the reference to *'āwen*, a noun normally meaning 'sin' or 'evil'. While such a place name is possible, referring to some terrible past event happening at the site, one also may consider that the name is a homograph with a very different nuance—strength, wealth. This latter makes good sense in that the one who is strong is threatened with being cut down.

The verb 'cut off/down' also serves the second half verse, so the *'one who holds the sceptre'* could also meet that fate. The Hebrew noun *šēbeṭ*, can refer to a staff or truncheon, a symbol of authority and power, but also available as a weapon. Again, the singular form is probably collective. The locative *Beth-'Eden* has been connected often to a city north-east of Damascus, but again there is no certainty. The two geographical references presumably imply that the whole of the Aramean kingdom would be under this threat.

Then, the entire population of Aram stood in danger of going into 'exile' to *Kir*, an unusual possibility, in the sense that that is the locale from which they are said to have originally come, according to 9.7! *Kir* is thought to be a region east of Aram (see Isa. 22.6) in southern Mesopotamia. While the location itself may not be so vitally important, the fact is that Amos envisaged exile—perhaps a return home?—as the fate of the Aramean enemy; whichever it was, that was surely good news for Israel. According to 2 Kgs 16.9 Tiglath-Pileser III destroyed Damascus in 732 BCE and deported the population to Kir, although as the LXX version of the text omits 'Kir', there is some question about the accuracy of the statement. What in fact happened was that Israelites were exiled in that general direction when overrun by the Assyrians in 721 BCE, shortly after Amos's mission in the north.

1.6-8

6 *Thus has Yahweh spoken:*

For three transgressions of Gaza, and for four, I will not resile from punishment because they carried into exile entire communities, to hand them over to Edom.

7 So I would send a fire against the wall of Gaza, fire that would devour its strongholds.

8 I would cut off the one who lives in Ashdod, and the one who holds the sceptre in Ashdod; I would turn my hand against Ekron, and the remnant of the Philistines would perish,

Says my lord Yahweh.

1.6 The second oracle relates to the Philistines, traditional enemies of both Judah and Israel. The oracle is specifically directed against the city of Gaza as representative of the whole Philistine community; it was one of five major Philistine cities, the others being Gath, Ashdod, Ashkelon and Ekron, the latter three also identified in the oracle. The Philistine region covered the southwest corner of Canaan along the seacoast, with Gaza of particular significance in the trade between Egypt and points north in Israel, Syria and beyond. The form of the oracle follows that of the first in 1.3-5, and vocabulary is repeated in v. 8a.

The accusation against Gaza, and presumably all of Philistia, was that they forced entire communities into exile, especially noting Edomite involvement. The exact nature of the charge depends on the understanding of the Hebrew verb *sgr*, which has a basic sense of closing up or shutting in, thus, sending into exile, or enslaving. This seems to imply that the Philistines became known for trading in human flesh or at least enslaving peoples by 'selling' them to the Edomites, who occupied the region farther east beyond the Dead Sea. As with the other oracles in this collection, details of an actual event or occurrence are of no matter because the charge is generalized. Some commentators, however, have spent much time and paper suggesting possible situations and historical connections; but the very nature of the oracles' language defies such precision. What the editor's report highlights is Amos's (and his southern colleagues') overall perception, a traditional Israelite characterization of the Philistine and other communities.

Edom to the east of the Dead Sea was a kingdom at times friendly with Israelites, at times not so, and traditionally descended from Esau, a brotherly relationship for Judah and Israel, the origin of which was the stuff of family legend (Gen. 27).

1.7-8 The oracle continues, as did 1.4, with the threat of *fire* that would *devour* Gaza's defences, its strongholds, meaning that it could never resist the divine plan. Verse 8a reuses the language of v. 5b with the operative verb being 'cut off', a common expression for bringing an end to something. Here it is the people who live in Ashdod, and those in power in Ashkelon who will be 'cut off', understanding the singular participles as collective. Both cities are within the pentapolis of Philistine territory.

As for Ekron, the threat is that God would 'turn a hand' against it—the verb is the same as that used in v.5b. The cumulative result would be that *anybody remaining* in Philistia would perish, perhaps a reference to the other city not listed, that is, Gath, or the countryside more generally.

The entire oracle is bracketed as usual with the '*Thus has Yahweh spoken, ... says Yahweh'*, a slight variation on the form imposed.

1.9-10

9 *Thus has Yahweh spoken:*

> *For three transgressions of Tyre, and for four, I will not resile from punishment because they sent entire communities over to Edom, forgetting the covenant of kinship,*
>
> 10 *So I would send fire upon the wall of Tyre, fire that would devour its strongholds.*

The third oracle is directed against Tyre (Heb. *ṣor*, 'rock') and is the shortest oracle in the group. As with the preceding oracle, the same charge is leveled with regard to selling people to Edom, and as a result, Tyre and its *strongholds* could be devoured by fire, the formal component of the destructive divine action envisaged. *Tyre* was the Phoenician seaport originally on an island south of Sidon, to the north of Israel. The island later became joined to the mainland as the waters between the island and mainland became silted.

Down to the late-eighth century BCE, good relationships between Tyre and the Israelites were maintained as both benefitted from trade: Israel provided oil and grain, while Tyre brought in a variety of imports from other parts of the Mediterranean. It was this mutual benefit that may lie behind the phrase *'covenant of kinship'*. If this was the covenant in mind, then it seems to presume that the Tyrians were taking and trading Israelites to Edom in contravention of their covenant. The fact that the text does not specify who the Tyrians captured and sold prevents a final decision.

At a later date, Joel refers to the selling of Judah to the Greeks (Joel 3.6-7), not Israelites to Edom as here. Selling people into slavery to foreigners seemingly was a common practice. Some commentators see the charge

1.3–2.5 Yahweh and the Nations 33

against Tyre as referring to that post-587 BCE situation when the Edomites assisted the Babylonians in their attack on Jerusalem, but is that what the generalized statement *'entire communities'* (Heb. *šᵉlēmāh*) refers to? If so, it would mean, of course, that it is a charge that postdates by almost two centuries the mission of Amos, a conclusion that is deeply problematic.

The point that I have sought to make regarding these oracles is that positing a specific historical circumstance that gave rise to each of these challenges is generally a blind alley as the text in each case merely offers the most vague of references, suggesting that the charges represent a common negative characterization of each 'enemy'. Repetition of vocabulary and phraseology dominates, supporting the view that the presentation is deliberately generalized rather than specifying one historical event or situation.

1.11-12

11 *Thus has Yahweh spoken:*

> *For three transgressions of Edom, and for four, I will not resile from punishment because he pursued his brother with the sword and cast off all pity; he maintained his anger perpetually, and kept his wrath forever.*
>
> 12 *So I would send fire upon the wall of Teman, to devour the strongholds of Bozrah.*

Like the previous oracle, this has a formal introduction, but it lacks the closing formula. Its object is Edom, represented by two named locations, *Teman* and *Bozrah*. The latter was regarded as the capital of Edom. It was a strategic city not far from its border with Judah to the west, and elevated on the escarpment above it. *Teman* was a clan name that became synonymous with the Edomites. As a general name for the region as a whole, a precise location is irrelevant.

The charge was that *he pursued his brother with the sword and cast off all pity*. Here 'Edom' is representative of Esau, and the reference appears to hark back to the traditional story of the dispute between the two brothers. Esau's anger with his brother Jacob was so intense that he sought to kill him, and his father Isaac characterized his life as living 'by your sword' (Gen. 27.41-45). The tradition of this enmity provides the vocabulary used here.

In another tradition recorded in Gen. 33.1-11, it was Esau who sought reconciliation with Jacob. In this Amos version the enmity and hostility remained, so the imperfective verbs have a frequentative or on-going cast, together with the adverb *lāʿad*, stressing permanence. The Hebrew verb used (*wayyiṭrop*) to describe Edom's anger is a particularly strong one, likening Edom's attitude to that of a wild animal tearing its prey. This more dramatic picture represents a very different and more negative version of the relationship between Judah and Edom, a relationship that clearly ebbed and flowed. The oracle's purpose is to suggest that the Edomite enemy would be overcome despite it having been a 'perpetual' enemy.

For many commentators this section contains echoes of the events of 587 BCE when Edomites joined the Babylonian attack on Jerusalem, long after Amos's actual mission. As noted, however, the text does not require that it be read in light of that later episode. In other words, the basis of the oracle is the historical tradition of hostility between the two brothers rather than some current or much later event.

1.13-15
13 *Thus has Yahweh spoken:*

> *For three transgressions of the Ammonites, and for four, I will not resile from punishment; because they have ripped open pregnant women in Gilead in order to enlarge their territory,*
>
> 14 *So I would kindle a fire upon the wall of Rabbah, fire that would devour its strongholds, with shouting on the day of battle, with a storm on the day of the whirlwind;*
>
> 15 *then their king would go into exile, he and his officials together,*
> *says Yahweh.*

The fifth oracle targets the Ammonites, leveling serious accusations against them for an attack on Gilead. In this respect, this oracle echoes material in the oracle against Damascus (1.3). While the previous oracles related to Israel's immediate neighbours, this section refers to a community that lay across the Jordan and to the north, with mention of the city of Rabbah. Rabbah was located where Amman, the present Jordanian capital, is sited. The oracle threatens exile for the king and officials of Ammon.

The accusation against Ammon sounds horrendous—they are accused of *having ripped open pregnant women in Gilead in order to enlarge their territory.* Ripping open pregnant women assured the deaths of both mother and child, and regardless of the precise nuance of the verb in this case, attacking women and children has always been a feature of warfare. Such despicable activity itself, however, was not what gave the Ammonites a larger territory, so the connection between that act and gaining territory is merely a general illustration of the evils of warfare with territorial expansion as its intent.

1.13 The Hebrew verb *bqʻ* describes the action of breaking something open, or breaking into something, so while here the rendering 'ripped open' (NRSV) is acceptable, if it was a matter of 'breaking into', then the

1.3–2.5 Yahweh and the Nations 35

charge concerns the rape of pregnant women, also a heinous crime. Again, it depicts the general savagery inspired by war.

On *Gilead* see the location note at 1.3.

The purpose of their attack on Gilead was '*in order to broaden their border*', a land grab.

1.14 Against the main city, Rabbah, representing the whole Ammonite community, the threat was that '*I would set fire against the walls of Rabbah*'. The use of the Hebrew verb *yāṣat*, 'set (fire) to', is unusual, breaking the pattern of the form that in all other sections uses the verb *šālaḥ*, 'send', but it is one used in a number of passages in Jeremiah—Jer. 17.27; 21.14; 43.12; 49.27; 50.32—in the similar context of using fire as a form of absolute punishment against a city and its people. Here the form repeats the metaphor of 'eating' to describe the result of destructive fire upon the fortifications.

Two additional adverbial phrases supplement the description of the attack: *shouting on the day of battle, with a storm on the day of the whirlwind*. Both metaphors, 'battle' and 'whirlwind', picture in parallel scenes the chaos, noise, the destruction associated with war. The noun *day* carries its broad sense of a moment in time, an occasion when an event takes place; it does not refer to a set or projected moment.

1.15 The fate of the Ammonite king and of his leaders as they literally 'walk' or go into exile is the final humiliation envisaged by Amos. No agent of Ammon's demise is named, nor an exilic destination given, as happens in 1.3, 6. In the context, this merely expresses what happens to all leaders of a defeated community who aren't killed in battle (as in 2.3)—they are captured and taken away humiliated.

The section then is closed with an abbreviated '*Yahweh has spoken*'.

2.1-3

1 *Thus has Yahweh spoken:*

> *For three transgressions of Moab, and for four, I will not resile from punishment; because he burned to lime the bones of the king of Edom.*
>
> 2 *So, I would send a fire upon Moab to devour the strongholds of Kerioth, and may Moab die amid uproar, amid shouting and the sound of the trumpet;*
> 3 *I would cut off the one who judges from its midst, and kill all its princes with him,*
> *says Yahweh.*

The sixth oracle is directed against Moab. It was a small kingdom to the south of Ammon on the eastern side of the Jordan valley opposite Judah. Moab occupied the high plateau area east of the Dead Sea in a narrow strip of arable land extending from the Ammonite border south to the Arnon river valley. It was along this narrow strip that the King's Highway passed from Egypt and the Gulf of Aqaba to points north. On Moab's southern border was Edom.

Relations between the Israelites in Judah and the Moabites were generally hostile, but there was at least one period when relations were more friendly, as is noted in the book of Ruth. Relations with the northern kingdom of Israel were less close. In this oracle, however, it is the relationship between the Moabites and the Edomites, both of whom were in Transjordan, that is the topic of concern. Information regarding the specific charge described in the oracle is unavailable, but it does reflect the frequent conflict that arose between each of the occupants of the Transjordanian territory. There is no reference to relationships between Israel and Moab in this oracle, a distinctive feature of the collection.

2.1 The formal introduction to the oracle follows the set x, x+1 pattern, followed by the reason for the charge against Moab. That reason was that 'he', using the singular and thus laying blame on every Moabite, *burned to lime the bones of the king of Edom*. We can note that the charge is general in the sense that the king is not named, while the specific allegation was that the bones of an Edomite king who had presumably died or been killed were burned to ash, thus producing lime. What was the sin? Was it the burning of the bones or the production of lime? Probably it was the former, being the desecration of the dead king's body and/or tomb. In 2 Kgs 23.16-18 there is mention of Josiah burning bones and thus desecrating the Bethel sanctuary's altar, so such activity was known. Mention of the burning 'to lime', however, might imply that the lime was to be used in some manner, further humiliating the Edomites. As noted, this charge does not relate to Israel in any manner.

2.2 As a result, Amos envisions fire being inflicted on Moab, destroying the strongholds of Kerioth, a town or city now unknown, but presumably one of significance at the time as representative of all Moabite strongholds.

Further examples are given of the end of Moab as seen by Amos: each relates to war, though again the description is general, namely uproar, shouting, and the sound of the ram's horn trumpet, the *šôpār*, calling to battle. Who the aggressor or agent might be is, of course, unspoken. Assyria is the more likely enemy in mind, given that there was a long history of Assyrian

1.3–2.5 Yahweh and the Nations 37

aggression into this region during the late-eighth century BCE. If so, then the Assyrians would have already traversed and overcome all areas to the north of Moab.

2.3 The metaphor of 'cutting off' is repeated here (see 1.5, 8), as the lives of the tribal leaders (Heb. *šôpēṭ*, 'judge') and its princes/officials (Heb. *śārîm*) are to be taken. This time there is no reference to the deportation of the leadership; rather, all would be killed. The use of the participle *šôpēṭ* recalls the function of the tribal leaders between the time of Moses and the establishment of the kingdom; each *šôpēṭ* was a local leader in the days before the tribal system morphed into a kingdom that embraced all tribes (see the book of Judges).

2.4-5
4 *Thus has Yahweh spoken:*

For three transgressions of Judah, and for four, I will not resile from punishment; because they have rejected the law of Yahweh, and have not kept his statutes, but they have been led astray by the same lies after which their ancestors walked.

5 *So, I would send a fire upon Judah and devour the strongholds of Jerusalem.*

The seventh oracle targets Judah, northern Israel's southern and minor partner. The charge against it differs from that lodged against the preceding entities, which focused on war and aggression. The threefold charge against Judah, however, is based on its alleged religious failures, with 'Jerusalem' the eponymous name for the entire southern kingdom and its religious tradition centred on the Temple. The charge is specific, but the punishment is abbreviated, confined to setting fire to Judah and it devouring the strongholds—that is, Temple—in Jerusalem. No mention is made of the fate of the king and leadership.

This survey of northern Israel's traditional enemies comes to a head with a vision of Judah's troubles. Nothing would make the northerners feel relaxed more than to hear that their 'brothers' in the south would come under divine judgment along with their traditional opponents. We assume that this clever presentation was the brainchild of Amos, even if the actual form in which it now exists was one provided by a literate editor.

There is no closing element '*says Yahweh*' for the section.

2.4 The charge against Judah arises from their rejection (Heb. *mā'as*) of Yahweh's Torah/Instruction, emphasized as failing to keep/obey his 'statutes'. The language is that of the Deuteronomic cohort, the main religious community in the southern kingdom. It was this community that was responsible for the Deuteronomistic History, written or compiled using their established set of values, especially that of blessings for obedience to those statutes and curses for disobedience (Deut. 28-29). It was this version of the faith that underpinned Amos's message throughout—he was an emissary of this cohort. There is something unusual about this challenge, however, as Amos from Judah accuses his own Judaean community of religious apostasy. It points to his mission as wider than just the northern kingdom.

The charge accuses Judah of being *'led astray by their lies'*, that is, what the Deuteronomists regarded as the false religion followed by their ancestors. The 'ancestors' is a vague term in that readers cannot know how far back the reference here extends, but, in reality, there had always been religious apostasy within Israel, as is evidenced in Josh. 24.14-27. The call of the Deuteronomists had been for religious purity, as defined by them, and for Yahweh-only as the one to be worshipped, with true or pure worship located only in Jerusalem's Temple. Here, however, Amos is said to have noted that the Israelite story had been compromised from the outset. The religion of the ancient forefathers clearly was pre-Yahwistic and not that of the post-Mosaic era. Furthermore, religious life in Israel, both north and south, was never as 'pure' as demanded by the religious elite—popular religion had always been 'corrupt' and syncretistic—for example, the golden calf incident.

In view of this charge, the question of Amos's mission to the northern kingdom has to be raised again. If such religious failure was endemic in the south, why was Amos not called to speak to his own community? Why send him, a southerner, to the north to represent southern values when there was the same need in Jerusalem?

2.5 Fire is again used as the formulaic metaphor of destruction threatened; what reality might have been envisaged by Amos is unknown here, as in the preceding oracles. It would 'devour' the strongholds of Jerusalem, another generalized expression for the city as representing the southern kingdom.

Like the oracle against Edom, this oracle also omits the final *'says Yahweh'* as the closing bracket.

2.6-16 Yahweh and Israel

6 *Thus has Yahweh spoken:*

For three transgressions of Israel, and for four, I will not resile from punishment; because they sell the righteous for silver and the needy for a pair of sandals—

7 *they who trample the head of the poor into the dust of the earth, and push the afflicted out of the way; father and son go into the same girl, so that my holy name is profaned;*

8 *they lay themselves down beside every altar on garments taken in pledge, and in the house of their God they drink wine bought with fines they imposed.*

9 *Yet I annihilated the Amorite before them, whose height was like the height of cedars, and who was as strong as oaks; I destroyed his fruit above and his roots beneath.*

10 *Also, I brought you up out of Egypt and led you forty years in the wilderness to possess the land of the Amorite.*

11 *And I raised up some of your children to be prophets and some of your youths to be nazirites. Is it not indeed so, O people of Israel?*

Says Yahweh.

12 *But you made the nazirites drink wine and commanded the prophets saying, 'You shall not prophesy'.*

13 *So I would press you down in your place just as a cart presses down when it is full of sheaves.*

14 *Flight would be removed from the swift, and the strong one not retain his strength, nor the mighty save his life;*

15 *the one who is skilled with the bow not stand, and the ones swift of foot not escape, nor would the one who rides a horse save his life;*

16 *and let the stout of heart among the mighty flee away naked in that day.*

Says Yahweh.

This final and climactic oracle in the series targets the northern kingdom of Israel itself. In its current form it comes as an unexpected accusation, taking Israel by surprise and removing all earlier joy in hearing of the demise of its enemies (1.3–2.5). The entire presentation is a very special and creative literary achievement with psychological impact on its northern Israelite audience.

In terms of its structure, the section consists of three component parts: vv. 6-8 list the many social and/or ethical problems Amos saw; vv. 9-12 remind the nation as a whole of God's previous assistance; vv. 13-16 threaten divine pressure that would strip all power from the strong, especially from the warrior class, whenever 'that day', the day of Yahweh, might come. Throughout, the message is conveyed by use of contrasts—what the people are alleged to have done contrasts with what Yahweh had done, a contrast made more obvious rhetorically with the repeated first-person address in vv. 9, 10 and 13.

An inserted '*says Yahweh*' at the end of v. 11 is clearly out of place, interrupting the chiasm in vv. 11-12, but the speech bracket is finally closed with the formula '*says Yahweh*' at the end of v. 16.

The focus of the charge is mainly on the social and ethical failings of the people, along with a socio-religious failure in v. 12 as they are also accused of disrespecting the nazirites who had taken the vow, and of attacking prophets whom God had raised up, preventing them from fulfilling their mission. As a consequence, Israel was threatened with military and mental weakness from which there would be no escape. No agency by which God might inflict these ends is mentioned. What is significant here is that the historical review in vv. 9-12 relates to the entire nation and is not confined to the northern 'rebels', meaning that the divine response in vv. 13-16 should apply nationally and not just to the north. See further in Introduction, **Literary Features A**.

2.6-8 Following the formal introduction, the reason for the threatened punishment is noted—'*selling the righteous for silver*', and its parallel, '*selling the needy for a pair of sandals*'. Both focus on those in power who take advantage of the poor and needy, perhaps by forcing them into some form of domestic slavery. The notion of figuratively 'selling' a person involves either a monetary or material exchange considered to represent the value of an object, here as 'silver' or 'sandals'. When it is the 'righteous' (Heb. *ṣaddîq*) who are being 'sold', there is clearly implied that those doing the selling or taking advantage are the unrighteous, the unscrupulous among those who hold power.

The charge is further described as '*trampling the head of the poor* (Heb. *dallîm*) *into the dust of the earth*'. Those described as 'poor' are the weak and powerless, not just the financially poor. The imagery portrays cruelty directed toward those who were unable to resist. The following charge is more institutional oppression of those who seek justice—they

2.6-16 Yahweh and Israel 41

are simply 'pushed away', their cases ignored or supporting evidence dismissed.

The next charge claims that there is a sexual practice that also offends, as a father and a son both 'go into' (Heb. *yēlkû*, 'go') the same young woman. In the context of oppression of the poor and needy, the woman concerned may well be a domestic servant girl. Whether this implies incest or some other aberration is difficult to establish, but Amos's peculiar perspective is that such conduct brings dishonour to the divine name—what about the girl? While there were numerous laws surrounding sexual relationships (see Lev. 20–23), just how the situation noted here might be understood to dishonour God's name probably depends on the statement implying incest, or more probably, cultic worship involving foreign gods (Lev. 20.3).

A small grammatical issue here is that Hebrew *lᵉmaʿan* usually expresses purpose, but here can only mean 'result'.

The next charge (v. 8) relates also to taking advantage of another. In the first instance it could be priests who are the target since they are *'lying down beside every altar'* on garments that have been given them as a pledge against a borrowing, or for some other reason. Clothes taken in pledge must be returned by the end of the day (Exod. 22.25-27), but here instead of being returned they are appropriated for personal use. The phrase 'house of their God/gods *('ᵉlohêhem)*' is ambiguous and could in fact refer to those who worshipped non-Israelite gods. Whether priest or judge, they also have been purchasing wine for their private enjoyment, using the money that they had imposed as a fine for some offence committed. The money should have gone to the treasury, but instead it has been pocketed for personal pleasure. How many priests were involved in such practices is unclear, but the hyperbole brands them all as guilty. No wonder Amaziah took offence!

These sweeping charges are being made against actions that contravene Israel's law, making it clear that Amos's concerns were primarily of a socio-religious nature, where inequality and lack of concern for the disadvantaged neighbour were allegedly a feature of life. Justice had broken down, a not uncommon and perennial problem (see Hab. 1.2-4).

2.9-12 This section moves from charges against what the people had done to what Yahweh had done in the past; it is a historical retrospect as Amos reminds the community of basic elements in the nation's story. It is presented as first-person speech by Yahweh, and the contrast between what the people have done and what Yahweh had done is made obvious by the repeated and emphatic first-person pronouns '*But I ...*' in vv. 9 and 10. The order of divine interventions is perhaps unusual; rather than beginning with the traditional reference to the exodus as a starting point, it lists dispossession of the Amorite population from Canaan as the first such act. Could it be that this is a reference to the period in which Israel's ancestors, the Abrahamic family, first emigrated from Haran to enter the region they were later 'given', rather than a postexodus reference?

What is remarkable here is the relationship in time between the situation described in 2.6-8, the present, and that of the historical review. The review speaks of what God had done in Israel's distant past, the original national tradition, the divine interventions that were understood as bringing it to birth and sustaining it. It appears then as a charge that Israel, both north and south, has forgotten where it came from, the how and the why, and what obligations that involvement placed on the community. The initial *waw* conjunction in v. 9 is not then a simple 'but'; it could be better understood as meaning: 'This is what you have become despite what I did for your ancestors. ...' As a 'historical' review, along with 3.1-2, the reference is to both kingdoms, not just the north.

'Amorite' is a general term for the many tribes in early Canaan. They were remembered in the tradition as giants—see, for example, Num. 13.31-34—recalled in 2.9b, and no reason is offered for their annihilation other than that they were the original inhabitants of the land. The second great act was the exodus itself, followed by the years of wandering, again without explanation as to their view that it was their God who so acted to rescue Israel, or their belief that Canaan was his 'gift' to them. The third act had nothing to do with the national journey *per se*; rather, the focus shifted to the appearance of prophets and nazirites, two important cohorts in the community, and said to be the gift of Yahweh. Why Amos would choose to highlight these two roles in particular is not clarified. What we read here is Israel's strong belief or claim that these past events were directly related to Yahweh's intervention in their life for their exclusive benefit.

God is said to have 'exterminated' (Heb. *šāmad*) the Amorites, a particularly forceful statement, clearly hyperbolic given the evidence of Judges 1 and the very limited success Israelites had in driving out the locals. The Amorites were annihilated *'from before them'* in which the pronominal suffix in the third person refers to Israel, not some other group. Grounded in the Holy War notion, Israel believed that Yahweh had led their troops to victory over the Amorite inhabitants. The following two relative clauses relate to the Amorites, to their reputed height and strength, using cedar and oak trees as the metaphors. Divine power and violence continue the figurative picture (see 1.2) as God is said to destroy (Heb. *šāmad*) the fruit as well as the roots of the tree, meaning complete annihilation of the Amorites with no chance of recovery.

2.10 Traditional language about 'bringing up' and 'leading' is used in v. 10 to refer to the exodus from Egypt and the subsequent occupation (Heb. *yāraš*) of Canaan, here called the 'land of the Amorite'. The language is very much part of the Deuteronomistic vocabulary—see Judg. 2.1; 6.8.

The divine initiative is further exemplified in God *'raising up'* prophets and nazirites. No mention is made of priests or kings or even judges, perhaps reflecting Amos's personal concerns. As for 'prophets' (Heb. *nᵉbî'îm*), much evidence exists for their role whether as 'seers', early versions of religious roles such as that of Elijah, or later proclaimers of what they believed were messages from God, including those who became 'sons of the prophets' and as students helped keep alive the message of their prophetic masters.

Nazirites were of a very different category, being individuals who voluntarily took personal vows (Heb. *nāzîr*) to abstain from drinking wine, to shave the head, and have nothing to do with corpses (Num. 6.1-8). To say that Yahweh raised up such individuals is clearly a manner of speaking given that taking that vow was an individual decision with a considerable and lasting impact on one's personal life. They were a community who 'separated themselves' by these actions 'to the Lord', in which such separation was an expression of 'holiness'.

2.11-12 The concluding note is a rhetorical question that calls Israel to recognize just how much Yahweh is said to have done for Israel's benefit. Placing the *'says Yahweh'* form here is probably a copyist's error, because it breaks the chiastic pattern that is vv. 11-12 (prophets-nazirites-nazirites-prophets).

In v. 12 the editor returns to the challenge or accusation against all Israel. Although Yahweh had 'provided' both prophets and nazirites, the Israelites are charged with forcing them to break their nazirite vow, and with demanding the prophet refrain from speaking. The command 'Do not prophesy(?)' in v. 12 is echoed in Amos's encounter with Amaziah in 7.13. On the Hebrew verb *nb'*, see Introduction.

2.13-16 The divine response to the situation described in 2.6-8 now follows; it is highly poetic and redolent with warfare imagery. The root *'āmaṣ*, 'be strong', occurs twice, and the root *mālaṭ*, 'slip away, escape', is used three times in the negative in reference to Israel's strong and mighty ones (*gibbôr*). They combine to highlight what could happen to Israel's warriors. Despite this, many commentators seek to link it with the earthquake mentioned in 1.1.

The section begins with the attention-getting *hinnēh*, 'Look!' It continues with the participle *mē'îq*, 'pressing', a threat that God would soon, or was about to, pressure Israel (only the north?) and strip it of every power; it pictures the contest of one power against another, with only one certain outcome, namely Israel's emasculation.

The use of the Hebrew verb *'wq*, 'to press', which occurs only in this verse (v. 13), is often questioned, but in the context of dealing with power it is entirely appropriate—remember the point in 1.2! The associated preposition phrase 'in your place' is an attempt to render the Hebrew *taḥtêkem*. The preposition itself carries a basic sense of '(that which is) beneath', but here is more abstract—'with you underneath'. That pressing down is exemplified as like that of a cart weighed down when fully loaded with harvested sheaves of grain. Such a cart would move slowly, an image then applied to the normally swift and strong; when that day dawns, they trundle along like an overloaded cart and cannot save themselves despite their physical skills and power.

Verse 15 focuses especially on the warrior class: those who are skilled at handling the bow will not be able to 'stand' (Heb. *'āmad*), usually with the sense of 'stand against' or 'resist'. Those who can run fast, seeking to escape capture, will not succeed, nor would those riding horses escape unharmed from the battle. No matter what physical skill or agency one might have, the 'day of Yahweh', implying untold disaster, is inescapable.

2.16 The final warrior group, identified as *'those who are brave (stout of heart)'*, is characterized as abandoning all its protective gear in a rushed attempt to escape; they would flee naked on that 'day'. The notion of being 'naked' refers not only to the removal of clothing and weapons; it carries the further cultural dimension of being publicly shamed.

The phrase 'on that day' uses the vague future expression, an undefined moment or occasion in time. There is something unusual about 'that day' as found here, however, for no agent, no enemy is identified as inflicting this loss of power on Israel. Nor is any divine appearance specified; rather, a generalized threat hangs over the northern kingdom for the charges laid in vv. 6-8 and v. 12. Though the concept of the 'day' is used here, the manner in which it is referred to is not typical of prophets—this is the visionary's volitional application of the notion of things and events that would/could happen.

The section 2.6-16 is closed by means of the formal *'says Yahweh'* phrase.

3.1–5.17 'Hear This Word...'

With ch. 3, we meet the first of three chapters each of which is introduced by the call to *'Hear this word ...!'* (3.1; 4.1; 5.1), along with an abbreviated call to *'hear'* in 3.13. In the reading being offered here, chs. 3–5 constitute the second major division of the book, and as such, 3.1-2, the opening two verses, serve to introduce the section as a whole, in the same manner as 1.2 served as an introduction to the initial section of the book, 1.3–2.16, and to the book as a whole. The two verses with which this section begins have also been seen as the Prologue to what many commentators consider to be the four central chapters of the book, namely chs. 3–6, embracing 5.1-17 as its core.

The call to *'hear'* is a rhetorically significant one; it is spoken by prophets (Isa. 1.10), sages (Prov. 4.1) and priests (Deut. 5.1; 6.3-4) when calling the people to attend closely to what was about to be said. It is not confined to prophetic speech.

3.1-15 'I Will Punish'

3.1-2

1 *Hear this word that Yahweh has spoken concerning you, you children of Israel; it concerns the whole family whom I brought up out of Egypt:*
2 *'You alone of all the families of the earth have I known so intimately; therefore I would bring upon you all your wrongdoing'.*

This Prologue in v. 1 echoes material in 2.9-12; it retells in briefest form the exodus story that was foundational for the whole people of Israel, both north and south, a reminder as to the addressees of this report. It moves then to a quotation of words said to have been spoken by Yahweh (v. 2). The two-part statement is crucial to an understanding of Amos's message more generally—because of (a) the intimate relationship of Yahweh with his Israelite 'family', (b) *therefore* Israel's 'sin' is the greater. As for the Prologue's function at this point, in its concise form with v. 2a stating a fact and v. 2b stating its consequence, it is a perfect introduction to the following examples in 3.3-8, 9-11 and 4.6-13 of events or states and the logical or assumed explanation for each.

46   *Amos*

It is the quote of v. 2a that reflects the language used in the DH—see, for example, Deut. 6.21; Judg. 2.1; 6.8, but especially Deut. 10.15. As covenant language under the guise of family relations, it forms the basis of Israel's claim to have been chosen by God and given the land of Canaan as a permanent possession. What is of special interest is that Amos's charge is not confined to northern Israel. This is true also of other parts of the report, which means that Amos's message was not directed solely at the northern kingdom; it was inclusive of the whole Israelite 'family'. Amos may have been physically present in the north, but for how long is unknown, while his vision and message encompassed the south as well.

The reference to *'the whole family'* in this context relates to both parts of the kingdom as one unified family, while in v. 2 they together are set over against *'all the families of the earth'*. This latter aggregation should be kept in context; it is far from global, being confined to the region occupied by those foreign nations noted in 1.3–2.5 rather than extrapolated to cover what that phrase represents in a modern context.

The Hebrew verb *'know'* has a wider semantic range than simply being aware of facts or having general knowledge; as in Gen. 4.1, the verb can portray the closest of human relationships, hence it is used to apply to the human-divine relationship.

It was the claimed exclusive relationship alluded to in v. 2 that then became grounds for the judgment or threat expressed in v.2b, with *'therefore ... I would punish ...'*. Amos's perspective on the special relationship emphasized the national responsibility, making Israel more culpable should it fail to live by what was regarded as an exclusive arrangement—one to be seriously questioned later in 9.7.

3.3-8

3 *Do two walk together unless they have made an appointment (to meet)?*
4 *Does a lion roar in the forest if it has no prey? Does a young lion cry out from its den if it has caught nothing?*
5 *Does a bird fall into a snare on the ground if there is no trap for it? Does a snare spring up from the ground if it has caught nothing?*
6 *If a trumpet is blown in a city, are the people not afraid? If disaster happens to a city, is it not Yahweh who has done it?*
7 *(Actually, my lord Yahweh does nothing without revealing his secret to his servants the prophets.)*
8 *The lion has roared; who would not be afraid? My lord Yahweh has spoken, who would not prophesy?*

This sub-section of six verses begins with a series of five rhetorical questions in 3.3-5, followed by two conditional clauses in 3.6, all in poetic form.

Verse 7 is in prose, making a statement about the divine manner of working, with 3.8 returning to poetic form in two additional rhetorical questions. As rhetorical questions, they equate to five strong negative statements. The topics that are the subject of the questions are varied, referring to friends out walking, lions roaring, birds and traps, trumpets and natural disasters. The variety makes difficult any argument as to their ascending to a climax, but that the section concludes with a reference to a prophet speaking may suggest that each question in 3.3-6 and 3.8a is preparatory for that ultimate focus on a 'prophet' speaking in v. 8b.

The initial five questions begin with the question marker (Heb. h^a) followed by a verb expressing a commonly occurring fact or situation, then a possible result or consequence cast in the negative. In the case of the two conditional clauses in 3.6, the initial *'im* introduces a potential event— 'if ...' or 'whenever ...'—as the second half asks a question in the negative as to its expected response. Two further rhetorical questions are asked in v. 8 with the question form appearing as the second half verse following a description of a state of affairs. It is the prose form in v. 7 that causes some discussion in the literature about its provenance, with many scholars considering it a later intrusion. Apart from its connection with the reference to 'prophets' and to 'speaking' in v. 8, there is no immediate explanation for its presence, however; see my note below. The overall thrust of the section relates to events or observations that are part of common experience and that have a cause in, and/or effect upon, those involved.

As an identifiable unit, it is clearly composed of four discrete examples from everyday life set around a general theme of causes and effects or responses. The story of its formation is probably complex, but in its present edited form it serves as a way of emphasizing that every action, whether of divine, human or animal origin, occurs within a context and that context is what validates the action. Each saying can also be turned around to say that a situation observed can only come about in given circumstances; for example, if there is no trap, then no bird is going to be snared in it; if it has not caught any prey, then a lion won't roar. These are all known and predictable realities, illustrative of the principle that every situation/event has its cause or explanation. It then concludes with the challenge in v. 8: just as one is fearful when the lion roars (example), one must 'speak out' (response) because Yahweh has spoken (cause). This principle is then illustrated in 3.9-11 and beyond.

3.3 The first question imagines two people walking together, a most common sight. The fact that they are walking together implies, at least for the purpose of this illustration, that there had been a mutually pre-arranged time, place and purpose leading to that scenario (though in some other contexts that may not have been the case). The rhetorical-question form in the negative is used, its point being to make a strong statement to which the answer is obvious—'No, of course, they are not walking together purely by chance—they obviously have made a prior arrangement to meet!' The Hebrew *nô'ādû* refers to some time or place agreed upon. The question is not an absolute example, but one that fits a context.

3.4 The next two questions draw on the lion and young lion and their respective habits of roaring in relation to hunting their prey. The lion only roars when it has been successful and caught its prey. While hunting, it is totally silent, but when it has caught and killed its prey, it roars to alert the family that it has caught something, and at the same time warning other lions to keep away. Likewise the young lion, here a neat parallel example, remains silent in its den as it has nothing to roar about, not having caught any prey. Hearing a lion roar is a sound that is linked directly with a particular event; it is not haphazard. The drama of lions roaring echoes the metaphor of Yahweh as the roaring lion in 1.2, though readers should not over-interpret the metaphorical language used in either case.

3.5 Here the examples are of birds and traps or snares. The question form states baldly that no bird falls from the sky into a trap if there is no trap (Heb. *môqēš*) there on the ground, presumably baited to attract the bird. It is an obvious fact supported by experience; it can be demonstrated as true. In v. 5b a related image of a ground-based snare (Heb. *paḥ*) 'jumping up' as its spring is released is not possible unless a bird manages to trip it and become caught. The two images are down-to-earth and indisputable. Using the rhetorical-question form emboldens the statement. An observable event always has a cause or contextual explanation.

3.6 Two potential or conditional situations are outlined. The first refers to the blowing of the *šôpar*, the ram's horn trumpet that serves as an alarm signal, or as a call to war or worship. Ancient cities usually had a watchtower, or series of watchtowers, on the walls, and these were manned in order to alert the inhabitants to persons approaching, be they friend or foe, as well as to observe signals that carried messages from nearby cities. Armies also used the distinctive sound of the shophar blast as a call to arms. Hearing the shophar being blown immediately alerts residents of a city to anticipate news of some kind. Whether it strikes fear or not depends on other factors, but the immediate response to the sound itself could be momentary fear, or at the very least, to wondering about its purpose and significance.

The second half of the verse moves the scenario to activity described as 'trouble/calamity' (Heb. *rāʿâ*). The noun form here implies some kind of catastrophic event or disaster befalling a town. That possibility is contextually clear. It is the second half of v. 6b that raises some issues, for it asks: *'Yahweh has not done/caused it?'* Generalizing from this question, as some commentators do, suggesting that every misfortune striking a city is the result of some divine intervention or punishment for sin, is obviously going too far, especially when no reason for the misfortune is here offered. Yet, one has to acknowledge the principle of a direct link drawn in the Deuteronomic ideology between meeting disaster and divine action as punishment. That seems to be the assumption operative in this example; otherwise the sensible response to the question would be, 'No, not necessarily!'

3.7 As for the prose statement that God does nothing without forewarning his spokesperson, it appears as a completely general statement of principle. As noted, many commentators agree that this is a late insertion that breaks the flow of the text. As such, I would prefer to read it as a quite separate aside or comment on the previous verse's claim, set in prose rather than poetry, to make it explicit as a comment. For translation purposes I place it within brackets.

If one actually accepts and agrees with the sentiment expressed so baldly in v. 6b, then v. 7 can be read as a concession or expression of hope that no matter what the disaster God plans to bring upon a city and its people, at least he might forewarn the inhabitants and explain why it is happening. How God might do that is not entertained. The thesis could be made clear by rendering the initial *kî* as an explicative, 'Actually, …', or 'But in fact, …', softening the extreme view that v. 6 appears to suggest. On the other hand, if one takes the Deuteronomic position and affirms that what v. 6 states is incontrovertible fact, then any attempt at explanation is pointless.

We note the use of the noun *dābār* as 'matter, thing' rather than 'word', and the unusual noun *sôdô* that refers to his counsel or advice, rendered in NRSV as 'secret'. The statement appears to be an all-embracing one, hyperbole at work. The verb *gālâ* speaks of uncovering something to make it evident and clear. Thus, the text makes the assertion that God reveals his intentions to his prophets/spokesperson—here also described as 'servants', an honorific title—to forewarn his people of a coming crisis. It is a statement of belief, whether true or not.

3.8 The structure of this short verse differs again by virtue of it placing the rhetorical question at the end of each half verse, while beginning each verse with a statement of fact. Both half verses are in strict parallel, the second half verse beginning with the question form *'who would not (verb) ...?'* (Heb. *mî lō'* ...), signaling the assertion that everyone would so do. The first half returns to the imagery of a lion roaring (3.4), as the second half elevates the discussion to that of a prophet responding to a divine word. The parallel forms mean that there is an analogy between them: just as the lion's roar causes fear, so the word of Yahweh induces those who are prophets to speak.

The core question is then, Is this merely a generalized pronouncement by Amos, or is it far more personal? Does it state a principle, or is it, as some wish to see, Amos's justification for his call to an irresistible 'prophetic' mission? If the latter, then it contrasts sharply with his denial in 7.14-15 that he was ever a prophet. For this reader, the entire section 3.3-8 has a single focus, that is, it focuses on situations that can be said to have a recognized cause or obvious explanation. Verse 8 is no exception; it offers yet another general statement of cause and effect, just as the principle stated in 3.2 makes plain.

The fact that the metaphor of the lion roaring recurs here has led some to link it closely with the character of Yahweh, and especially with Yahweh as presented in 1.2. This has led some to suggest that Israel is Yahweh's prey! For this reader, such an equation goes well beyond the scope of the metaphor as an attempt to particularize a general principle.

3.9-11

> 9 *Proclaim to the strongholds in Ashdod and the strongholds in Egypt, (and say) 'Gather together on the mountains of Samaria and note the many tumults within it, and the oppressive acts (done) in it'.*
> 10 *They do not know how to do (what is) right, says Yahweh, those who store up violence and devastation in their strongholds.*
> 11 *Therefore, thus says my lord Yahweh: an adversary will surround the land and strip you of your power and your strongholds be plundered.*

This short sub-section is reminiscent of those in 1.3–2.16, here as words directed to Ashdod, representing the Philistines, and Egypt, nations that were traditional enemies of Israel. Neither nation would get to hear these words, so what is the point? In the case of the earlier foreign nation oracles in 1.3–2.5, the intended audience was Israel itself, given a message that Yahweh would deal with its opponents. In this case, however, the two foreign nations are called to Samaria as witnesses; they are summoned to see and bear witness to what Yahweh would do against Israel itself, reversing the usual more hopeful message that the enemy would be overcome. Here the foreign nation oracle is once again turned against Israel rather than offering it comfort. The nations are summoned to witness the violence and injustice that is being charged against Israel. Then the specific punishment is outlined in v. 11, namely a stripping of Israel's power and the plundering of its strongholds. The reference to 'strongholds' connects to the formal features of the earlier oracle.

3.9 The text implies that this is Amos's address summoning Israel's enemies in Philistia and Egypt to come to the capital Samaria and bear witness to Israel's failings. Once again readers will note that the language is generalized. The imperatives used require everyone in Israel to issue the call, an obvious exaggeration, to be understood as a challenge to the nation. It is not to be taken as a literal invitation but as an indirect way to emphasize the nation's obvious failures. It was not expected that there would be formal delegations from Philistia and Egypt coming to see what was transpiring in Samaria. It is, after all, a literary device.

'Samaria' was the name of both a region, the mountainous area south and west of the Galilee and west of the Jordan Valley, and the main city that under Omri in the ninth century BCE became the northern capital; it was located between the mountains of Ebal and Gerizim. Major trade routes passed through the region. With its good soils and more plentiful rainfall there was an abundance of grassland for sheep, along with general cropping. Archaeology has revealed something of the architectural glory of the ancient city as well.

The use of 'strongholds' in reference to both Ashdod and Egypt is clearly metaphorical for the armies or delegations of both; a 'stronghold' is a defensive and immobile structure. Why these two entities are called to be witnesses is unclear but understandable as people representative of the two major southern fronts facing Israel. The text may be slightly problematic in that the LXX reads *Assur* (Assyria) rather than Ashdod, an understandable textual corruption since the Hebrew names as written may look similar and be mistaken—it wouldn't happen in an oral presentation—while Assyria was a common threat to the northern kingdom, actually capturing Samaria in 721 BCE. There is more than a touch of irony in inviting witnesses to come view the moral failings of the enemy.

The 'tumults' and 'oppressive acts' are summary terms for what Amos saw as the troubles in the north. Though vague and universal, they each represent a society that is profoundly disrupted by social divisions, corruption and injustice; this was the point of Amos's major criticism throughout. There is no specification here of what were regarded as religious failings, though that is made clear in other addresses such as 3.14 and 4.4-5.

3.10 Israel's problems are further stated as the people not knowing *'the deeds of straightforwardness'*, that is, honesty, as a result of which there is much violence and robbery, social breakdown. The picture is of these problems residing 'in their strongholds', in which case 'strongholds' is here a metaphor for the walled towns and cities throughout the land.

The addition of the phrase *'says Yahweh'* in mid-verse is probably a scribal addition that is unwarranted, especially as it breaks into the syntax of the sentence, separating the subject—*those who store up*—from the opening verb clause. Additionally, the fuller phrase follows in v. 11, making the insert here irrelevant.

3.11 Because of the problems listed in v. 11, Yahweh is said to be determined to act. The verse opens with a strong consequential link, *'Therefore ...'*, and speaks of the action to be taken as that of an enemy (Heb. *ṣar*) who will surround *the land*. Consistent with the generalized language used throughout, no enemy is nominated, but whether real or imagined, the implication is that the enemy will be sent and led by Yahweh. It will be the task of the enemy so raised to de-weaponize Samaria, weaken it, and plunder whatever was in its strongholds or palaces.

3.12
12 *Thus says Yahweh*

> *As the herder rescues from the lion's mouth two legs or part of an ear, just so shall the people of Israel who live in Samaria be saved by/with the corner of a couch or part of a bed.*

One of the more intriguing texts in this book is found here in a prose description of a rescue effort that saves a miniscule part of a herder's animal when taken as prey by a lion. It appears as an isolated text that has been placed in the general context of lions and their prey (3.4, 8), its function being to emphasize the extent of the de-weaponizing threat. It is obvious that when an animal is attacked by a lion, very little remains, and even less can be 'saved'. By 'rescuing' only a leg or two and part of an ear there is essentially nothing of the animal left, and, in any event, the animal having been killed, trying to 'save' half an ear is utterly pointless.

Scholars have wondered for some time about certain details in the text of v. 12, especially the prepositional phrases that speak of tiny parts of furniture items, of a couch and a bed. Presumably they could be items parallel to the small remaining parts of the animal, but the question is what are/were they used for? and how do they rescue from the lion's mouth? Nothing of any value remains seems to be the point.

Some commentators regard the two examples, the torn animal and the pieces of furniture, as similar, meaning that only a tiny piece of the furniture will be left—from what and for what?—just as little of the animal remains. But why choose a broken couch and bed as exemplars in such a context? To some readers, the *'corner of a couch and part of a bed'* suggest pieces of wood that were used as a weapon to drive the lion away in order to 'rescue' what was left of the animal, the preposition *b'* signifying agency, but that sounds utterly implausible to others. The imagery, whatever the precise sense, seems to relate somehow to the preceding threat to Samaria, a warning that the city could be almost completely destroyed, and with what does remain being of no value whatsoever. On the other hand, it is always possible that this analogy was an independent saying, or part of a saying, now editorially inserted at this point because of its reference to Samaria. We will never know for certain its significance, from where the verse originated, or where it might otherwise best fit.

Prefacing the verse with *'Thus says Yahweh'* but omitting the accompanying closing bracket happens often in these texts. As fixed *pro forma* elements, their use is more mechanical and literary than deeply significant theologically.

3.13-15

13 *Listen up and testify in the house of Jacob, says my lord Yahweh, God of Hosts.*
14 *On the day that I visit upon Israel its transgressions, I will punish the altars of Bethel, and the horns of the altar will be cut off and fall to the ground.*
15 *I will tear down the winter house as well as the summer house; and the houses of ivory shall perish, and the great houses shall come to an end,*

Says Yahweh.

The first question to be asked of this sub-section relates to the ones who are being addressed—it could well have originally been a message for Amos as the one who was to take note and then for him to testify, but given that the call to 'hear' is third-person plural—as is the call to testify—that seems unlikely, especially as each of the major sub-sections here (3.1; 4.1; 5.1) begins with the same plural imperative form, *šimʻû,* addressing an anonymous collective.

The focus is on punishment for Israel's transgressions (see *pešaʻ* in 1.3–2.5), in this case cultic or religious sins, with a second threat in v. 15 to demolish what appear to be its lavish houses. In fact, the noun 'house' is a keyword in this sub-section, suggesting its original independence as a speech unit, now placed in this wider block of material because of the opening call to 'hear'.

3.13 The call to listen and then testify implies that those called have been given a message to pass on, if Amos himself is not the one addressed. That message is intended for the 'house of Jacob', but the attached *b'* preposition is always flexible and context-dependent, so it could mean in/with/by/about, rather than 'against' Jacob as suggested by NRSV. The 'house of Jacob' generally refers to the entire Israelite community not just the northern kingdom (see also 9.8), and is frequent in exilic and postexilic books (e.g., Isa. 2.5; 14.1; 46.3; 48.1; Obad. 1.17-18).

In a reference to Yahweh, we find a unique complex phrase *'my lord Yahweh, God of Hosts',* adding to the special language used throughout this sub-section.

3.14 The text then refers to 'the day', a common notion in prophetic books, pointing to a moment or occasion at some undetermined but imminent time that could spell either rescue or punishment. Here it clearly signals a possible future punishment of Israel, but its practical outworking is directed at sacred objects rather than people—the altars in the royal sanctuary at Bethel will suffer desecration. Bethel, located north of Jerusalem, was the site of the north's royal sanctuary; it was regarded by the Deuteronomists as a rival to the Temple in Jerusalem and thus corrupted and corrupting. The 'horns' or projections on the four corners of the altars would be chopped off and left to fall to the ground. This threatened act of desecration essentially meant that worship at Bethel would no longer be possible or no longer effectual, as the 'horns' of the altar were often used in blood sacrifice ceremonies (Lev. 9.9), and were available to be gripped by anyone seeking sanctuary (1 Kgs 1.60).

3.15 Further destruction was threatened for 'the day', to result in houses being torn down. Four types of house are mentioned: winter houses, summer houses, ivory houses and great houses. It seems obvious that it was the wealthy who were targeted by this threat as they were the only ones who could afford a residence suitable in winter and another in a cooler region in which to escape summer heat. That it is the wealthy who are Amos's main targets here is further confirmed by the mention of 'houses of ivory', not that the house was actually made of ivory but that its appointments and decorations were of imported ivory. (Archaeological finds in Samaria attest to this feature.) The fourth type of house is described in Hebrew as *bāttîm rabbîm*, literally 'many houses' or 'great houses', perhaps on the basis of size or significance. It is obvious that Amos wants to place the blame for the social problems or inequity squarely on those with wealth, though displays of wealth *per se* were not necessarily justification for punishment—especially in the Deuteronomic worldview.

There is also an interesting play on words in the phrase 'summer houses' since the Hebrew *qāyiṣ*, 'summer', sounds like *qēṣ*, which means 'the end'. See also the vision in 8.1-2.

The sub-section closes with *'says Yahweh'*, an ending bracket despite missing an opening bracket.

4.1-13 'You Did Not Return to Me'

The fourth chapter begins another compilation of Amos's words addressed to the northern community; it too is introduced by the call *'Listen up!'* (Heb. *šim'û*). The section divides into three major sub-sections: 4.1-3, 4-5 and 6-13. The first is directed to the women of Bashan, the second more widely and with a religious focus, and the third sub-section reviews past actions that were intended to bring Israel back into a proper relationship with its God, each attempt having failed, so each verse or mini-section is concluded with the phrase, *'yet you did not return to me, says Yahweh'*, repeated six times. The final verse, 4.13, may be viewed as a doxology that closes the section, suggesting that the chapter has an identity of its own, that is, a collection of Amos's words that had been brought together before being included in the book's second major section in which *'Hear this word ...'* is the initial marker. Other doxologies are to be found in 5.8 and 9.5-6, all having similar wording.

In view of the threat of capture and exile in 4.1-3, the section can be presumed to relate to Amos's mission pre-721 BCE when the northern kingdom was overrun by the Assyrian enemy, Samaria decimated and many taken into Assyrian exile.

4.1-3

1 *Hear this word, you cows of Bashan who are on Mt. Samaria, who oppress the poor, who crush the needy, who say to their husbands, 'Bring something for us to drink!'*
2 *My lord Yahweh has sworn by his holiness: the time is surely coming upon you, when they shall take you away with hooks, even the last of you with fishhooks.*
3 *Through breaches in the wall you shall leave, each one straight ahead, and you shall be flung out into Harmon,*

Says Yahweh.

Amos directs this call to a certain female element of the population, the wealthy or privileged women living in Samaria. The region of Bashan was a fertile area, today known as the Golan Heights, east of the Galilee and famous for its agricultural produce and raising of cattle. The phrase *'cows of Bashan'* points to well-fed, quality animals, here used as a metaphor for fortunate, well-fed, wealthy or upper-class women. Whether this was a local and derogatory expression for the upper classes in Samaria at the time is uncertain, but it does have the ring of authenticity.

Three criticisms are levelled against these women. They are said to (1) oppress *the poor*, presumably by demanding more and heavier service of them, (2) crush *those in need* by making excessive demands of those who come to them for help or who work for them, and (3) demand they be provided with drinks. The *'poor and needy'* summarizes all those who were the objects of wealthier-class oppression. There is a little ambiguity here as the relationship between the women and those obliged to wait on them, in Hebrew *la'ᵃdonêhem*, with its masculine suffix is curious—the phrase could mean 'their own husbands' or 'their masters' (i.e. the masters of those who serve them). It is probably the former that is intended even though not strictly correct grammatically.

The pronouncement notes the division in Samaritan society, as in all societies, but here that harsh reality is exemplified in the way the wealthy then take advantage of the poor, and it is that that prompts Amos to rail against them. Amos was not against wealth *per se*, but against those who flaunted their wealth and easy living while oppressing the poor. The third charge, demanding drinks be brought, seems to imply their haughtiness and arrogance, requiring that others serve their selfish concerns.

Amos reminds his hearers that Yahweh has already sworn *'in/by his holiness'* that he would act. The swearing or pronouncing of an oath was one way to emphasize that what one intended to do would in fact be done. The basis of such a threat from the divine one is grounded in his holiness or uniqueness, the noun *qodšô* referring to the separate or unique quality of God, his 'godness'; 'holiness' is not primarily a moral characteristic in biblical terms but a cultic one. The imminent 'days' are always undefined, so the threat is a general challenge, in this case the women are threatened with being taken away into exile as captives. No agent is ever identified, so the threat just hangs there. The 'hooks' and 'fishhooks' are metaphors for instruments of torture, but the imagery does liken them to fish caught on a line. This was the fate Amos willed for every last one of the people he described as guilty of selfish living, literally 'those left behind of you'— this is hyperbole.

The women's threatened departure from Samaria to their eventual destination is described simply as through *'breaches in the wall'*, perhaps meaning that the people would be taken out through every place where the city walls had been broken through, though there is no mention of a possible attack on the city. The phrase *'each one* (Heb. *'iššâ*, 'each woman') *straight ahead*' implying that no matter where they were, *they*—the unidentified agents—would simply move the women out through the broken wall, with the adverb perhaps meaning that they would be tied together and led out in a line formation as was common. These details are deliberately vague.

The threat is that they could then be exiled toward Harmon. There is some question about the MT here as there is no known place Harmon, but there is a mountain, Hermon (Heb. *har harmôn*)—could this be a textual mistake, as LXX suggests? Hermon is in southern Syria, and north of the Bashan district, across the northern border of Israel. Regardless of its precise location, it speaks of potential exile for these oppressors of the poor.

4.4-5

> 4 *Come to Bethel—and transgress; to Gilgal—and multiply transgression; bring your sacrifices every morning, your tithes every three days,*
> 5 *Bring a thank-offering of leavened bread, and proclaim freewill offerings, publish them, for so you love to do, O people of Israel!*
>
> Says my lord Yahweh.

This brief sub-section reports another of Amos's interventions; it is deeply sarcastic and focused on northern Israel's religious life that, while apparently ordered and 'correct', was seen by Amos as corrupted. *Bethel*, as noted in 3.14, was the king's sanctuary, served by the priest Amaziah (7.10), who obviously was opposed to Amos's presence and activity in the northern kingdom. *Gilgal* is more difficult to identify as there were several places so named—one location was east of Jericho in the Jordan Valley (Josh. 4.19-20), another is on the northern border of Judah (Josh. 15.7), another north of Bethel (2 Kgs 2.1-4). In the present context it simply serves to emphasize that at any sacred site in the northern kingdom religious observance was an act of rebellion against God—that was the Deuteronomic standpoint.

Amos 'invited' everyone to go to their religious sanctuaries and there to 'sin', meaning that by participating in its 'false' religious or cultic activities, bringing their tithes, and making sacrifices and a variety of offerings as required. Rather than atone for their transgressions, however, coming to these centres to worship would compound their sin because it was illicit. In its present form the speech does not accuse the worshipper of any specific failure; it simply equates all formal cultic activity in the north's religious centres with transgression itself. It must be remembered that Amos was a representative of the Judaean or Deuteronomic perspective, according to which, by failing to worship in Jerusalem, the place where Yahweh 'put his name', and by worshipping elsewhere, the northerners were committing grave error. Setting up rival sanctuaries in the north and preventing his followers access to Jerusalem was the major 'sin' of Jeroboam I, founder of the northern kingdom—see 1 Kgs 12.25-33—and now it was the sin of its people. A second explanation is that the kinds of transgression listed in 2.6-8, 12, such as injustice and the oppression of the poor, made all religious activity null and void because it did not spring from an honest desire to seek God or to honour Yahweh by compassionate and just lives; cultic activity of every form became offensive because it was based in hypocrisy.

The section consists of a series of seven imperatives and is completely universal in its expression, embracing all in the northern kingdom. As a charge it is indiscriminate and reflects Amos's negative attitude toward all members of the northern kingdom—it is seriously overdone. He further generalizes his southern negative attitude by suggesting that the northerners participate happily in this kind of cultic romp that can have only a negative result.

A final form *'says Yahweh'* closes this sub-section, as it does all others in this chapter.

4.6-12
> 6 *I gave* you cleanness of teeth in every one of your cities and a shortage of food in each of your places,
>
> But you did not turn back to me,

Says Yahweh.

> 7 *I also withheld* rain from you while there was yet three months to the harvest; *I would make it* rain on one city but not rain on another; one field would receive rain while the one on which it did not rain withered.
> 8 Two or three towns would go to another town to fetch water to drink, but it was never enough.
>
> But you did not turn back to me.

Says Yahweh.

> 9 *I struck you* with blight and mildew, laying waste your gardens and vineyards; locusts ate your fig trees and olive trees,
>
> But you did not turn back to me,

Says Yahweh.

> 10 *I sent pestilence* among you in the manner of Egypt; *I killed* your young men with the sword; I carried off your horses; *I made you* smell the stench of your own camp,
>
> But you did not turn back to me,

Says Yahweh.

> 11 <u>I overthrew</u> some of you as God had overthrown Sodom and Gomorrah, and you were like a brand snatched from the fire,
>
> <u>But you did not turn back to me,</u>

Says Yahweh.

> 12 THEREFORE, this is what I would do to you, Israel. <u>Indeed</u>, this is what I would do to you:
>
> PREPARE TO MEET YOUR GOD, ISRAEL!

Once again Amos's words take the hearer/reader back to the past. This time the editor has compiled a series of five claims about divine intervention in the nation's past, reminding of the various events and ways in which God is believed to have imposed natural disasters (see 3.6b), in this case with a view to turning the people back to a right relationship with God. Each attempt, however, proved ineffective, failing to achieve its intended goal. Each case is expressed in so generalized a manner that no specific incident is identifiable. These examples are further evidence that Amos was not confining his comments to the north, for this catalogue of issues was the common experience of all in Canaan.

What impact such a vague description might have had originally is uncertain, but it does raise serious issues for any reader's concept of the divine one (see **Amos's Theological View** in the Introduction). It is difficult for most if not all readers to acknowledge that Amos subscribed to the view of God as one who deliberately and cruelly subjected his people to hardship in order to acquire their allegiance. It also assumes that the people could put two and two together and interpret their suffering as divinely driven and intentional.

The literary structure of the section is clearly observable, each event concluding with the repeated phrase '*But you did not return to me*'. This compilation may well reflect an original oral performance, with the final call in v. 12 an essential part of that oral delivery.

Amos's view of God conforms very closely with the Deuteronomic perspective. That perspective is set out in detail in Deut. 28.15-46, listing the many 'curses' that might overwhelm those who fail to keep God's commandments. They can also be seen in another form in 1 Kgs 8.33-40. What it reveals is the extent to which Amos reflects a theology in which God uses natural phenomena, and creation more generally, as a means of either blessing or cursing his people; God, as Creator, uses his handiwork as a tool to reward or to punish. What stands out initially is that these are statements of belief about a God who inflicts natural disasters upon his people, yet without here offering any explanation for them being inflicted on all indiscriminately. That theology is so characteristic of the Deuteronomists and their historical reporting that it remains one of the more dominant theological traditions in the Hebrew Bible. The examples of crises that Amos outlines here are what he and others believed signaled to Israel that there was something unacceptable about its relationship with the divine, and thus each crisis was a call for them to 'turn back/be restored' (Heb. *šwb*). This key verb, often calling for 'repentance', is better understood as a broader call for a *mutual* 'returning' to one another, to reconciliation, rather than just Israel turning to its God—see, for example, Joel 2.12-14.

Whether, as some suggest, this means that material like that in this section can therefore be dated as exilic, post-587 BCE, and thus from a later hand than that of Amos, is fundamentally wrong because although the Deuteronomistic materials in final form may be that late, the roots of the tradition have to go back much further. It is this reader's view that Amos and his editor were well aware of the perspective of the tradition in its incipient form from a date in the late eighth century BCE.

4.6 The first example speaks of a lack of food caused by divine intervention, that lack ironically presented as a 'gift'. The noun phrase *'cleanness of teeth'* is a cultural metaphor for a lack of food to eat—the noun *'bread'* being representative of all food. As is typical of these five examples, this first one is completely generalized and unidentifiable though the reality was that famine and food shortage was a frequent experience in Canaan, especially the farther south into Judah one moved.

The structure of the verse exhibits parallelism in vv. 6b and 6c, followed by the concluding v. 6d, *'But you did not return to me'* (Heb. *wᵉlo'-šabtem 'āday*).

4.7-8 This example is more developed literarily; it begins with the statement that God withheld *gešem,* a general term for 'rain' (e.g. Gen. 7.12). Following the gift of famine and food shortage (4.6), God now refuses to give rain. The verbs used in this sub-section are imperfective, indicating frequent occurrence.

Without rain all vegetation suffers, and such was a frequent experience in the Canaanite region, more so in the south than the north, due to natural geographic factors. The expanded description adds that this happened three months before the harvest, that is, during the most crucial growing period for any crop. Yahweh is then claimed to have selectively discriminated, making it rain in one location and not in another, with the inevitable result that crops in the dry zone withered and the harvest failed. Additionally, the water supply that sustains life was limited, causing people to go from one town to another in a vain search for enough water to drink. While this might well have been a regular experience for some parts of the region, especially in the south, to attribute this to a deliberate divine act presents God as cruel and inhumane, a natural outcome from the underpinning theological view of the Deuteronomic tradition. It should not be held up as definitive!

4.9 A further 'strike' from God was the onset of blight and mildew that ravaged the gardens in which cereal crops and vines grew. This was followed by a plague of locusts that devoured the fig and olive trees, impacting all basic food sources of the region. This too had failed to have the desired effect on the community, it was said.

4.10 Yet again, said Amos, God sent the pestilence or plagues just as had happened in Egypt. The reference takes the hearer/reader back to the exodus tradition in which numerous plagues, followed by the loss of Pharaoh's army and its horses, are used as examples of what had happened also to Israel at some unspecified point. There is no actual correspondence between the Egyptian loss by drowning and the loss of Israel's warriors by the sword, but the analogy can broadly serve. The reference to the stench of the camp could be a vague reference to the stench of decomposing bodies of the dead and dying soldiers on the battlefield. Despite these negative divine 'contributions', the repeated phrase again claims that these actions failed to achieve their intended result.

4.11 The last of the five strophes offers an even more vague reference as the nature of the particular 'overthrow' (Heb. *hāpak*) is simply likened to that of the cities of Sodom and Gomorrah, the two cities that, according to the tradition, were destroyed because of a shameful event said to have taken place there (see Gen. 18–19). In this new example, no particular city or region or event is identified, nor is there any way of telling whether it refers to the nation as a whole or just to the north. So once again we have to contend with a very vague generalization. What is intriguing is that as Lot and his family were the only ones rescued from 'the fire and brimstone' that were said to have engulfed Sodom and Gomorrah, so too here, only *'some of you'* were so fated to be overthrown, like sticks snatched from the larger fire. This tiny remnant idea appears to refer to a present group rather than to those spoken of in the earlier examples, all of which seem to be much further in the past. Nevertheless, whatever the action, it apparently did not have the hoped-for result of seeing the people 'turn back' to God.

4.12 Based on the preceding set of reminiscences and its catalogue of failures, the climax comes with its powerful threat. The introductory 'Therefore ...' (Heb. *lākēn*) is a regular feature of similar historical reminders (3.11; 5.11, 13, 16; 6.7). Here the threat is repeated for maximum effect: '*Thus* (Heb. *kōh*) *would I do to you, O Israel; So indeed* (Heb. *'ēqeb kî*) *this I would do to you*'. What is it that constitutes 'this' in such a threat? The threat is of an encounter with 'your God', the God who has just been spoken of, the one whose 'gifts' or 'withdrawals' have brought such hardship in the past. What form would that meeting take? Would it be a repeat of the divine acts of the past in a new generation? Or would it differ? More importantly, would it expect the same outcome, no fresh 'turning back'? While the threat sounds ominous, there is little but the imagination to guide interpretation. How would Amos's hearers react to this threat unless at the time he gave more of a hint as to what events or crises he was referring to?

4.13

> 13 *For behold!*
>
> *The one who formed the mountains, and who created the wind, who reveals his thoughts to humanity, who makes the morning darkness, and treads on the high places of the land,*
>
> *Yahweh, God of hosts is his name!*

The final verse in what I have argued is a complete unit (4.1-13) is the first of three doxologies in the book; the others are found in 5.8 and 9.5-6. Here it is in praise of the Creator, the lord, Yahweh, God of hosts. It is typified by participles describing five aspects of the divine power—'*maker of mountains, creator of the wind, revealer of ideas, maker of darkness, treader on the heights*'—and concluding with the expression '*Yahweh (the God of hosts) is his name*'. This ringing shout ends the doxology, as in each of the three examples. They also share a focus on cosmology rather than on any past historical activity involving Israel.

The Hebrew noun *śēḥô*—here rendered '*his thoughts*'—is a problem in that this is its only occurrence and its precise sense therefore is completely dependent on the context. In other words, we have only an educated guess at its meaning. There is a general consensus that it has something to do with thoughts, plans or ideas, but there remains an ambiguity—are they thoughts or ideas of humans themselves, or is the 'his' a reference to God and his plans? Further ambiguity—a feature of poetry?—is present in the phrase 'the one who makes the morning darkness' or is it 'darkness into dawn'? An unquestioned resolution is impossible, especially in light of the LXX's fourth-century BCE text with its forced link to a messianic idea!

5.1-17 'Seek the Lord and Live'

The structure of Amos the book that this reader is suggesting is most helpful incorporates these verses within the book's second major section. Its inclusion is based on the call to *'Hear this word ...'* with which each of its three chapters begins (3.1; 4.1; 5.1). In my reading I regard 5.18–6.14 as a separate and third major section of the book, organized around the formal phrase *'Woe to those who ...'* (5.18; 6.1, 4) and its concern with the 'day of the Lord'.

In the case of its opening call, the 'word' to be heard is a lamentation that brackets the section (5.1, 16), though the theme does also appear in 5.18-20 that has been appended. The lamentation is not a divine word but that of Amos (5.1), despite the editorial addition of the *pro forma* markers of divine speech. A deep concern with the twin issues of 'justice' and 'righteousness' is central (5.7, 24), along with a theme of 'darkness' and 'light' (5.8, 18, 20), suggesting that the editor has brought together a number of Amos's comments that he was anxious to have the community 'hear'.

The section, as noted, offers another 'word' from Amos that is characterized as lamentation (Heb. *qinah*). His lamenting is general, since the lament itself does not follow any of the fixed literary forms that are found throughout the lament literature, or such as are present in the Psalms collection. For example, there is no questioning as to 'why?' and 'how long?' an innocent person might suffer, nor is there any appeal for rescue, nor a priestly word of assurance that the request has been heard, nor a concluding thanksgiving. There is a general reference to public mourning and wailing in 5.16-17, but this merely describes the community's reaction to what appears to be an agricultural problem, and it ends with divine inattention—the Lord will merely *'pass you by'*—hardly what Amos would have wanted. Additionally, there is no explanation offered for this divine passby. The *pro forma* 'tags' that begin and close reported divine speech appear surrounding the 'lament' in 5.16-17, which is attributed to the Lord, but its content notes that it is the people who lament and wail, rather than Amos, and certainly not the Lord who merely passes on. Confusion is obvious in the details of the text as presently reported.

The section 5.1-17 can be further divided as:

5.1-3 Amos laments that Israel has 'fallen' with no hope of recovery;
5.4-7 a call to 'seek the Lord and live!';
5.8-9 a doxology;
5.10-13, 14-15, 16-17 lamenting the lack of justice 'at the (city) gate' where all matters were negotiated.

The calls to *'seek the Lord and live'* (5.4, 6, 14) surrounding the doxology of 5.8-9 and leading into a final component describing the lament in 5.16-17 provide the two keywords—*seek, live*—in this core section of the book. It becomes evident on closer examination that the section is a collection of shorter sayings, each of which is marked by its own ideas and vocabulary, but now set within the broader call to 'Listen up!'

For some time now the suggestion that 5.1-17 has a chiastic structure forming the book's core has become a widely accepted view despite the fact that 'it does not all fit neatly', as its original proposer himself admits (de Waard and Smalley, *Handbook on the Book of Amos,* Appendix, Fig. 2). This reader prefers to view the section as a compilation of various sayings of Amos that do not have a great deal of linkage one to the other.

5.1-3
1 *Hear this word that I raise against you, a lament, O house of Israel:*
2 *Fallen, never to arise again is the young woman Israel, forsaken on her land with none to raise her up.*
3 *Truly, my master Yahweh spoke thus: The city of which a thousand went out shall have a hundred remaining, and that of which a hundred went out shall have ten remaining, for the house of Israel.*

As noted, the opening words initiate a call addressed to a community, the 'house of Israel', normally a term applied to the entire Israelite people. The words are those of Amos in the mode of lamentation, a cry to God from the heart, yet lacking every formal component of the established lament forms. It conveys a sense of hopelessness as the community is decimated (v. 3), but for what cause is left unspoken, unless the following added sub-sections are intended to provide the reasons. The general tone seems to presume a military defeat, though the verb simply speaks of 'going out' (exile?), from which there will be no recovery. Those who have fallen would have none to help raise them up again, and the remaining 10 percent are imagined as powerless to assist one another. As a statement it lacks any appeal for help such as one might expect in a lament. This initial unit uses a traditional '10 percent left' model (5.3) to describe the hopelessness of the situation.

Israel is referred to three times using two metaphors—'the house of Israel' (Heb. *bêt-yiśrā'ēl*) and 'the young woman Israel' (Heb. *bᵉtûlat yiśrā'ēl*). It is typical to use a feminine metaphor when speaking of cities and nations. Using the metaphor of a young woman, even a girl, perhaps evokes an unfulfilled life, but unfortunately the text gives no explanation for her hopeless situation other than what has been charged elsewhere against the whole of society.

Verse 3 is introduced by one of the many *pro forma* editorial inserts, '*my master Yahweh spoke thus*', to give Amos's words a greater gravitas. The final phrase, '*for the house of Israel*', is awkward, and many translations omit it, but it can in fact be viewed as an inclusion with the opening v. 1.

5.4-7

    4 *Indeed, my master Yahweh spoke thus to the house of Israel:*
       Seek me and live!

    5 *Do not seek Bethel (the house of El) nor go into Gilgal, neither cross over into Beersheba, for Gilgal would certainly go into exile and Bethel come to nothing.*

    6 *Seek the Lord and live! Lest he ... like fire (on) the house of Joseph, and it devour with none (able to) quench it, for Bethel.*

    7 *Oh the ones who overthrow justice for wormwood and leave righteousness lying on the ground.*

The first thing to notice about this sub-section is that it has nothing to do with the issue in the preceding verses; also, it has little to do with formal lamentation. It does seem to stand alone with two imperative calls to *seek* and *live*. Additionally, vv. 4-5 present as a chiastic structure—Bethel-Gilgal-Beersheba-Gilgal-Bethel—though the precise function of that is unclear as there is no focus on the central component, Beersheba. It does seem odd that two southern centres, Gilgal and Beersheba, are noted if Amos's address actually concerned only the north, to which he was supposedly called. Beersheba was a border town in the far south of Judaea. It was not a prominent religious centre, but is here included as a place to be avoided for fear of being exiled, though no exilic destination is mentioned. In the case of Gilgal and Bethel, it is obvious that Amos views any cultic activity there as counterproductive.

The notion of 'seeking' the Lord is a common religious or cultic expression, a focused intentional desire to do as God requires, a manner of living in the covenant relationship (see Deut. 4.29; Prov. 8.17; 28.5). Combined with the verb '*live*' it offers a result, the promise of a life that enjoys all the blessings that God is able to give. Here 'live' is practical, everyday living, and as the verbs are plural, reminds that this is not some individualistic or spiritual concept; rather, it is collective, communal and social.

In 5.6, however, the call seems more like a threat, but the meaning of the Hebrew verb ṣlḥ in the expression *Lest he ... like fire (on) the house of Joseph* is problematic. Translators have guessed at a meaning that they think may be contextually adequate, and the LXX is of little help—I have opted to omit the verb for the simple reason that its meaning here is unknown. The use of fire as a metaphor for complete destruction echoes that in 1.3–2.16.

The frequent use of the noun *'house'* meaning 'people of ...' is an interesting element in the presentation, carrying as it does a slight on Bethel, the 'house of God', a sanctuary where God is dishonoured (4.4). The *'house of Joseph'* phrase is one normally applied to the northern kingdom, otherwise known as Ephraim and Manasseh, the tribes said to descend from the two Egyptian-born sons of Joseph. It is more than possible that the name 'Joseph' here carries a pejorative tone, given that the sons were known to be half Egyptian (Gen. 41.50-52).

Verse 7 takes up once again the theme of being overthrown (Heb. *hāpak*) seen in 4.11 and again in 5.24. It is a very descriptive way of speaking of the seriousness of trashing or subverting, in this case, the twin values of 'justice and righteousness' (Heb. *mišpāṭ ûṣᵉdāqâ*). The first, justice, is turned to wormwood, a poisonous plant, and the second, righteousness, 'thrown to the ground'. Both metaphors speak of the perversion of social and moral principles that should underpin Israelite society. In the context of calling the community to seek the Lord and living (or, coming alive), Amos was calling for those values to be restored; it would in reality mean turning back to the Lord, something that had failed previously (see 4.6-12).

5.8-9

> 8 *The one who formed kîmâ and kᵉsîl and overthrows/turns deep darkness into the morning, and makes daytime darken to night, he who calls the waters of the sea and pours them out on the surface of the earth,*
>
> *Yahweh is his name.*
>
> 9 *He who ... destruction against the strong and destruction comes upon the fortress.*

Like 4.13, the refrain in v. 8 is a doxology in praise of Yahweh as Creator with its climactic point being the cry *'Yahweh is his name!'*; the cry follows the listing of the divine one's cosmic powers, each identified using participles: they are, *'he who makes/creates ... he who overturns ... he who calls out ... he who pours out ...'*. While referring to God's creative powers that can change light to darkness and reverse, however, it also highlights God's destructive power in bringing floods upon the earth, good and ill, both deriving from divine action.

Along with the themes of darkness and light, morning and night, of the seas, and of God's control over them, is that of the overthrow of other cosmic powers, the stars Pleiades (Heb. *kîmâ*) and Orion (Heb. *kᵉsîl*). Its affirmation that *'Yahweh is his name'* is repeated again in 5.27.

Verse 9 has been attached, I presume by the editor, because of a similar focus on divine power, though its presence here has the air of an afterthought, suggesting that it was probably originally an independent statement. The verb in v. 9 is so uncertain that I have left it untranslated, though it is clear that it must have something to do with bringing destruction—cognate languages suggest it may relate to a flash of light, while some commentators think emending the Hebrew text is required.

The doxology and the attached description of Yahweh's power interrupt the flow of the discussion on justice and righteousness in vv. 6-7, a discussion that then resumes in v. 10.

5.10-13
> 10 <u>They</u> hate the one who judges at the gate, and abhor the one speaking truth,
> 11 <u>Therefore</u>, on account of your trampling on the poor and taking from them grain tax, you have built houses of dressed stone, but you will never live in them, planted wonderful grapevines, but you will never drink their wine.
> 12 Truly, I know of your many transgressions, and the extent of your sins, you who oppress the righteous and take a bribe, then turn aside the needy at the gate.
> 13 <u>Therefore</u>, should the wise one remain silent at this time, for it is a troubling time?

As noted above, these verses return to the lament theme of justice and righteousness after the doxological insert and its attachment, v. 9.

An initial issue in this sub-section is the mysterious use of an undefined third-person plural subject, *they*, before reverting to second-person in v. 11. That issue aside, the reason for the lament is that 'they' are full of hate for the individual who is charged with prosecuting (Heb. *môkîᵃḥ*) cases where the poor come seeking justice, whether they come as the offended party or as one giving evidence. In addition, their sin is greater because 'they' then take advantage of those whom their hatred treats so badly, while all the time enjoying an extravagant lifestyle at the expense of the poor. 'They' are obviously members of the corrupted elite of the community.

The phrase '*at the gate*' in vv. 10, 12 serves as an inclusion, focusing the threat on Israel's judicial process. Archaeologists have uncovered the remains of many cities throughout the region in which the entrance is marked by a series of what were rooms immediately inside the city's gate. Ruth 4.1-6, 11 reports on one of the purposes for which these rooms at the city entrance were used—legal matters were discussed and settled; also, taxes were paid on goods incoming and outgoing, social issues were negotiated, so 'the gate' was the social and administrative hub of the community.

Verse 10 thus makes the basic charge, defining that to which 'overthrowing the law' in v. 7 was referring.

Verse 11 is Amos's response, his explanation of what could result for them from this attitude that brings about such injustice. The one seeking to administer justice and the one giving testimony are the objects of 'their' hatred, then described as a *trampling on the poor*, stealing the money paid as a grain levy and using it for their personal benefit. The Hebrew text is not totally without problems in this verse, but the general drift of the *'therefore, because ...'* clause is clear. The 'they' whose hatred is the focus are accused of having built houses of 'dressed stone'. While most housing may have been of field/undressed stone, there were others who could afford dressed stone. Amos says they should not get to live in the homes they had built, while others who had planted vines on their land should never get to enjoy the wine that would eventually be produced. Both of these threats use hyperbole to make the point that this hatred, this attitude to the poor and to the justice process, could end badly for them. Amos's reasoning was that God knows how profound were their transgressions, their use of bribery and lack of care for those in need. See also 2.6.

Verse 13 is an interesting verse, technically the conclusion to 5.10-12, yet unrelated in terms of its content. That the *maskîl* or wise person, not necessarily a recognized sage, should *remain silent* (Heb. *yiddom*) in the face of injustice runs contrary to all that Amos represented. While it is true that wisdom may at times call for silence in certain circumstances (see Eccl. 3.7), that is not what Amos here was intending, surely. So, what is this verse doing or saying about responding to the circumstances reported? If v. 13 can be detached from its present location on semantic grounds and treated as an independent statement, this reader suggests that it presumably has been added to the text at some point in its journey to this final written form. Furthermore, as there are several books in the scroll in which the central verse(s) serves a structural purpose—for example, Joel 2.17 and Obad. 1.11—and as 5.13 is virtually the central verse in this book with 71 verses preceding and 74 following, this may explain its current presence and location.

What I am suggesting is that there is a more contextually appropriate reading and rendering of 5.13 in place of what appears so negative and incongruous a statement for Amos to have made in response to the situation. My translation of v. 13 above is based on the present Hebrew consonantal text and reads the *hammaskîl* not as a simple defined noun, 'the wise one', but reads the initial *he* as the interrogative particle. Thus, I read it as, *'Therefore, would a wise person remain silent at such a time ...?'* As a rhetorical question implying reflection and denial of fact, it would be a fitting conclusion to the matter raised by vv. 10-12 and offer an appropriate core statement for the book as a whole.

5.14-17

14 *Seek <u>good</u> and not <u>evil</u>, that you may live, and then may Yahweh, the God of hosts be with you, as you have said.*
15 *Hate <u>evil</u> and love <u>good</u>, and ensure justice in the gate; perhaps Yahweh the God of hosts will show mercy to those who remain of Joseph.*
16 *Therefore, thus says Yahweh the God of hosts, my master, 'In every square let there be wailing and in every street let them say "Oh! Oh!"'*
And let them call the farmers to mourning, the specialist lamenters to wailing,
17 *In every vineyard wailing, because I will pass by in the midst of you,*
Said Yahweh.

Once again we encounter the 'Seek ..., and live ...!' formula, the third such call in this section of the book. Here it is precisely 'seek good' in contrast to seeking evil, both rather abstract notions, but in the context defining the 'good' as Yahweh, as well as all matters that are so qualified, including the best way to establish a more just society. Amos offers the community the assurance that God's active presence was available, and a chiasm emphasizes that message—good–evil–evil–good. This is not a 'prophetic' statement but simply one based on Amos's theology and the people's own confession. The section is characterized by conditional expressions such as 'perhaps Yahweh will ...' (v. 14b) and Hebrew *'ûlai*, 'maybe' (v. 15). Repetition of the phrase 'in the gate' (vv. 10, 12, 15) further links the calls to seek Yahweh.

In v. 14 the call to 'seek' (Heb. *diršû*) returns—see notes on 5.4. The 'good' in this context refers to all that relates to following Yahweh, living in a manner that is just and compassionate, in contrast with 'evil' (Heb. *rā'*), which can only refer to the kinds of transgressions already outlined. This style of good living will lead to 'life', that is, being part of a society in which justice determines the values and relationships of all classes. This manner of living equates to the divine presence with and within the community. The phrase *'just as you have said'* seems to imply that the community has either a vague notion or even a more formal confession in which all claim to depend upon some sense of the divine presence to sustain them. It hints at a situation in which Amos was speaking with a group who responded to his challenge with an affirmation (or was it an excuse?) that they believed God was present with them. The divine presence with his people was a basic belief within the Israelite community as a whole, a belief linked with the exodus tradition (Exod. 6.1-9) and later pushed back as far as the Abraham tradition (Deut. 4.1).

The divine title *Yahweh, God of hosts*, is one of several slightly variant forms used throughout this book.

Verse 15 focuses on the call for justice to be administered faithfully. The verb speaks of establishing a principle, setting something in place, namely *mišpāṭ*, 'justice'. The phrase '*in the gate*' (as in vv. 10, 12) points to the communal gathering place just inside the city gate where all formal business was transacted. If this were to happen, then Amos expects (Heb. *'ûlay*) God would continue to show mercy to the community, here referred to as the '*remnant of Joseph*'. This 'remnant' (Heb. *šeʾērît*) phrase should not be read as though the remnant was just the 'left-overs', an English term that is pejorative, but as a way of referring to the surviving descendants of Joseph, as in 5.6, though some commentators prefer to read it as mercy extended only to a limited number, and that to the few who might survive the destruction of Samaria in 721 BCE.

Verses 16-17 seem not to be directly dependent upon the preceding vv. 14-15 as the introductory '*Therefore* ...' turns to a scene in which the whole community is lamenting, as in 5.1-2. It can be regarded as the conclusion to the sub-section 5.1-17, rather than just that of the third call to *seek Yahweh*. What it does do literarily also is, it serves as an introduction to the following collection of '*Woe* ...' forms (5.18–6.14), what this reader considers as transitioning to the fourth section of Amos the edited report.

Following the expanded reference to 'Yahweh, God of hosts, my Master', the key-word '*wailing*' (Heb. *mispēd*) appears three times to emphasize the lamentation that would potentially sweep the community. '*Alas, alas*' heard in the town squares, its streets, farms and vineyards, involves ordinary and specialist wailers (see, e.g., Jer. 9.16-17), as all join voice together. The cause of such community-wide lamentation is that they would see God as having passed them by, meaning that God has abandoned them. Some commentators have sought to link the closing phrase with that of Exod. 12.12 and God's 'passing through' the Egyptian community, devastating Israel's oppressor. That context differs considerably from the Amos 5 context where oppression of the poor by the wealthy is the setting. Here it is the entire community that is called to wail and lament its own transgressions.

The editor rounds off the section with a closing formula, '*says Yahweh*', despite Yahweh being referred to in the third-person (5.14), indicating that the speech itself belongs to Amos, not Yahweh.

5.18–6.14 'Woe to Those Who . . .'

5.18-27 The Day of the Lord

This is what I have suggested is the third section in the book, a collection of Amos's messages gathered around the theme of wailing or lamenting. It begins with 5.18, though anticipated by 5.16-17, and features a key phrase referring to the day of Yahweh as *'darkness and not light'* (5.18, 20), with a second lament collection at 6.1-7

It is composed of two shorter sections (5.18-27 and 6.1-14) with some parallel wording. The tone of the whole section is one of warning and doom, with the repeated expressions *'Woe to …'* (5.18; 6.4) and *'I hate, I despise ... I take no delight in ...'* (5.21), and *'I abhor ... and hate ...'* (6.8). The alternative is the demand for justice and righteousness (5.24; 6.12). The language is mostly poetic, but there are two inserted narrative notes, 5.25-27 and 6.9-10.

5.18-20
> 18 *Woe are those of you who are longing for the day of Yahweh; what on earth is the day of Yahweh to you? It is darkness, not light.*
> 19 *It is as though a man fled from a lion and was confronted by a bear, or entered a house, placed his hand against a wall and was bitten by a snake.*
> 20 *Is it not darkness, the day of Yahweh, and not light? Or gloom with no brightness in it?*

The clear focus here is the nature of the 'day of Yahweh' as something not to be so eagerly anticipated, for it represents that which is dark, not light. The nouns 'darkness' and 'light' are metaphors for a wide range of negative and positive values, and together they provide an *inclusio* for the sub-section 5.18-20. Here the doublet *'darkness and not light'* represents a set of circumstances or events that are far from positive; 'the day' was not something to which to look forward. Yet it appears that the community was so expectant—why? There has been nothing in the text to date that would suggest that Amos had anything positive to say about the community's prospects for a bright future; rather, the message has all been about their failures and transgressions, which put them under threat of divine punishment. The 'day', as Amos foreshadows it, could be a dark one.

I have rendered v. 18b as 'What on earth is the day ... to you?', a rhetorical question that uses the strong pronoun *lāmmāh-zeh*, 'Why (is) this to you ...?' or 'For what to you (is) this?' to draw out the emphatic nature of the question. It is then followed by the two examples (5.19) of terrible misadventure—quite literally, 'out of the frying pan and into the fire'! Escaping the lion only to be met by a bear, or entering the safety of one's home only to be bitten by a (poisonous?) snake, is illustrative of the people's misplaced optimism with regard to the day—it will be even more severe than they could imagine, and certainly not a day to rejoice on seeing enemies defeated and one's own rescued, as it is often portrayed. These two examples, especially that of the snake, could well be traditional wisdom-related examples known throughout the community (see Eccl. 10.8, 11).

Verse 20 then sharpens the point with the rhetorical question: '*Is it not, the day of Yahweh, darkness and not light ...?*' The structural change, placing the subject first, adds power to the repeated assertion that the 'day' is one of darkness, of punishment, rather than of rejoicing.

5.21-24

21 *I hate, I despise your festivals, nor do I enjoy your solemn assemblies,*
22 *Even if you offer up to me burnt offerings and offerings of grain I won't accept them, peace offerings of fatted animals I will not look upon,*
23 *Take away from me the sound of your songs, and I will not listen to the tunes from your harps,*
24 *But let justice roll down like water and righteousness like a perennial stream.*

Much in this sub-section is cast in the most general and negative of tones, covering all festivals and cultic gatherings: there are three '*I will not ...*' phrases that follow the two initial verbs '*I hate ..., I despise ...*', until the conclusion rises to one of the highest moments in the book altogether—the call for justice and righteousness to overflow in the life of the community. It is one of the most significant moments of Amos the book, charged with deep emotion. Amos's core message was that justice and righteousness throughout society were far more important to God than any religious devotion—a very contemporary reminder. Again, the statement can be applied to the whole nation, not just the north, but perhaps particularly relevant to the north since the Deuteronomic view was that ANY worship outside of the Jerusalem Temple was false.

Beginning this speech with the two verbs 'hate' and 'despise' makes a powerful statement, something that Amos's audience would not forget easily as he denounced the present state of affairs in northern Israel. It bears all the hallmarks of oral speech—short, sharp statements in the imperative, culminating in the climactic demand for justice and righteousness. Readers can imagine Amos speaking thus at the royal sanctuary in Bethel and its inevitable consequences for him as he applied the language of the Deuteronomic perspective to the nation's cultic life.

The unit introduces a number of Israelite religious terms: *ḥag*, or Hajj, which refers to a pilgrimage festival that often involved dancing; *'aṣrot*, solemn assemblies, such as on the day after the Feast of Weeks (Neh. 8.18); *'olâ*, offerings burnt on the altar; *minḥâ*, an offering of grain after the harvest; *šelem*, a peace offering. At Israel's various festivals there would have been much feasting, music, singing and dancing in celebration. None of this was acceptable, no offering was accepted, says Amos, if society was lacking in justice and care for others. This begs the question, 'How does a people know whether God accepts or rejects an offering?' Under normal circumstances, it is assumed that if the offering itself conforms to all the priestly rules, it is an acceptable offering, and thus the priest can confirm that God will accept it; there is nothing mysterious or objective like a sign from the heavens about that process—God's acceptance of any sacrifice or offering is entirely dependent on priestly say-so. Amos's words here, however, reject the certainty of any offering being accepted, for no priest can guarantee that God has heard and accepted anything ritually offered, he says, even those that meet all priestly and cultic requirements, if the community or individual lacks justice and righteousness.

The call for justice to flow (*gll*, roll along) like water may also involve a play on words since the root is also that which lies behind the place name Gilgal, an alternative shrine (see 4.4). There is a suggestion that rather than a perennial stream, the phrase *naḥal 'êtān* describes a stream that is fast-flowing, as after heavy rain, when the water flow is strong enough to roll stones and rocks downstream.

5.25-27
> 25 *Did you <u>bring me</u> sacrifices and offerings during the forty years in the wilderness, O house of Israel? (No!)*
> 26 *But you took up Sikkuth (as) your king, and Kiyyun, your images, your star-god that you made for yourselves.*
> 27 *So I would send you into exile beyond Damascus, says Yahweh. The God of hosts, is his name.*

This sub-section has been a challenge for some interpreters, primarily because the exodus wilderness-wandering period was seen by many as an ideal time in the Yahweh–Israel relationship. That view was supported by texts like Jer. 2.1-3, which idealized the period, despite other texts like Exod. 16.1-12 or 17.1-7 that are contrary. Also, it is clear that there actually was some kind of cultic activity during that forty-year period (see Num. 7.1-88; 16.1-35). Interpretation largely depends on the function of the connecting particle *waw* of 5.26; it is for this reader a 'But ...', marking the alternative fact. However, some read it as a simple continuation of the question in v. 25, while NRSV assumes it is independent and leaves it untranslated, turning the verse into a future 'promise'! The syntax is ambiguous, but not so uncertain as to permit the future orientation. It is to be noted again that the focus of the historical review is on the whole nation, not just on the north.

The initial question in 5.25 is clearly rhetorical, making a strong accusatory statement to the effect that the people did not bring offerings and sacrifices during the wilderness period of the exodus—whether that was true to fact or not. The following verse gives the reason that they so failed—it was because they had made other gods for themselves. In other words, the issue raised here was whether they brought offerings specifically to Yahweh or not (Heb. *higgaštem-lî*), rather than simply engaging in cultic activity more generally. It was that specific failure that was being highlighted.

In v. 26 the initial verb relates to lifting or carrying something, or as metaphor, it could describe them as 'taking up' something, in this case images (Heb. *ṣelem*) of these two gods, Sikkuth and Kiyyun, described as '*your*' images', the plural referring back to both. The two gods are of Mesopotamian origin, celestial gods in the Assyrian and Babylonian cults with which the northern kingdom contended. Alternatively, it could refer back to the gods brought into Canaan by people such as Rachel (Gen. 31.19-32). This would suggest that v. 26 has little to do with v. 25 and its reference to the earlier exodus motif.

Translating and interpreting the initial *waw* conjunction in 5.27 is a further challenge. The NRSV sees it as introducing a result, so '*Therefore* ...'; others as less clear, 'So ...', linking the divine response to the people's use of foreign images. The threat spoken by Amos was that God would react by sending 'you'—presumably a representative or collective 'you'—into exile '*beyond Damascus*'. This vague locative phrase is understandable given that at the time the north was coming under pressure from the Assyrian leader Tiglath-Pileser III.

The sub-section then ends with the *pro forma* phrase, 'says Yahweh. The God of hosts is his name'.

6.1-14 'Woe to Those Who . . .'

The collection of Amos's sayings, his words relating to the lamentation theme that began in 5.18, continue here in 6.1-3. The third grouping, 6.4-7, and a fourth saying at 6.13-14—though both lack the initial 'Woe ...'

marker—complete this third major division of the book, that is, 5.18–6.14. Amos's lamentation, his distress, is clearly directed at those who indulge themselves with their privilege and wealth, who see themselves as better than others, lack all compassion, and as a consequence, should pay the ultimate price—exile. Given that Amos is a visionary, not a traditional prophet, I read the verbs here as volitional, that is to say, they express what Amos believed should happen to such individuals; they are not predictions as to what will happen to them.

While 6.1-7 is readily seen as a unit concluding with a 'therefore' in v. 7, the remaining verses, 6.8-14, are essentially a collection of loosely connected disparate oracles, while vv. 13-14 I read as a further unmarked Woe-oracle, bringing the survey to an end.

6.1-7
1 *Woe to those who feel safe in Zion, and to those feeling secure in Samaria, distinguished leaders of the nations, to whom the house of Israel goes.*
2 *Cross over to Calneh. and see (for yourselves), go on from there to Hamath-Rabbah, thence to Gath of the Philistines. Are you any better than these kingdoms, or are your borders more extensive than theirs?*
3 *You who deny the day of disaster, and bring closer a reign of violence!*
4 *(Woe to) those who lie/sleep on ivory beds, lounging on their couches, who eat lambs from the flock and young calves from their stall,*
5 *Who sing idle songs to the tune of their harp just as did David as they thought up for themselves musical instruments.*
6 *Who drink from bowls of wine, anointing themselves with the finest oils, but do not grieve over the ruination of Joseph.*
7 *Therefore, now let them be the first to go into exile, and may the revelry of those who lounge about come to an end.*

As is typical of the Woe-form generally, so here, participles are used extensively to describe the kinds of people and actions that are the reasons for lamentation. Such individuals are addressed directly in v. 1, followed by a series of four imperatives ordering or advising the Israelite elite or leaders noted there to look at and compare themselves with others to get a proper sense of proportion—to acknowledge how insignificant they really are. While there is no Woe-marker at the head of v. 4, the reality is that the lament against the 'notables' continues, again with participles describing their extravagant lifestyle. Finally, Amos longs to see them meet their just end—exile, and a passing away.

6.1 The verse opens with parallel phrases identifying the object of lamentation—the self-satisfied or arrogant (Heb. *ša'ănān*) and the self-confident

(Heb. *boṭeḥîm*), also described as 'notable ones', the elite, in both Zion and Samaria. The reference to Zion has caused many readers to wonder why suddenly Amos would include the southern kingdom in his lament. Some commentators suggest it is a textual error and excise 'Zion', but in doing so they destroy the rhetorical parallel. That is unhelpful. There seems no explanation for this double reference other than to recognize that Amos did not speak exclusively to the northerners. One can conclude that whatever the problems Amos encountered in the north, similar issues were present in the south; what Amos had seen in the north was also true of the elite in Judah.

The final clause, literally, 'they come to them, the house of Israel'—that is, people from all over Israel— is most unclear. It would seem appropriate to read the verb 'they come' as referring to the people of 'the house of Israel' coming to the elite, but for what purpose is uncertain. Both third-person references are so vague as to render any guess with regard to identities a futile endeavour. What can be said is that the issues he confronted in the north were also issues in the south, and so his words applied more broadly.

6.2 Instructions are given to 'them', the elite or notable ones, to figuratively 'go' to Calneh, Hamath-Rabbah, and Gath for the purpose of noting the power and extent of their kingdoms relative to that of Israel. Calneh and Hamath-Rabbah were city states on the Orontes River to Israel's north, while Gath, one of the five main Philistine centres, was to Israel's south and southwest. Four short but strong imperatives are used —'cross over', 'see', 'go' and 'go down'—calling people from all over Israel to figuratively consider these cities for comparison with themselves. What particular features or aspects of those cities are relevant is not stated, other than size. To do this implies that there was a certain body of local knowledge about these places, or knowledge of their reputations, though probably not so widespread. How Amos from the back-blocks of Judah knew so much about the regional geography is also an interesting question to ponder.

This is followed by a rhetorical question enquiring whether Israel is any '*better*' (how?) or holding more territory than any of the three cities named. 'Better' is such a vague adjective when it comes to defining its semantic value with regard to a community—morally, economically, size, power, etc.? The question clearly implies that Israel was no match for these cities, for on any scale Israel is said to be the lesser. The intention behind the words seems to be to remind both Judah and Israel that they were inferior in the world of international politics and power. However, there remains the question of the real purpose of such a reminder; where does it fit in Amos's message calling for justice and righteousness (5.24)?

6.3 The verse, in my reading, refers to the 'you' of v. 2b, so, *'You who deny the day of disaster, and bring closer a reign of violence'* are all those who are arrogant and self-satisfied in either kingdom. It is obvious that the elite in both kingdoms were not expecting or anticipating any upset to their lifestyle; it is far from their minds. Here, however, they are threatened with some disaster that they can neither avoid nor delay, described as *'the day of disaster/tragedy'* (Heb. *rāʿ*)—it is not a day of 'evil', in view of the parallel *ḥāmās*, 'violence'. That *'reign of violence'*, though undefined, may well be the advance, then conquest, by the Assyrian armies, one contextual iteration of the 'day of Yahweh', which they are accused of inciting.

6.4 The phrase 'Woe to those who …' is missing from the Hebrew text but nevertheless it is clearly implied by the continuing use of participles describing the elite and their lifestyle; hence my translation supplies the Woe-marker. The rich are accused of lying about on their ivory-inlaid beds and lounges, enjoying sumptuous meals of lamb and beef, items not on the ordinary person's menu more than a few times a year, and often then only as the left-overs from the animals they offered sacrificially. The beef is described as veal from the fattening pen (Heb. *marbēq*), so seemingly choice animals, indicative of their wealth. There is a hint of hyperbole in all these descriptions.

6.5-6 Another aspect of a lavish lifestyle was that they had time to entertain themselves and others with their music. The comparison made with David picks up the tradition that he was allegedly an expert and talented musician. Additionally, the accused were hearty drinkers of wine, apparently using bowls rather than smaller drinking vessels or cups, implying excessive drinking. The Hebrew noun *mizrāq*, rendered 'bowl', suggests that they drank from the larger vessel in which wine was stored, implying excess—hyperbole again. Anointing themselves with expensive ointments or fragrances further paints a picture of an indolent life, for fine quality oil would not be used if one was heading out to work in the field or working at some other demanding task; it is as preparation for the banquet. And for all this lavish living there was no remorse over the situation throughout the community, a general criticism of their lack of concern for the rest of the kingdom. Here 'Joseph' serves as a term for the whole northern kingdom.

Interestingly, the elegant lifestyle pictured is one that would have been read by the Deuteronomic cohort as evidence of divine blessing (see Deut. 7.12-16). So the criticism in this lament must be grounded on the fact that the elite, though materially blessed, are to be condemned for not caring about the community, the poor and needy, that is to say, the sin of omission.

6.7 There is irony here in that the 'first' (Heb. *rē'šît*) among the people (6.1) are now to be the first to be taken into exile (Heb. *bᵉro'š-golîm*)! At the head of the line of exiles will be 'those who are at ease', the ones lounging about; no more revelry. In terms of the rhetoric, the concept of first/head (*ro'š*) functions as an inclusion for this Woe-oracle, while this final verse opens with an unusual '*Therefore, now ...*', which is not actually a time-marker but rather a forceful way of stating what should happen to the self-satisfied elite of Israel.

In light of Amos's role as visionary, the translation here offered renders the verb 'go into exile' not as a promise but as volitional, that is, expressing what should happen to those who are so self-serving and arrogant. For Amos, the ultimate punishment he can imagine is to be sent or taken into exile, away from the land God was said to have given Israel, its very birthright, according to the Deuteronomic viewpoint.

There is a further rhetorical element in this verse with assonance highlighting the fate of the elite for which Amos is said to have longed—*yiglû, golîm* and *sār mirzaḥ sᵉrûḥîm*. The noun *mirzēᵃḥ* is thought to refer to the feasting by the elite, though in Jer. 16.5 it seems to have a different context, that of lamenting. In the present context of Woe-oracles it is this latter that fits the context

6.8-14

8 *(My master, Yahweh, has sworn on his life, <u>says Yahweh the God of hosts</u>, 'I abhor Jacob's pride, and its strongholds I hate, and I would hand over a city and all within it'.)*

9 *If there were ten men remaining in a single house, they would die,*

10 *And if his relatives and cremator were to pick him up and carry him out of the house and say to someone inside the house 'Is anyone else with you?' the answer will be 'No', then the relative would say 'Quiet! We must not mention the name of Yahweh!'*

11 *Look, Yahweh commands, may the great house be smashed to pieces and the small house to rubble,*

12 *Can horses run on rocks, or does one plow (them) with oxen? Truly you have turned justice to poison, and the fruit of righteousness to wormwood.*

13 *(Woe to) those who rejoice for Lo-dabar, who say, 'Have we not in our own power taken Karnayim?'*

14 *Indeed, behold I am raising against you, house of Israel, <u>says Yahweh the God of hosts</u>, a nation, and may they oppress you from Lebo-hamath to Wadi Arabah.*

Apart from the possible inclusion '... *says Yahweh the God of hosts*' in vv. 8 and 14, this sub-section consists of a collection of what seem to be random 'words' of Amos that echo some of his concerns expressed earlier: the *'hate/abhor'* theme in 5.10 recurs here in 6.8; the pairing of justice and righteousness in 5.7, 24 recurs in 6.12 along with the verb *hāpak*, 'turn/ overturn'. References to *'fortresses'* or *'strongholds'* that are found frequently earlier in the collection recur here in v. 8. Verses 9-10 present a completely independent and difficult to understand conditional statement. The possible connection between the 'ten' remaining (5.3) and the 'ten' referred to in 6.9 seems likely because the verb 'remain' is involved in both, but the nature of the connection is unclear. There is a seemingly isolated proverb in question format in 6.12a, whose meaning in this context needs investigating. Then there is the real probability that v. 13, like v. 4, implies a Woe-oracle from which the opening cry 'Woe to …' (Heb. *hôy*) has been omitted; the participles that feature in vv. 13-14 are consistent with their use in laments. The sub-section is obviously an exegetical 'can of worms'.

6.8 The verse begins with a report that Yahweh, my master/lord, swears an oath, followed by a strange marker *'says Yahweh/my Lord, God of hosts'*. It appears to be irrelevant at this point and is missing from the LXX, so the story of its inclusion may be complex. Its prose form also suggests that it is an independent item, hence the brackets in the translation above—so also NRSV. Yahweh swears 'by his *nepeš'*, that is, on his own life, his own powerful being. The phrase intends to stress certainty and independence, that the oath taken will without doubt be actualized.

What the verse does is to return to the theme of *'hate'* and *'abhorrence'* (5.10, 21) with the focus this time on what is referred to as the *'pride of Jacob'* and *'his strongholds'*. The reference to Jacob as a code name for the northern kingdom is something readers have already seen in 3.13, though here it is Jacob's *'pride'* (Heb. *gᵉ'ôn*) that is the target. In Prov. 8.13; 16.18 and Nah. 2.2 the term is used as a parallel to 'arrogance', an implied feature of the northern elite and their lifestyle, according to Amos, though in Ps. 47.4 it speaks of positive value. A second target is the *'strongholds'*, mentioned frequently in earlier verbal attacks (see 1.3–2.6). Because of this basic human failing, Amos would wish to see God *'hand over the city and everything that it contains'*, a comprehensive threat to its survival. No city is specified, so it would appear to be representative of cities in general, not necessarily Samaria only.

6.9-10 These verses are in prose, suggesting that they are independent, and their having a different theme adds to that possibility. The basic problem is knowing what they intend to address. There is a rhetorical link with 5.3 via the reference to 'ten' people along with the verb 'remain', though the specific context here differs in other respects. Here there is no future for the 'ten', all will die, so perhaps the description and dialogue are intended to add emphasis to the loss of everything in the city noted in v. 8. The subsection contains a tantalizingly brief dialogue, but the editor has not identified the speakers, nor is the purpose of the question obvious, with a final imperative that is meaningless.

The scenario posited is that of a house in which there are ten individuals who have died due to some unspoken cause. Then a relative arrives to remove a body (or bodies?) in order to burn 'it'. While most commentators read the suffix 'it' as referring to the body, it is also possible to link it to the house; that is what was to be burnt, since burning of bodies was not a traditional Israelite way of dealing with the dead. Others suggest $m^e s \bar{a} r p \hat{o}$ (Heb. *srp*, burn) refers to burning incense in preparation for embalming the body. Having removed the body, someone asks whether there were any others 'with you', suggesting that there might have been at least one survivor who could answer the question. He knew, somehow, that there were no others left (alive?) in the house, to which this person would reply 'No', no others remaining. The relative bearing the body requested the remaining one to be silent in order not to invoke Yahweh's name. The significance of this command is lost forever!

Readers may never know what this possible scenario intended. If it ever had a part in Amos's oral message, it is now frozen in such a garbled written version that it defies attempts to unlock its mysteries. Guessing its meaning or significance opens the door to individual fancy and untestable possibilities. Readers need to acknowledge that often an ancient text like this can throw up problems for the interpreter, and no amount of ingenuity can reasonably resolve them.

6.11 Any potential connection between this verse and the preceding is via the noun 'house', in this case large and small houses, all would suffer the same fate—destruction. No reason or agency is revealed, but such destruction follows from a divine command. Presumably it is a foreign army invading that causes such complete destruction, though some commentators have even suggested a link to the earthquake noted in 1.1—quite a stretch! The adjectives 'great' and 'small' may refer to size as well as importance.

The next question has to do with the relationship between this verse and what follows, and while some suggest there is a connection, it is difficult to draw as there are no rhetorical indicators or evidence of same.

6.12 The verse consists of two rhetorical questions, an important device used throughout by Amos. Both here are equivalent to negative statements, noting two actions that could not possibly occur: horses cannot run over rocks; oxen cannot plow—whether rocks or sea is yet to be determined. The first question seems completely logical if Hebrew *sl'* means boulders or large rocks rather than just rocky ground. Horses are not capable of running from one large rock to another. The second question it would seem asks whether oxen can plow on those rocks. However, the suggestion that the Hebrew text *babbᵉqārîm,* 'with the oxen', should be emended by separating the final two consonants and read *yām*, 'sea', has much support among commentators, so the question becomes about oxen possibly ploughing the sea. Whatever the textual solution, it is of course another absurd suggestion; it is clear that the intent is to indicate that there are actions or situations that are beyond possible.

The question then becomes how does this connect with the statement in v. 12b that speaks of matters that have indeed happened, but should never have happened? It connects back to the theme of justice and righteousness in 5.7-15, so the statement here is thus full of irony: Israelites have managed to do what was thought impossible—they have overthrown and reversed justice and righteousness, turned them into poison and wormwood. This was a serious indictment of society in the northern nation as well as in the south.

6.13-14 I read these two verses as a unit and would argue that an opening 'Woe to ...' has been omitted, as in 6.4. The following series of participles lists the ones who are being referred to. Those addressed are rejoicing about a presumed victory over a place called Lo-Davar, a name that is ambiguous and ironic, meaning 'no thing'. They are also proudly celebrating their victory in their own power over Karnayim. Interestingly, their response to the 'Woe ...' pronounced against them is by way of a rhetorical question of their own.

Lo-dabar was an Ammonite city in Transjordan; *Karnayim*, an Aramean/Syrian city to their north. Does their boast simply evidence their pride in their achievements? That may be the case, but Amos's response was to remind Israel that God could or would raise against them a nation that would oppress them and so deal with their pride. That threat warned of potential oppression from *L'bo-hamath* to *Wadi Arabah,* both place names together representing the northern and southern extent of the kingdom, in other words, the full extent of the northern kingdom could fall under this foreign pressure. Wadi Arabah, the Rift Valley, is a diverse region stretching from the Sea of Chinnereth down the lush Jordan River to the Dead Sea and then on to the Gulf of Aqaba. There is dispute, however, about the actual location of Lebo-hamath. See 2 Kgs 14.25 for a reference to Jeroboam's victories that incorporated these two outlying centres.

Inserted into the text of this sub-section is another *'says Yahweh the God of hosts'*, the purpose of which is unclear, especially as it separates the object *'a nation'* from the initial participle *'raising up'*. Both uses of this speech marker are irrelevant to the immediate context and so are considered editorial inserts at the beginning and end of the sub-section 6.8-14.

7.1–9.10 Amos's 'Visions'

With ch. 7 the report in Amos takes on a different cast. In place of collected reports of Amos's 'words', the report focuses on a series of five so-called visions that Amos is said to have had (7.1-3, 4-6, 7-8; 8.1-3; 9.1-4), together with the reported dialogue with Amaziah the priest (7.10-17) and a concluding reference to a Davidic restoration in Judah (9.11-15). It includes also another *'Hear this …'* message (8.4-8), together with a detail concerning *'that day'* in 8.9-14, and smaller units in 9.5-6, 7, 8-10. However, it is the collection of what have been called 'visions' that have attracted most attention. See **Amos's Visions?** in the Introduction.

The first four 'visions' are presented in two separate forms: 7.1-3 and 7.4-6 are similarly structured as:

a. *This is what my lord Yahweh showed me, and behold he was (+ participle) …*
b. *Then I said, …, I beg you.*
c. *How can Jacob stand? He is so small*!
d. *Yahweh relented …*
e. *It shall not be, said my lord Yahweh.*

The second pair, 7.7-9 and 8.1-3, use a slightly different structure:

a. *This is what my lord Yahweh (he) showed me -*
b. *Yahweh (he) said to me, 'Amos, what do you see?'*
c. *And I said …*
d. *Then the lord Yahweh said (to me) …*
e. *… I will never against pass them by.*

The fifth 'vision' (9.1-4) differs yet again:

'I saw my master standing beside …, and he said:
though they …, from there shall my hand take them … (or, there I will …)
– repeated five times.

While there are differences in the forms used to report the 'visions', there is also an important tonal difference between the first two recorded and the following three: the message changes from impending dangers that were withdrawn as God was challenged by Amos in the first two listed, while threats of utter destruction are affirmed in the remaining three.

There is no way of knowing how, or if, these 'visions' are related, or when they occurred relative to one another or relative to Amos's mission; they are simply gathered into one space by the editor without any comment.

What was the nature of these 'visions'? Were they ocular events, visible sightings of material 'things'? That would apply perhaps in the case of 8.1, as Amos was possibly frequenting a market; but in the case of the other experiences he had, the 'visions' were more esoteric. It is vital that readers note the language used; each of the reports uses the Hebrew verb *rā'â*, 'see', in a causative form, 'caused me to see', 'made me see', or 'showed me', except for 9.1, when the plain form is used—'I saw'. The verb 'see', as any native speaker is aware, can cover a broad semantic range, from ocular vision to comprehension and understanding. The objects 'seen' in these 'visions' were not physical objects that became visible to the eye, apart from 8.1, so the figurative sense of the verb 'see' is clearly intended in each.

These 'visions' were matters going on in Amos's head; they were like his musings, his reflecting on circumstances in Israel. What the musings do suggest, however, is that whatever Amos 'saw' he has attributed to a divine source or prompting. We can picture Amos engaged mentally in a dialogue with his God, pleading with God—'Please God, don't ...!'—to change his mind about summoning a locust plague, or raining down fire, or laying waste to his people. Amos claimed that in the first two 'visions' reported, he was able to convince God to withdraw the threat of destruction, but in his other 'visions' he saw that destruction was absolutely sealed—recalling the image of Yahweh in the introductory 1.2.

Some commentators suggest that there is some kind of progression, a development, as one reads through these 'vision' reports. There is absolutely no reason to believe, however, that these experiences were sequential, that God was initially swayed by Amos's plea, then hardened his stance subsequently. These individual 'visions' are simply placed as they appear editorially in the text on the basis of the similarity of forms used. This cannot be called 'progressive revelation' as some suggest, for they present truly conflicting outcomes; to suggest progression is to read far too much into the editor's reporting. What it does leave, however, is the challenge of understanding and/or explaining the very different divine responses as reported. While the first two 'visions' end with Yahweh deciding not to punish or destroy, the third and fourth 'visions' speak of Yahweh completely demolishing Israel and its king, one has to ask, What was the point of the first two 'visions', if real, when the other visions contradict them? They are in conflict, perhaps because Amos was not able to reconcile them in his own mind? Tying the 'visions' to historic moments or outcomes is not called for, nor is it even helpful in terms of understanding what is being reported.

The report breaks after 7.9 with the conclusion of the third 'vision' serving also as a link to the inserted dialogue in 7.10-17 via its references to Jeroboam and the sword, the sword being the means by which he could be dispatched. The 'visions' report then resumes in 8.1-3.

Some commentators have drawn the conclusion that these 'visions' are from the time of the exile or even post-587 BCE by linking the 'little Jacob' notion in 7.2, 5 to Isa. 40.27. This reader sees no reason to seek specific historical connections for the 'visions', for it was the overall social and religious contexts that were important to Amos rather than their relating to specific historical moments, as is seen in his use of generalized language throughout.

7.1-9 Three Visions

7.1-3 First 'Vision'

1 *This is what my lord Yahweh made me see: behold, he was creating locusts at the time when the latter growth was about to sprout; it was the latter growth following the king's mowings.*
2 *What if they finished devouring the vegetation throughout the land, I said, 'O lord Yahweh, please forgive, I pray you! How can Jacob resist when he is so small?'*
3 *Yahweh relented on this matter and said, 'Nothing will happen'. (Yahweh has spoken.)*

The report presents Amos as the speaker, telling of something that Yahweh has enabled him to 'see'. The formula *'This is what my lord Yahweh made me see: behold ...'* is used to introduce each of four 'visions'. As argued above, these are not matters visible to the eye, for the verb 'see' here is figurative for insight and understanding. In 7.1 that understanding relates to Amos acknowledging that God has created or shaped (Heb. *yṣr*) a plague of a particular kind of locust (Heb. *gobay*), a rarely used word (but see also Nah. 3.17). The various insects in that category always represent a destructive force, and in Joel 1.4 are used also as a metaphor for an invading army. A specific time marker is indicated, namely when the vegetation or crops were beginning to sprout, here identified as *'the latter growth'*, presumably the final burst of growth before harvest. Was that the time of year when Amos had this 'vision', or was it an element in the 'vision' itself? A locust plague of course would be devastating for any farming community. The 'vision' is also identified as following *'the king's mowings'*, a more uncertain activity for which there is little or no information available, though plenty of unsupported guesses.

Did the insects devour all vegetation throughout the land—an exaggerated description? The Hebrew *wᵉhāyāh 'im killâ leʾᵉkôl* is generally rendered as past or fulfilled (see, e.g., NRSV)—all the vegetation was 'seen' to have been devoured, making Amos's plea useless or irrelevant. On my reading of the Hebrew, however, it is better to render the phrase as 'What if they finished devouring ...?', a potential disaster rather than an actual one. Then, in 7.2b, Amos imagines a dialogue with God in which he commands God to 'pardon' or 'forgive' (Heb. *sᵉlaḥ-nāʾ*)—the verb is imperative—whom and for what is unspoken, and obviously this is not a call for Israelite repentance. The attached *-nāʾ* particle does add a note of pleading that softens the imperative, so Amos calls for God to end the locust plague. Amos's rhetorical question is actually a negative statement to the effect that none could stand against any such plague, especially Israel, which is said to be *'so small'*. The phrase *mî yāqûm*, literally 'who can arise?', is used again in 7.6 and interestingly is also found in Nah. 1.6 in a similar context. In the face of its international setting Israel was quite small—is that what was in mind? No other justification is offered for the plea.

Amos's plea was heard, according to Amos's description of the 'vision' (7.3), and God, he says, relented (Heb. *nḥm*) or 'repented' (see also Jon. 3.9-10), ending the plague. God then states that 'It will not happen', or perhaps better, *'Let it not happen!'*, reading the imperfective as a jussive.

What is the point being made? There is so much that is enigmatic about this text. Amos was musing about an outcome for Israel in light of its failure in justice and righteousness, failures that would have been as destructive as a locust plague, but in the end nothing happened? The looming threat about which Amos 'interceded' did not arrive, seemingly because Amos challenged God and God changed his mind—that was obviously how Amos has understood the process in his mind. What did Amos actually learn from this 'vision' other than that God might be swayed, convinced not to proceed with a plan? How such a change of heart relates to the very negative picture of divine threats of punishment that dominate the other 'visions' in the book is difficult to imagine. Some commentators see here a message of divine forgiveness, to this reader a view unsupported by the text and more evidence of a reader's imposed perception. The real problem is that this and the following 'vision' in which the Lord also relents are then overturned in the other three, yet without providing readers with an explanation for the divine change of heart other than that of Amos's imploring.

The appended *'Yahweh has spoken'* is a *pro forma* note that can be bracketed out.

7.4-6 Second 'Vision'

> 4 *This is what my lord Yahweh made me see: behold, my lord Yahweh he was calling for a judgment by fire that it should devour the great deep and (also) devour the land.*
> 5 *Then I said, 'O my lord Yahweh, cease I pray you! How can Jacob resist, for he is small?'*
> 6 *Yahweh relented on this matter, also he said, 'Nothing will happen', my lord Yahweh.*

The second 'vision' is edited to follow the same pattern and use the same vocabulary as the first. The focus here, however, is fire that seems to be figurative of judgment via destruction, though the Hebrew phrase *rîb bā'ēš* is problematic. There is a root *rîb* that speaks of disputation, and it is possible that it is the one used here to express the purpose of the fire. Again, we note that it is driven by God, but its cause is unexplained; and the fact that it is to devour the deep sea (Heb. *tᵉhôm*) means that it relates to the cosmos rather than any human object, certainly not specifically Israel—see Deut. 32.22. Again, Amos claims protection for little Jacob in face of this overwhelming figurative fire, and God supposedly changes his mind and relents. No reason is offered for that sudden change of heart, so Amos remains mystified.

Like the preceding report of a 'vision', this too is difficult to comprehend—a planned divine destruction is averted by Amos's simple intercession. Commentators note the enigmatic nature of the 'vision', but attempt to locate it in a historical setting in the period, generally concluding that it is probably related to some time after the late-eighth century BCE. This reader finds the text so concise, enigmatic, and lacking in detail that no conclusion as to any historical context can reasonably be drawn. Moreover, it is not an ocular sighting, rather something in the mind of Amos, more in the nature of a musing, but in what regard is unclear.

At the level of the text, the poetic reference to the 'deep', the primeval ocean, removes the 'vision' far from reality, but it does have some relationship to Amos's theology regarding Yahweh as Creator (Gen. 1.2). The other noun in 7.4 is *ḥēleq*, here rendered as 'land', but with a narrow and specific reference to the land of Canaan as Israel's 'inheritance' (e.g. Josh. 19.2). The sea and the land are both saved from the threatened conflagration.

7.7-9 Third 'Vision'

> 7 *This is what my master made me see: behold, my lord standing on a vertical? wall with a plumbline/tin in his hand,*

> 8 *And Yahweh said to me, 'What do you see, Amos?' And I said, 'A plumbline/tin', and my lord said, 'Look, I am placing a plumbline/tin in the midst of my people Israel; I will never again pass it by'.*
> 9 *The high places of Isaac will become desolate, and the sanctuaries of Israel become a ruin,*
>   *And I will raise the sword against the house of Jeroboam.*

We have noted above that there is a similarity in the form of the 'visions' reported in 7.7-8 and 8.1-2, a variation on that used in 7.1-3 and 7.4-6. The 'vision' in 8.1-2 may well be the only one that can be considered ocular as Amos, possibly while visiting a market, spies a basket of fruit that triggers another insight.

Here an unnamed agent, obviously Yahweh as in 8.1, makes something known—the verb has no direct object. It entails a 'vision' of Yahweh standing on or against a wall described as *ḥômat-'ᵃnāk*. There is some confusion as to this phrase, which has often been thought to mean the wall was 'vertical'. God is standing there—on or by—the wall with something in hand, an *'ᵃnāk*, preparing to apply the device to the people of Israel.

What is this thing called in Hebrew *'ᵃnāk*? The word appears only in this text, and although in the past it has been regarded as a 'plumbline', more recently it has been largely agreed that linguistically it means 'tin', the plain metal, not a tin can. That, in fact, makes the sense even more opaque as an instrument for placing in the midst of the community. However, there is operating here a play on words, as happens in the fourth 'vision' also. The term *'ᵃnāk* sounds very much like *'ᵃnāq*, 'moaning', and relates to threats of coming disaster (see Isa. 24.7; Joel 1.18). Yahweh will not relent this time but will destroy, causing much 'moaning' or 'groaning', whether in anticipation or after the fact.

Yahweh in 7.8 is presented as initiating a dialogue with Amos. He puts a question to Amos asking what he thinks he is seeing. Amos imagines that he can see an *'ᵃnāk*, to which God responds that it will be set or placed in the midst of *'my people Israel'*, and he will never again *'pass them by'* (Heb. *lo'-'ôsîp 'ôd*). Was it an object to serve as a sign or memorial? That *'never again passing by'* here implies a divine action that could have had dire consequences for Israel. The result of this divine action in 7.9 indicates that it would destroy the high places and other religious sanctuaries, including the royal one, and that Jeroboam would die by the sword. This threat involves another play on words as the two lines in 7.9 end with reference to the root *ḥrb*. The verbal form in v. 9a refers to desolation; the nominal form ending v. 9b, *ḥereb*, is a 'sword', the means by which Jeroboam should be dispatched—whether that means dying in battle or in a palace revolt is deliberately vague. Importantly,

Amos makes no intercession to plead for Yahweh to change his mind and relent—why not?

So, the third 'vision' report involves a neat paranomasia, as happens in the report of the fourth 'vision' also. This is editorial rhetoric. It should not be forgotten, however, that the text is reporting on Amos's inner reflecting; these were 'visions' in his head, not something concrete and visible to the naked eye. As a visionary, Amos was expressing what he believed could and perhaps should happen in Israel and to Jeroboam in particular.

The reference to *Isaac* in v. 9a is most unusual as a way of speaking of the northern kingdom because the Isaac tradition was more associated with Beersheba in the south, but it provides a neat parallel with the name 'Israel' in v. 9b.

7.10-17 Amaziah Encounters Amos

10 *Now Amaziah, a priest of Bethel, sent (word) to Jeroboam the king of Israel. 'Amos has conspired against you in the midst of the house of Israel. The land is not able to tolerate all his words.'*
11 *'Here is what Amos has said: "By the sword Jeroboam should die, and Israel surely go into exile away from its land"'.*
12 *Then Amaziah said to Amos: 'Seer, go, get out to the land of Judah! Earn your keep there, and do your talking there!*
13 *'Don't stay around in Bethel any longer to speak, for here is the royal sanctuary, the home of the kingdom'.*
14 *Amos replied, saying to Amaziah: 'I am not a prophet, nor am I a member of the prophetic guild. I am a herdsman and a pruner of sycamores.*
15 *'Yahweh took me from being one who followed the herd, saying to me, "Go speak to my people Israel"'.*
16 *'Now, hear Yahweh's word: "You are saying, 'Do not speak about Israel, nor preach about the house of Isaac'".*
17 *'So this is what Yahweh says: "May your wife become a prostitute in the city, and your sons and daughters fall by the sword. May your land be divided with the measuring line, and you yourself die in an unclean land. May Israel go into exile from its land."'*

This section intrudes unexpectedly into the reports of the 'visions'. It is evidence of the editorial gathering of material in which availability is more important than plot development or chronological placement. It is the only part of the book where the editor has reported something of a biographical nature. Why here and not elsewhere, such as at the beginning of the book, is a question one can ask, but there are no answers. Presumably the editor was dependent on Amos for the details, or the oral accounts of Amos's mission contained sufficient detail for a late editor to include.

Amaziah the priest at Bethel, the royal sanctuary, is said to have sent a message to Jeroboam the king charging that Amos's message in the north included negative 'words' about the king himself and about the nation generally, Amaziah calling them a lie or treasonous words. It was too much for the country to bear, he told Amos, so 'Get back to Judah and do your speaking there!' Amaziah pulls rank on the lowly herder from Judah. Amaziah is clearly failing, according to Amos, in ensuring Torah's demands for justice and righteousness in the community are met. There is another unspoken issue, however, namely that Amaziah is rejecting the specific Deuteronomic claims that worship at any site other than in the Temple in Jerusalem was 'false' worship'. He is actually saying that Amos's southern perspective is something to be kept there, not brought north, Thank you!

Amos's response to Amaziah's put-down was to claim a divine calling. He denied being a prophet or a member of the prophetic guild. He was a herder and a part-time pruner of sycamore trees. (See **Amos and his Background** in the Introduction.) The only reason he was in the northern kingdom was to speak as God had ordered him to do. Amos's reaction to Amaziah's charge was to tell him what he wished for him and his family, and to threaten the nation with exile if they failed to hear and respond to what he had to say.

7.10-11 Amaziah was seemingly the chief priest at the Bethel sanctuary (see 1 Kgs 12.25-33). That sanctuary was no doubt one of the buildings in the north that had been constructed with the finest of materials, typical of many homes (see 3.15). Amaziah is said to have 'sent' (i.e. a message) to Jeroboam the king. We have only a general summary of its contents that Amaziah claimed threatened the future of the royal house and kingdom. How the king reacted at the news can only be surmised. It was Amaziah himself who took Amos to task, sneeringly calling him a 'seer' (Heb. *ḥōzeh*), but accurate in his description. That there was tension between the priests and prophets within Israel is well known and documented. For the most part it was the prophets who criticized the priestly class for their failures, as they were the ones who bore major responsibility in teaching the community, calling them to live by the laws that were integral to their covenant with Yahweh. Amaziah, no doubt stung by unsophisticated Amos's criticisms, wanted Amos out of the way, and his 'words' with him.

7.12-13 Amaziah, asserting his priestly authority, issued commands to Amos, ordering him to return to Judah. The orders are expressed in peremptory fashion—'go you, flee you, ..., eat your bread there, and there *tinnābē'*, reflecting the priest's status and arrogance. The phrase *'eat your* *bread'* refers to one's earning a living. On the verb *nbʾ* frequently but misleadingly rendered as 'prophesy', see the Introduction. Here the imperative from Amaziah carries a condescending tone, or he is just being plain rude—implying that Amos is really no prophet but is playing at being one, and one from the 'inconsequential' south, the 'rump' of the kingdom and its self-serving views.

7.14 Amos's response to Amaziah is as forceful as was Amaziah's sneering command. He asserts: *'I am no prophet, nor am I a son of a prophet'*. The Hebrew text is clearly implying a thorough rejection of the priest's arrogant order. By placing the personal pronoun in the full form *'ānokî* following the two phrases *'not a prophet'* and *'not a son of a prophet'*, it becomes an emphatic. Repetition further stresses the point that he neither has nor has had a connection with the prophetic movement—as is borne out in 1.1. So first, Amos denies any claim to being a prophet; he then states positively what he was before being 'called' to his current responsibility.

Some commentators want to divide the Hebrew phrases rendered *'I am no prophet, nor am I a son of a prophet'* differently, separating the initial *lo'*, 'not', and have Amos say to the priest *'No! I am a prophet ...'*. The 'No!' in that context means that he will not return to Judah and *hinnābê'* there, but he will remain in northern Israel and continue his work as a prophet. That reading of the text does not comport with Amos's statement about his true identity and work as a herdsman. Reading Amos as a prophet is a long-standing but inexcusable error! He was a visionary, an important difference that must be acknowledged and understood.

Amos was and remained a herdsman (Heb. *bôqēr*) who also pruned sycamore trees, or dealt with their fruit in season. See the Introduction for more details on the background to Amos. I have noted that the region in which Amos grew up, Tekoa, was very dry and marginal, so his herd was most likely to have been goats, not sheep, and it was a region in which sycamore trees almost certainly could not be grown due to poor soils and lack of moisture. Amos probably had to travel seasonally to more fertile regions such as Jericho in the Jordan Valley or to the western slopes (Shephelah) to prune the trees when such was required. He was no agribusinessman or agricultural consultant as some wish him to have been!

7.15 Amos now relates how it was that he came to be in the north and to be speaking as he did. He has used the verb *lāqaḥ*, 'take, pick up', claiming that it was Yahweh who literally picked him up while he was herding his flock and ordered him to go *'to my people Israel'*. The imperative *'go ...'* is literally understood, but where was he to go? There is no textual evidence that the order meant only 'go north'! Almost entirely, the tradition has assumed that '*to my people Israel*' meant only the northern kingdom, on the grounds that at some point he was present there in Bethel. But, the ambiguity of the phrase '*to my people Israel*', and the evidence in the text more widely, indicates that '*Israel*' in this report is a broader term, not confined to the northern kingdom.

Amos's statement, if it were to be limited to the northern kingdom, is interesting for two reasons: (a) northerners, the majority population, are still recognized as within God's covenant people despite all the failings that have been exposed, though no different from the situation in Judah, and (b) the claim functions literarily as an equivalent to the call-component in traditional prophetic books. That Amos is said to have described the moment of his call as being '*from following the flock*' lends support to the notion that his flock was of goats rather than sheep—or a mixed flock—because the harsh marginal conditions of his home were more suitable to goats, and they were usually followed rather than led.

Included in Amos's call was the command to *hinnābê'*, traditionally rendered as 'prophesy!' See the discussion of this verb in the Introduction. Although the nominal form *nābî'* refers to one who is/was a prophet, acting in unusual trance-like ways and hallucinating that prophets sometimes did when speaking, including running about naked for years as did Isaiah (Isa. 20.2-4), the fact is that the semantic content of the verb or root has more to do with speaking out, whether they were one's own thoughts or those of another. Thus, Amos could say he was no weird prophet; he did not act like a prophet, but could and did speak out words that he 'saw' about what he observed in Israel (1.1).

The use of the phrase '*my people Israel*' is significant for its ambiguity, not to be confined to those Israelites of the northern kingdom; it embraces Israel as a whole, as is clear from 2.4-5.

7.16-17 Amos moves the discourse on, ordering Amaziah: 'Now, you listen to what Yahweh has to say …!' He is peremptory, as was Amaziah. 'You say, "Don't speak up against Israel; and do not preach against the house of Isaac…"'. The latter expression, which occurs only here, cannot be confined to the north either. Amos then launches into an angry threat against the priest. I read the verbs in this response as volitional, expressing what Amos was desperate to see happen rather than, as is customary, to read them as predictive certainties. These words introduce a curse. Amos was a visionary, not a prophet, so this word is his own, not some revelation received from God, despite the editorial addition of the *pro forma* 'thus says Yahweh'. That addition is intended to add authority to Amos's words that now move from prose to poetry.

Amos's angry words are directed at Amaziah's wife, his children and land—though priests should not have held land—then at Amaziah himself, before mentioning the kingdom. Each of these objects is placed first in the clause, to give prominence to each, with the verb in final position. It is a powerful challenge from Amos, one that helps further define what the verb *nb'* means in this context; it is not predictive but volitional.

Whether Amaziah's wife became a prostitute in the city, his children killed by the sword, their land-holdings divided up, whether Amaziah himself suddenly died and the whole nation went into exile is hardly the main point—it was Amos's way of cursing and demeaning the priest, his family and the northern kingdom. All were being cursed in Amos's response to the priest's sneering dismissal.

The reference to an 'unclean' (Heb. $t^e m\bar{e}'\hat{a}$) land is a way of speaking here about both the northern kingdom and any foreign territory; such land was 'unclean'—a purely cultic term—because it was the land of people considered ritually unclean as defined by Judaean religious tradition. Three times in this brief statement the word 'land' has been used, each with slightly different nuance but together emphasizing the gravity and extent of the threat.

8.1-3 Fourth 'Vision'

1 *This is what my master Yahweh made me see: Look, a basket of summer fruit.*
2 *He said, 'What do you see, Amos?' and I said, 'A basket of summer fruit'. Then Yahweh said to me, 'The end has come upon my people Israel; I will no longer pass it by.*
3 *Let the temple songs turn to wailing, in that day', says my master Yahweh, 'there will be many dead bodies cast out everywhere. Silence!'*

This fourth 'vision' begins as did the preceding reports. As was the case with the third 'vision', the format presents Yahweh asking Amos the question *'What do you see?'*, to which he replies that he can see *qāyiṣ*, 'a basket of/for summer fruit'. Whether the basket was actually full of fruit, or the kind of basket used when harvesting the summer fruit, is interesting to ponder but in the end immaterial.

The 'vision' uses a play on words—Hebrew *qāyiṣ* speaks of the summer time (see 3.15), and here refers to the kind of fruit available in summer. One can presume that Amos was either at a local market or in a field where people were harvesting the summer fruit. The sight of the *qāyiṣ* prompted in Amos a homophonic recall of the *qēṣ*, the end that he believes has come upon the people. Assonance emphasizes that 'the end' of the kingdom has indeed already arrived, but attached is an assurance that God will not *'pass by'* again. Here the verb 'pass by/over' seems to imply that God will never again turn away from his people or from his intended action (see 7.8, 13 and notes on *lo'-'ôsîyp 'ôd*).

This 'vision' is most probably one sparked by an actual sighting of the summer basket, but the dialogue with Yahweh, an important element in the form of report, was in Amos's head. It recalls the situation described in 5.1, 16 in which Amos wailed and lamented over the nation; it was as if the nation had already died, and temple singing had turned from joy to lamentation. Mention of 'the day' was not indicating some far-off potential calamity; it was now a present or imminent circumstance.

The calamitous 'end' has given Amos a vision of dead bodies lying everywhere, though one has to presume that they are Israelite corpses, and in place of hymnic cultic singing, wailing and lamentation end in silence (Heb. *hās*) descending on the scene. See also 6.10.

8.4-14 'Hear This . . .'—a Famine of Words

4 *Hear this, you who trample on the needy and cause ruin to the poor of the land,*

5 *who say: 'How long before the new moon is past so that we may again sell grain; and the Sabbath, so that we can put wheat on sale, to shrink the ephah measure and increase the shekel coin, and cheat with false scales?*

6 *So that we can purchase the poor for cash, and the needy for the price of sandals, and sell the left-overs from the wheat?'*

7 *Yahweh has sworn by the pride of Jacob, 'I will never forget everything they have done'.*

8 *'Is it not for this that the earth shakes', says my lord Yahweh, 'and everyone in it mourn? Let all of it rise like the Nile, and sink like the Nile of Egypt.'*

9 *'On that day', says my lord Yahweh, 'I would make the sun set at noon and darken the earth in the daytime light.*

10 *I would turn your feasts into mourning and your songs into lamentation; I would clothe each of you with sackcloth, and each head become bald. I would make your mourning like that for an only son and its ending like a day of bitterness.'*

11 *'The days are coming', says my lord Yahweh, 'when I would send a famine on the earth; not a famine of food or a thirst for water, but rather (a famine) of hearing Yahweh's word'.*

12 *'They stagger from sea to sea, and wander from north to east in search of the word of Yahweh, but do not find it.*

7.1–9.10 Amos's Visions 95

13 *On that day beautiful young women and young men faint because of thirst.'*

14 *Those who swear by Samaria's shame, saying, 'As your god lives, Dan', or who say, 'as the way of Beersheba lives', let them fall and never rise again.*

Verses 4-14 return to the '*Now, hear this ...*' formula found in the second major section of the book, at 3.1; 4.1; 5.1. It picks up again the trope of the poor and needy (4.1). In this sub-section we find five loosely connected but individual reports of Amos's 'words'—vv. 4-6, 7-8, 9-10, 11-12 and 13-14, with various interconnecting ideas such as the time reference '*On that day ...*' and the keyword '*thirst'*. There is a general theme of mourning in vv. 8 and 10 that link back to 8.1-3. For some commentators these verses offer diverse reflections that develop themes and ideas presented in the earlier chapters of the book. While there is good evidence for that view, it should not then be taken to mean that they are later than the preceding 'words' as they almost certainly were comments that were contemporaneous if Amos spoke often about his key concerns. I read these as alternate versions of Amos's 'words' as remembered, with vocabulary repeated, for example, 'trampled', 'poor' and 'needy' in 2.7a and 4.1, and now here in 8.4. They read as individual items rather than as elements in a closely integrated plot development.

The introductory verse to the second section of the book that focused on 'Hear this word ...' (see 3.3) can be considered the context in which this sub-section also operates.

8.4-6 Oppression of the poor was a major concern within Amos's purview. In this sub-section the focus is on those traders who cannot wait to demean the poor and needy in order to further their own greedy ambitions. The text here is so well written as it paints a picture of traders venting their frustration at having to wait for community celebrations to end and for normal religious restrictions to be lifted so that they could resume trading. The Hebrew particle *mātay,* 'how long ...?', frequently found in lament psalms, gave voice to that frustration. The editor has created a quote to evoke an emotional response to the traders' intentions.

The '*new moon*' refers to the cultic celebration on the first day of the lunar month. It probably was a one-day-only celebration, but these grain merchants were so eager to see it pass. Likewise the day of rest ordered for the Sabbath when no work was allowed was, for them, a further annoying interruption. The question form used in this created quote emphasizes their desperation to get back to business.

The *'ephah'* was a dry measure of weight of roughly forty litres; a *'šekel'* was a piece of silver used as coinage and weighing about sixteen grams. These grain dealers planned to cheat both on the weight of grain sold by using false weights on their scales and also by increasing the price demanded. At both ends of the transaction they intended to cheat, thus making more money.

The phrase *'buying the poor for silver'* is presumably a figurative expression for making money from the poor and powerless, though many take it literally as a reference to buying and selling slaves. The parallel phrase *'(buying) the needy for a pair of sandals'* is similar. Sandals were the cheapest form of footwear, so again it shows how little value these traders are said to have placed on the poor and needy in the community. The power imbalance worked entirely in the traders' favour. As if that wasn't enough, they also planned to sell the last remaining grains they swept up from the floor. Whatever grain fell to the floor in the process of doing business was swept up together with any contaminant that lay on the ground.

8.7-8 These verses relate directly to the preceding quoted material, this time quoting Yahweh's supposed reaction to the traders' scenario; this too is an imaginary form of the issue running through Amos's head. Yahweh, he says, has sworn an oath *'by the pride of Jacob'*. The name 'Jacob' as a substitute for Israel has been used in 3.13; 6.8; 7.2, 5. See the notes on 6.8. Here it probably refers to the same people and the sense of pride that the nation has (see also Nah. 2.2[3]), pride that is attached to its land. Swearing an oath emphasizes the seriousness of the commitment to act, in this case, never to forget what these traders have done and intend to keep doing.

8.8 then is presented as a rhetorical question in the negative, which means that its answer is affirmative. 'Yes! The whole land will tremble, and its inhabitants mourn.' This threat is another example of hyperbole unless the traders and the poor are mourning for different reasons—the one for not being able to rob the poor, and the poor for being robbed.

What seems a strange reference to Egypt and the Nile follows. Its annual flooding, its rise and fall, are used as a metaphor, though the point of the metaphor is not so clear. The annual Nile flood was the source of moisture in a very hot and dry land, and it carried with it nutrients to replenish the arable soil on the Nile flood plain. From that point of view it was a very important and positive element in Egypt's climate regime. The river may have occasionally become a destructive flood, but for the most part Egyptian agriculture was heavily dependent on the flooding to revitalize the soils. The example here of rising and falling does not imply anything negative. See the 'rise and fall' imagery again in 8.14.

8.9-10 *'That day'*, says my lord Yahweh, will see a cosmic upheaval. On the one hand, the rise and fall of the Nile portends something uncertain; on the other hand, cosmic events that see the sun setting at noon and the bright sunlight darkened apply a common theme when portraying disaster. The threat to overturn (*hāpak*) things—the verb used often in 4.11; 5.7, 24 turning feasting to mourning, singing into lamentation—using the light-to-darkness trope in 5.18-20 reappears here. Wearing sackcloth, the textile associated with lamentation, and shaving of heads to demonstrate the depth of sorrow are actions linked to deep mourning, here likened to that of mourning the loss of an only son. It is abundantly clear that 'the day' will be a truly bitter (Heb. *mār*) moment in the community's life. The *'end of it'* (Heb. *'aḥᵃrîtāh*) may have a slightly different sense than *haqqēṣ*, 'end' (8.2), pointing more to the aftermath of the day—that is, the 'day' will have an on-going impact that will be 'bitter'.

8.11-12 Another reference to the 'day' and what it will portend speaks of it as approaching, as imminent. Amos envisages an on-coming crisis. It features a figurative use of the notion of a famine (Heb. *rā'āb*), clarified as not a material famine of food or lack of water but one of hearing (Heb. *lišmoᵃ'*) *'Yahweh's words'*. The specific content of those 'words' may refer to the Law or perhaps, in this specific context, Amos's 'words'. Not having access to Yahweh's words is clearly presented as a terrible loss, as something negative. Like literal famines it will grip the entire country—from one sea to the other, Dead Sea to Mediterranean, from north to east, the entire country will endure this 'famine'. Again, one notes the use of hyperbole when describing the 'day' and its overwhelming impact.

While the picture Amos presented was a very generalized one of a nation that was so recalcitrant, the likelihood of people everywhere seeking a word from Yahweh seems unreal. What the text seems to point to, however, was that priests, prophets, sages, visionaries would either cease to be or, if they were present, would have nothing to say; and even if people were to enquire of any one of them, running about in search of 'words' from Yahweh, there would be no answer or explanation—*'they will not be able to find one'* (Heb. *lo' yimṣā'û*). Whether this is related to Amaziah's comment that the land could not tolerate Amos's 'words' and demanded he stop (7.10-13) is uncertain, but in any event, the threat was that such an absence would become a much wider reality. Communication with and from Yahweh and his agents could come to an end.

8.13-14 When the crisis of vv. 11-12 arrived, Amos is said to have also envisaged a famine or 'thirst' causing even the young, men and women, to faint. There is a play on the word 'thirst' here if read figuratively in light of vv. 11-12, but some commentators read it here as literal thirst, a situation that makes no real sense in the context. Verse 14 speaks of people making oaths in the name of other gods, though the nature of these oaths, their purpose or intent, is not specified. Does it mean that they have assured the alien gods of allegiance if their metaphorical 'thirst' was to be assuaged? Even the young would 'faint'(?)—the Hebrew verb used here is in a form that pictures one covering oneself as with a shroud—before they ever found those words.

Oaths taken in the name of Ashimah of Samaria, literally 'Samaria's Shame', may refer pejoratively to an idol or image of Baal or even an Asherah apparently being worshipped in the north. Two versions of the oath are given: both use the form 'As your god lives …' (*hê* …) with the name of the gods specified, one revered in Dan in the north and the other revered in Beersheba in the south. These latter towns mark the extreme ends of Canaan, so serve as points that embrace the whole land and its people. Furthermore, these people will *'fall and never rise again'*. The metaphor recalls the rise and fall of the Nile river, but what is intended here is figurative for the end of the people of Israel, especially those who took advantage of the poor and needy. Amos's threat was that their imminent downfall is so close; they never will be able to rise again.

9.1-4 Fifth 'Vision'

1 *I saw my lord standing against the altar and he said: 'Strike the top of the pillar so that the thresholds shake. Cut them off at the head, all of them, and the left-overs let me kill with the sword. No fugitive shall escape, not one of them shall flee.*
2 *If they were to dig down to Sheol, from there my hand would pluck them up; if they were to go up to the heavens, from there I would bring them down.*
3 *If they were to hide themselves on the top of Carmel, from there I would seek them out and take them; and if they were to hide themselves from my sight at the bottom of the sea, from there I would command the sea-serpent (naḥaš) to bite them.*
4 *If they were to go to exile before their enemies, from there I would command the sword, and it would kill them. I would set my eye on them disaster and not for good/benefit.*

Formally, this fifth and final 'vision' is independent of the preceding four: Amos 'sees' someone, *ᵃdonāy*, 'my lord', rather than being shown some-

7.1–9.10 Amos's Visions 99

thing; *ᵃdonāy* asks no question but gives an order; the pronoun 'them' does not specify who is being addressed nor why; the divine monologue is lengthy and is structured as five conditional sentences, each beginning with *'im,* 'if they …' + verb, followed by *miššām,* 'from there, I would …' + verb; an inclusion, *'I will kill them by the sword'*, binds vv. 1, 4. Overall, it is a very vaguely expressed 'sighting'.

Although there is no mention of the 'day' in this 'vision', it would seem appropriate to think of the text as referring to it as either present or imminent, a 'day' or time that was inescapable, and thus its fearsome impact unavoidable. In colourful poetic imagery and style the editor emphasizes that nowhere is one safe from the imminent judgment. The image of God that this 'vision' projects is not a pleasant one, for 'my lord' *ᵃdonāy* is bent on destruction, recalling the opening image of Yahweh in 1.2. It is a fate that the final line here hardly softens—my lord's 'eye', that is, his intention, is on them, but not to offer something good, rather to bring pain and suffering (Heb. *rā'â*). There is no question of God relenting in this text.

Verse 1 pictures 'my lord' standing, as in 7.7, but on this occasion by the altar. If this were an ocular vision, then it might be in Bethel or some other northern sanctuary, but it seems that this is another imagined scenario, so to think of an altar in an unnamed temple is appropriate. Amos is ordered to strike the tops of the support pillars, the capitals, so that their bases shake and they crash down on the heads of all people present (present for what?) and presumably including any officiating priests. If there were some who survived the crash and tried to escape, then God would kill them with his sword, another figure of speech. This is hardly an encouraging vision, and one so different from the God who relented in the first two reported 'visions'. When speaking of those who may try to escape, the language is powerful: two parallel clauses stress that escape is not possible. Death awaits all without distinction. Such a 'vision' of Yahweh's total destruction of that community for whatever reason is deeply troubling to most readers, but one can only acknowledge that this was a dimension of the divine, consistent with the terrifying description of Yahweh with which the full report opened (1.2).

There follows a set of five conditional clauses—*'even if they …, then I …'*—depicting the divine response to any attempt to escape. The potential avenues of escape are expressed in exaggerated form—digging down to Sheol, the place of the dead; climbing up to the heavens; hiding on a mountain top; diving to the bottom of the sea; going to some foreign country. No matter where people seek to run to avoid the imminent disaster, 'my lord' *ᵃdonāy* can find them and deal with them. God's hand can reach into Sheol, and pluck them out; if they rise to the heavens, his dwelling place, from there he will expel them; if they were to dive to the very bottom of the sea (*Yam*), the mythical serpent *nāḥāš* will bite them at God's request; and those who seek exile in a foreign land will be found, and the sword will kill them. Death in one manner or another awaits—while the reader awaits an explanation, a reason, for such comprehensive destruction. The focus on death and destruction is presented without any specific context, meaning that they are and were independent items.

The final clause summarizes what Amos believed to be God's attitude to Israel—he will do harm, not good. There is no room here for 'turning' (Heb. *šwb*) as in 4.8-11! This is not a message that offers hope to the nation. There is also possible a play on words in 9.1, 4: what Amos 'saw' (*rā'â*) would prove to be *rā'â* (distress).

But what is Amos's concept of God as evidenced in this text? Readers are most probably left with the impression that his God is cruel and demanding, especially when no reason is offered for such a disaster being imposed. Readers are supposed, it seems, to recall that Amos's vision for the community was to see justice and righteousness established throughout—its failure must surely be the grounds for the disaster that is threatened. As such, it is so unlike the face of God in the first two 'visions' where God's mind can be swayed by a trifling intercession.

9.5-6 Yahweh the Creator

> 5 *My lord, Yahweh of hosts, he who touches the earth and it melts and all in it mourn; all of it rises like the Nile and recedes like the Nile of Egypt,*
> 6 *who builds his high places in the heavens and founds his storeroom on the earth, who calls forth the waters of the sea and pours them out on the face of the ground, Yahweh is his name!*

These two verses are generally regarded as a doxology, similar to those in 4.13; 5.8-9. Both also highlight the response, 'Yahweh is his name!' It is clear that these two verses are focused on the power of Yahweh as Creator and on his interaction with the material world. It is poetic language that paints a picture in short brush strokes. If/when God 'touches' the earth it melts, and those who live on it mourn for what has been lost; the annual rise and fall of the Nile river provides an analogy for the rise and fall of the land, perhaps suggesting earth tremors and earthquakes unless the 'rise and fall' are metaphors for political ends.

Verse 6 turns to the heavens and earth metaphors as God 'builds' structures in the heavens (Heb. *ma'ᵃlât* is literally his ascents) while on earth he establishes storehouses. Both references are vague and do not allow further clarification. The mention of 'seas' may describe flooding, though some suggest it is rain storms. The real point is that these are imaginative poetic descriptions to heighten the presentation of divine power exercised over the natural world. And the one who is responsible for all this—*his name is Yahweh*! It is like a triumphant shout from an awestruck poet, whether Amos or more likely perhaps, his editor.

What might be the function of a doxological insert at this point in the text? The triumphant shout *'Yahweh is his name!'* celebrates the national God as Creator, as one who uses that power in a manner that can bring destruction on the material and human world. Within the hymn-like celebration there is also a threat, a warning that if justice and compassion are not made the foundations of a society, then it is doomed to destruction.

9.7-10 Yahweh, the Lord of History, Shakes Israel

> 7 *'Are you not to me like the Cushites, O people of Israel?' says Yahweh. 'Did I not bring Israel up from Egypt, and the Philistines from Caphtor, and the Syrians from Kir?'*
> 8 *'Look, the eyes of my lord Yahweh are on the sinful kingdom, and I would destroy it from the face of the earth, except that I would not completely destroy the house of Jacob'*, says Yahweh.
> 9 *'For look, I command and shake among all the nations the house of Israel just as one shakes a sieve, but no stone falls to the ground'.*
> 10 *'By the sword they will die, every sinner among my people, those who say, "May the disaster not come near nor confront us!"'.*

As I read these questions and statements that follow the doxology of v. 6, it is clear that v. 7 is independent of the three verses that follow, vv. 8-10, in the sense that v. 7 applies to the entire nation, north and south; it is not confined to Amos's audience in the north.

What intrigues this reader is that v. 7 is presented in the form of two rhetorical questions. Why choose this form? The form itself is generally regarded as a way of making a strong positive statement, similar to the strong statements implied in the rhetorical questions in 3.3-8. Here, the two rhetorical questions would expect Israel to answer 'No, we are not!' (or 'Yes, we are not!' in some languages!) denying the possibility, whereas Amos's point is to assert resolutely his thesis that there is no distinction between Yahweh's attitude to Cush and his attitude toward Israel.

The first question concerns Yahweh's relationship with an alien community, the Cushites, and the second question relates to the migration of Philistines and Syrians. Both questions are equivalent to positive statements that must have come as a complete surprise and profound challenge to Israel and its self-image. Both questions speak to the way Yahweh views the world. So, did Yahweh really think and act like this? From where did Amos get this perspective on Yahweh's wider involvement?

Cush may refer to the tribes who lived in the area generally known as Ethiopia today. It was known as a fabulous land where jewels might be found (Job 28.19). What was it about the Cushites, a Nubian people south of Egypt's border, that lies behind this statement of Yahweh's relationship with them? Some have suggested that, like Israel, they were under Egyptian domination and enslaved, but this is all an arbitrary guess. In Gen. 2.13, however, 'Cush' appears as the name of a region in Mesopotamia, so it is quite possible that 'Cush' was simply a local 'dialect' term used to represent any remote, distant and alien people, regardless of location. The important thing to note is that the question implies a stripping away of whatever Israel thought of its privileged relationship with its God, Yahweh.

Even more important is it to ask, In what way or manner were these people said to be *'like Israel'* to Israel's God? Is it a case of the Cushites being compared to the Israelites, that is, as a people in covenant with Yahweh, as was Israel? Or is it that the Israelites are being compared to the distant and 'unchosen' Cushites? The syntax suggests the latter, that Yahweh's relationship with Israel is no different from that which Yahweh has also with the Cushites. And if that is the case, then Israel is not especially 'chosen', for being 'chosen' was merely Israel's perspective on the relationship, not necessarily Yahweh's. If that is how the text is to be read, then Israel's tribal and religious self-confidence is more than just threatened. Questions must surely have arisen in any Israelite mind upon hearing or reading this 'word', but it is so terse that one is simply left to imagine its specific content. It remains a live question for any religious tradition that sees or claims itself to be special!

Amos appears therefore to be indirectly dismissing Israel's claims about its being a uniquely 'chosen' one, as claimed by the Deuteronomic cohort, a belief based on understanding the escape from Egypt and journey to Canaan as the concrete proof of their privileged position with 'their' personal and covenanted God. Amos then represents a view on this issue that differed from that of the strictly orthodox Deuteronomic cohort, a fact that must have caused some angst.

It is interesting to note also that it is the national exodus tradition that is promoted here in 9.7b rather than the Abrahamic tradition; bringing the Jacob tribes from Egypt is highlighted, rather than the earlier calling of Abraham from Haran to Canaan (Gen. 12.1-3).

The verse continues, via rhetorical questions again, with the astounding claim that the migration of the two traditional enemies of Israel, the Philistines around the twelfth century BCE and the Arameans in the eleventh century BCE, to their present locations was the work of Yahweh, just as was Israel's own return migration from Egypt. There is a sense in Amos the book that everything that happens on the face of the earth is entirely attributable to Yahweh, so inevitably the movement or migration of peoples is simply another example of Yahweh being powerfully active in his world; it is one aspect of the event–cause relationship set out in 3.3-8. It does, however, need to be balanced against the statement in 3.1-2, here attributed to Yahweh, an unqualified statement of Israel's privileged position with their God. Is the conflict between these two notions inevitable if Yahweh is the awesome Creator of all and director of all human history? Or is the analogical use of the exodus motif simply a literary device for speaking about the way God works, not to be taken literally? Could or should the analogy be applied even more widely, perhaps even universally? If not the exodus analogy, can other elements in Israel's story be applied analogically to the rest of history?

Caphtor is probably what is now known as Crete, the island in the Mediterranean (LXX suggests Cappadocia), while *Kir* is uncertain. No matter who and where they have moved, Yahweh is here said to have been responsible for their migration. No detail is offered as to when, how or under whose leadership that might have occurred. Is that the point of this statement—that Yahweh is the one lord of national histories as well as of creation? Given that the preceding doxology draws special attention to the name Yahweh itself, 9.7-10 provides concrete examples that support the claim that Yahweh is lord of hosts as well.

While 9.7 looks back to the past, 9.8-10 looks forward. Based on the thesis that Amos was not a prophet forecasting some future event, but that as a visionary he spoke of what could happen, my translation renders the imperfectives as volitional forms—they speak of what God could or would do—for there is potential now for a change as not all would be destroyed, only the 'sinner' element.

In v. 8 Yahweh is said to *'fix my gaze on them'*, similar to the thought in v. 4. There it was a threat of harm; so also here. It is directed against *'the sinful kingdom'*, though identifying that kingdom is not absolutely certain. It could refer to northern Israel, to all Israelites, or to the enemies, but from Amos's Deuteronomic perspective there could only be one object and that was the north. There may be a measure of comfort, however, in that the destruction would not be total; some may survive. No information is provided as to who, how many and why some would survive apart from the very general identification of death for the 'sinners' in v. 9.

The metaphor of the sieve and the sifting of stones appears in v. 9. Details are far from clear, partly because the Hebrew noun $k^eb\bar{a}r\hat{a}$, 'sieve?', is a *hapax*, and its precise meaning uncertain. The shaking of the house of Israel among all the nations appears to imply that Israel will be lumped together with the nations and shaken around for the purpose of separating one from the other. Insofar as they are already separate, what is the logic in putting all together in a sieve for separation? Surely the main idea is to separate the 'sinners' from the rest within Israel, not separating Israel *'from among the nations'*! What possible action could be in view that achieves any such separation, and how are 'sinners' identified? If no pebble falls to the ground, then the sieve has failed to fulfil its function, as all remain within the sieve. How does it relate to the statement that not all Israel will be destroyed, only the 'sinners'? The figurative language is so opaque that whatever it might have meant originally is now a complete mystery. Arbitrary guesses as to its precise meaning depend on one's preconceptions and are not generally helpful.

What is clear, however, is that the final verse, 9.10, refers to those who believe that they are safe from any threatened destruction, wishful that such may not come anywhere near them. Only 'sinners', presumably the oppressor and unjust elite spoken of earlier, will be *'put to the sword'*, the metaphor of death noted in the 'vision' and in v. 4.

It is apparent that this particular section raises difficult theological issues for all readers, but particularly so because of the lack of clarity in the text itself and the implied image of Yahweh's use of unbridled power.

9.11-15 Judah's Fortunes Restored

11 *'On that day I would set up the booth of David that has fallen, repair its broken parts, raise its ruins, and rebuild it as in the distant past.*
12 *So that they may possess what was left of Edom and all the nations that are called by my name,' says Yahweh who does this.*
13 *'Behold the days are coming', says Yahweh, 'when the one who plows will catch up to the one who reaps and the one who treads grapes will catch the one who sows seed; the mountains will drip with grape juice and all the hills will flow with it.*
14 *and I would bring back my people Israel and they would rebuild the ruined cities and live there, plant vineyards and drink their wine, and they will plant gardens and enjoy their fruits.*
15 *And I would plant them on their land and never again uproot them from their land that I gave them,' said Yahweh your God.*

This closing section of the book has been the focus of much study with the general consensus that it represents a late, that is, postexilic, addition, for it relates to a historical situation well beyond Amos's time and concerns. The most obvious evidence of its late date is the complete turn away from the negativity of the preceding messages to something positive—the return and restoration of the Davidic dynasty (Zerubbabel?) and the restoration of abundant life for the community. It would seem also to imply that the two parts of the divided nation could reunite as before. Furthermore, using hyperbole again, an assured(?) future for Judaea is given, one that would mean never again going into exile; so clearly it is a postexilic note. Who might have contributed this material and what relationship it bears to the concerns of Amos himself is uncertain; it may simply be a completely independent and anonymous 'prophetic' note that somehow has become attached to the book before it was stitched into the scroll. The language is again general, so there is no mention of Jerusalem as its centre, only a vague hope for restoring what had been lost.

In v. 11 the 'booth of David' (Heb. *sukkat dāwîd*) is read by some as Sukkoth of David, thus referring to a town from which David launched attacks on Edom (Ps. 60.8-11). This interpretation has some logic since the *sukkâ*, or temporary booths set in the fields at harvest time, would probably not have 'broken parts' requiring repair, though that is not impossible. On the other hand, a booth being a temporary hut may suggest only a temporary restoration—or is that too literal? For others, the metaphor of repairing breaches relates to the broken walls of Jerusalem being repaired in Nehemiah's time (Neh. 12.27). Whatever reading of the Hebrew is correct, it does not detract from the metaphorical reference to the resurrection of the Davidic dynasty, the kings of the southern kingdom of Judah, from which Amos originated. The midrash in Acts 15.16-17 is irrelevant to our task here.

The thought in v. 12 is that this renewed Davidic house would control Edom and the nations 'that are called by my name', that is, God's name, Yahweh. What does this hyperbolic statement convey? The phrase is literally *'all the nations over whom my name has been called'*, and it means that Yahweh is their overlord. Which nations were they? Perhaps it was all those nations noted in 1.2–2.5. By adding the formula *'says Yahweh who does this'* the editor has tried to emphasize divine intention in this restoration.

The future that is envisaged in this closing section turns to the theme of abundance, both agricultural and material, as a consequence of the restoration. It fits closely with the Deuteronomic vision of blessing. Again, it is expressed in hyperbolic terms: as soon as seed is sown, it is ready to be harvested; as soon as grapes are planted, the treader of the fruit can harvest and tread out the wine—food and wine in an overabundance. The message in v. 14 appears to abandon the hyperbole and resume more normal description. Damaged cities can be repaired or rebuilt, and people can return to live in them as before; like home gardens they will be planted, but unlike the plants that can be quickly pulled up, the people will *'never again be plucked up'* out of their homeland. The use of hyperbole is fundamental when describing wide-ranging visions for the future.

Who might have added this conclusion and when? If the date relates to a hoped-for restoration of the Davidic dynasty, it may recall the period after Cyrus of Persia captured Babylon and in 538 BCE signed a decree allowing those who were in exile to return to Jerusalem. Zerubbabel, who was said to have Davidic lineage, was appointed 'governor' after Sheshbazzar. Could it relate to certain Judaean hopes in this late-exilic period, even between the appointment of Sheshbazzar and that of Zerubbabel? Certainly it would be consistent with the hopes of a man like Haggai or his contemporary Zechariah. What remains a problem is that from 538 onward, Judah was never a kingdom in which a revived Davidide was king; rather it was for the next two centuries a Persian dependency, with the northern kingdom already lost to history.

Within this section can be noted the 'knitting together' of Amos with the following book in the scroll, Obadiah, as Amos 9.12 relates closely to

Obad. 1-2, via the references to Edom and the nations. These clearly are a case of an addition to Amos in the postexilic period. Of course, the date at which the book is incorporated into the scroll does not affect the date of the material within it; that remains consistent with the period of its origin. What we can never know unequivocally, however, is its moment of origin; we can only take its contents as a late expression of a longing for a better and restored future in the south for those who survive the judgment of 'that day'.

Postscript

God, Israel and Humanity

The book of Amos contains within it, as noted, two perspectives on Yahweh's relationship with Israel, one affirming Israel's belief in an exclusive relationship (3.1-2) and the other that places Israel as merely one among a group of nations or peoples whose story was said to reflect God's work in the world. See the exegesis of 9.7 above.

More broadly, it is clear that within Israel of Amos's day there was a firm belief that its God, Yahweh, was omnipresent in all human history, not just that of the Israelites, even though in reality that view could be applied only to those few nations of which it was aware around the eastern Mediterranean some 2,500 years ago. Israelites obviously retained a memory of people movements throughout the region, and in Amos there was the claim that Yahweh was directly involved in them, just as he was believed to have been in their own story. Using analogy, Amos the book presents the migrations of Syrians and Philistines into the region as on a par with Israel's own exodus. Implicit in that is the possibility that similar divine interaction held true for all other nations in the region.

The foreign nation oracles in the opening chapter (1.3–2.16) and those throughout Isaiah and Jeremiah were further examples of the Israelite belief that Yahweh was actively engaged in the life of other nations, though usually it was for Israel's advantage! Isaiah, a near contemporary of Amos, spoke of the Assyrians as the *rod of God's anger* (Isa. 10.5-12), an agent with which to flay a disobedient Israel. One of Isaiah's followers later spoke of Cyrus, the enlightened Persian ruler, as Yahweh's *messiah* (Isa. 45.1), and of his exploits as planned to accomplish Yahweh's objectives. Thus we can be confident that at least some well-regarded Israelite figures had a vision of their God similar to that of Amos, a vision that was wider than the tribal. While Israel's claim to having a special relationship with Yahweh was just that, a private claim, it was a claim that gave the people its sense of unique identity. If this same Yahweh was so deeply involved with the nations around Israel, both friend and foe, however, it presented a *theological conundrum* as the two theses then involved a deep and unresolved tension: How could Israel claim an exclusive relationship with Yahweh their private God when Yahweh shared his interests around?

On the other hand, Israel's Wisdom tradition, its sages, held a much more international outlook, balancing it with their national identity. It maintained its own tribal expression of *ḥokmâ*, 'wisdom' (Prov. 1.7), while having that broader experience and outlook. The Israelite sages, it seemed, abandoned the exclusivist position, freely interacting with and sharing ideas across national boundaries, especially with Egypt, while still affirming some form of a national identity. That is one explanation for Wisdom's preferring to use *'elôhîm* when referring to God, rather than the specific 'name' YHWH, or Yahweh. There arises an inevitable tension then between the 'theologian'—if that's what Amos epitomizes—and the sage, because each had a different worldview.

Israel's wisdom tradition was fundamentally different from other tribal instincts, for it looked not only to an internationally shared body of material, but more importantly, to a shared approach to what it was to be human, all sages pondering issues that were vital to personal wellbeing and communal harmony. The book of Proverbs, Qoheleth and a plethora of non-biblical Israelite materials all testify to the way Israel's sages deliberated on those countless issues and situations that arise in personal and social life, as well as one's religious understanding. Conclusions reached by the sages across the cultural or tribal divides were inevitably similar, if not identical, given that the experience of being human is and was a shared one. Whereas a group like the Deuteronomic cohort spoke in absolute terms, the sages all worked from the relativity of different personal experiences and with a measure of uncertainty—see Qoheleth—as not all questions humans have can be readily answered.

For one who has spent most of his working life outside the Western cultural world, this aspect of God-in-history is fascinating, especially when considering Christian mission, which has most often viewed other histories, cultures and religions so negatively. It has done so on the premise that it is only in the Christian biblical context—OT and NT—and from a traditional Nicaean viewpoint that the God–humanity relationship can be understood. It reads the OT in a specific manner that views Jesus as the goal, the *telos*, of the Israelite story, a reading method that certainly is not one shared by those for whom the Hebrew Scriptures continue to represent their own pre-Christian story. Prioritizing the church's own worldview and history, grounded in that of Israel, and seeking to impose it on another and far more ancient cultural world under the guise of an exclusive biblical truth is a form of rape. Assuming that by adopting the Israelite story and reading it in light of the NT developments the church offers the unique and true story of the God–humanity relationship is seriously problematic.

Can one really 'borrow' another nation's—for example, ancient Israel's—history and perspective, use the biblical example analogically and apply it universally, or substitute a select reading of the biblical history for one's own? If one considers the biblical record to be THE source of all truth, or accepts the thesis that God intervenes in all human history regardless of time and place, then one must seek whatever is 'of God' in other ancient cultures, not deny them. Claims to uniqueness do not equate to exclusivity or negate the value of differences.

Just as Israelite wisdom demonstrates links with the wisdom traditions of its neighbours, especially that of Egypt, through a shared humanity, so it stands to reason that the wisdom of, for example, Confucius, and sages from the various cultures of South and East Asia, of Africa or the Americas, the Pacific and even Australia, needs to be taken seriously as the wider historical canvas of God at work there and incorporated into an overall theology. What would be the criteria for such a search? The wisdom of other cultures, Greek, Chinese or whatever, that predate the Christ must be valued as points at which the divine and human touch, if it touches anywhere at all. The national stories may differ wildly, but the underpinning wisdom within shared humanity offers a potential point of contact.

Jesus, an heir to the Hebrew wisdom tradition, was primarily a sage. He lived, taught and died as a sage, long before the human Jesus was elevated, in the mind of some followers, to that of the divine. He was a teacher whose pithy sayings and down-to-earth parables continued to exhibit the vital role of wisdom within that cultural world. He spoke of how to live a fully human existence, how to live in community where compassion, care and justice for all were priority values. In the same way, sages from other cultural communities have through the millennia offered the same advice and counsel as found in ancient Israel and in Jesus. Surely it is in these practical matters that there is a potential 'bridge' between the Hebrew Scriptures and the many ancient cultures known in our modern world.

Claiming that God has made himself(?) known in a 'special' revelation exclusive to the biblical community, that only there in the divinized Jesus, the Christ-figure, can one define what 'God' means, simply reveals the preconceptions of Western theologians with little or no experience of those other cultures, and with no regard for *homo sapien's* 300,000-year history that precedes. The Christ is not the fulcrum around whom all human–divine activity revolves; in his own time and community Jesus was not, nor is today, viewed as that exclusive point of contact; it is only within a Christianized and limited worldview that the Christ has been elevated to that position.

A relatively late Christ-centred worldview from the fourth century CE cannot represent the breadth of any alleged divine interaction with the world. This is not 2023, nor 5023, nor even 100,023. Whatever its modern practical value, a 'Christ-based' time scale and approach to global history such as our 'Common Era' represents only the tiniest fraction of the story of any possible human–divine connection. Acknowledging God in other cultures and their story is an essential element in a theology that has any validity; it also saves from 'spiritual arrogance' and narrow claims to exclusive truth. Surely Amos the book would agree that in the matter of the divine–human encounter one has to give more place to the wisdom tradition's emphasis on justice and righteousness, and to its universality, rather than to restrict it to any narrow Christology.

Selected Bibliography

Andersen, F.I., and D.N. Freedman, *Amos: A New Translation with Introduction and Commentary* (AYB, 24A; New York: Doubleday, 1989). Beware of information overload!

Barton, J., *The Theology of the Book of Amos* (Cambridge: Cambridge University Press, 2012).

Eidevall, G., *Amos: A New Translation with Introduction and Commentary* (AYB, 24G; New Haven, CT: Yale University Press, 2017).

Finkelstein, I., and N.A. Silberman, *The Bible Unearthed: Archaeology's New Vision of Ancient Israel and the Origin of its Sacred Texts* (New York: Simon & Schuster, 2001).

Stuart, D.K., *Hosea–Jonah* (WBC, 31; Waco, TX: Word Books, 1987).

Waard, J. de, 'The Chiastic Structure of Amos v 1-17', *VT* 27 (1977), pp. 170-77.

—, and W.A. Smalley, *A Handbook on the Book of Amos* (UBS Handbook Series; New York: UBS, 1979).

Waltke, B.K., and M. O'Connor, *An Introduction to Biblical Hebrew Syntax* (Winona Lake, IN: Eisenbrauns, 1990).

MICAH

A Commentary

Introduction

Micah, the book, is located in the Scroll of the Twelve, the so-called Minor Prophets, at no. 6, though in terms of its historical setting it should sit alongside no. 3, Amos, given that it relates to Israel during the Assyrian period. Micah shares the Israelite stage with Amos, Hosea and Isaiah in the latter half of the eighth century BCE.

How and why Micah came to be included in the scroll as part of what became known as the 'Latter Prophets' within the Hebrew canon is not now something that can be traced. It is clear, however, that Micah the man did retain some kind of reputation for his work in the oral traditions of the time, and was so remembered by a later generation (see Jer. 26.18). For further background, see 2 Kgs 15.32–20.21 in the Deuteronomic cohort's written version of those times (the DH) based on 'official' annals of the kings of both Israel and Judah.

Modern research into Micah the book has a rather checkered history. What is clear is that the many seemingly disparate elements of which the book is composed has challenged scholars to seek precise historical contexts for each, leading to a range of attempts to locate this or that section with Micah himself, or to link them to potential times and sources outside the mid- to late-eighth century BCE. This text-history search has had the general aim of identifying the supposed 'original' words of Micah as distinct from supposed later traditions about him. However, it has been far from a successful venture in the sense that researchers have never been able to arrive at a consensus. Such a failure is due no doubt to the disparate nature of the material itself, the very generalized language employed throughout and to commentators' personal and arbitrary preconceptions or methodologies, including seeing Micah as a 'prophet' when the term *nābî'* is never used of him. Consequently, some recent research has moved to prioritize the material's literary and rhetorical features as the more appropriate and fruitful means of unlocking something of the transmission and editing process that has brought us the book as we now know it.

One can from the text justifiably assert that Micah was a spokesperson, one who had a message, and that the message was orally delivered—the verb used is *ngd*, which conveys a sense of expounding, explaining or making matters conspicuous. There are sufficient oral markers such as

'Hear this ...' or 'Woe to those who ...' to substantiate this point. What we now read, however, is a written version of Micah's words that preserves what was remembered and talked about from his speeches in the community; they are now available only in this one 'frozen' written form. How close the written form is to that of the oral delivery may be argued but never proven, and scholars have diverged widely when it comes to decisions about the matter. What particular contexts Micah's numerous original speeches addressed can be seen in general terms, but never identified with the degree of certainty many would wish. Identifying genres, noting material differences between one unit and another, and the specific rhetorical devices used allow readers to appreciate how complex was the process of transitioning from oral speech to the editor's written format.

It is abundantly clear that the final work is that of an editor(s) who has assembled the material, provided the introductory Superscript (1.1), and arranged the material of which he was aware into some order, setting it within the framework he has constructed, namely a book-length chiasm. What is uncertain is to whom many of the words recorded were originally addressed, other than to 'Israel' more generally. Nor can we know how often Micah may have used or reused a particular speech or theme, and done so perhaps with slight variations as was often the case in an oral culture such as that of Israel at the time—we know that traditions can migrate (see the example in Gen. 12, 20 and 26!). Generalized language and pronominal references in Micah are never without questions as to their reference, so aiming to fix Micah's words to specific historical moments and situations is unwise.

Despite the challenges, most commentators are of the view that there are three main divisions in the material before us. The first question is then to determine what those three sections are—chs. 1–3, 4–5 and 6–7, or 1–2, 3–5 and 6–7. Most agree that there is a marked difference between the material in chs. 6–7 and the rest of the record. Within these sections, some suggest that there is an editorial balance established between units that focus on judgment and those that bring messages of hope, though the preponderance lies with the more negative messages.

Our challenge in this commentary is to see whether there is some way to resolve one or more of these issues and to submit them for wider attention and comment. The method to be adopted will be that of close attention to the rhetorical and literary elements of the book within its cultural and religious setting. That is not to say that others have failed to consider these two procedural matters, but that perhaps one can give more weight to them than has happened in some cases in the past.

Who and What Was Micah?

The title of 'prophet' (Heb. *nābî'*) is never applied to Micah in this book—that much is undisputed. The term *nābî'* is applied to others by Micah, but in a clear derogatory manner (3.5-7). Furthermore, verbal forms of the root *nb'* are not used to describe Micah's special activity, one that is 'declaratory'. Micah in 3.8 claims that he was *'filled with power, with the spirit of the Lord, and with justice and might'*, with the specific task of declaring (Heb. *ngd*) the nation's sin. The nature of Micah's mission thus requires a more nuanced understanding, rather than perpetuating the myth of a 'prophetic' role as has been and generally remains common practice. The simple fact is that, according to the text, Micah was not a *nābî'*, a prophet! See the Postscript **Micah, Amos, Isaiah and a Prophetic Crisis**.

The most telling evidence that Micah was not a *nābî'*, a prophet, lies in his denunciation of all *nᵉbî'îm*, characterizing them as those who lead people astray, speaking comforting words to any who would 'suck up' to them—see Mic. 3.5-8. Micah quite deliberately sets himself apart from such figures, all of whom he condemns, anxious that he is not mistaken for one. Micah was an iconoclast! His rather self-righteous claim that he was filled with 'the spirit of the Lord', while revealing something of his true personality, is his formal declaration that he believed himself to be superior to all who claimed to be prophets. Even allowing for Micah's hyperbole and generalized language, this claim reveals much about the man and his personality. His contemporary Amos likewise denied any relationship to the prophets and the prophetic movement (Amos 7.15-16), a scenario that suggests that during this mid- to late-eighth century BCE the prophetic activity of so-called *nᵉbî'îm* had lost much or all of its credibility because it had become corrupt. It is important to note that three contemporary spokespersons, Micah, Amos and Isaiah of Jerusalem (Isa. 9.15; 28.7), were Judaeans of the same generation and viewpoint and that they held a similar negative attitude to those who called themselves *nābî'*, 'prophet'. How the movement had reached this nadir is the question that needs to be explored. Was it brought on by broad social and/or religious decay itself, or was it merely some negative influence from the northern kingdom, as the DH would have us believe?

The editor has described Micah in 1.1 as (a) one with whom was the 'word of the Lord' and (b) as one who 'saw' (Heb. *ḥāzâ*) things that disturbed him. Both qualities are significant because he was a visionary. A modern reader's common understanding of what an Israelite prophet was and did is generally deficient, perhaps even distorted, by its focus on passing on a message received directly from God with regard to the future. That certainly was the Deuteronomic cohort's definition of a prophet (see Deut.

18.15-22), but it is far too narrow and sectarian a view to apply to Micah. A better and more nuanced definition of the term 'prophet' and of 'prophecy' itself is required. Hopefully, we can arrive at a more complete understanding of the ancient 'prophet' in general, of developments or changes both positive and negative that took place within the 'profession', and of Micah the visionary in particular. What we will find is that at the time of Amos, Micah and Isaiah the role of the *nābî'* was scorned by others in the community, especially by those social and religious critics who came to be known as visionaries, the *hôzeh* community whose personal insights were key.

Based on the first-person pronominal use in 1.2-7 and elsewhere, Micah, and those visionaries like him, was not a ventriloquist mouthing words deriving from an external source; rather, from his own keen observation, reflection and critique of his world, he came to have a view of Yahweh that he wanted to advance. Micah spoke about what he saw, and about how he saw it relating to Yahweh the national God. In light of this, the phrase 'the word of Yahweh' that opens the report in 1.1 has to be read as an objective genitive, words about, not from, Yahweh for they were words that resided in or were present with Micah (see my exegesis of 1.2-7 below). Perhaps this perspective, one that more closely resembles that of the wisdom tradition, could be applied more to all so-called spokespersons reported on in the Scroll of the Twelve, instead of lumping these various figures together as 'prophets' when they are denied such identity in the text. This would also apply to the *maśśā'* reports of Nahum, Habakkuk and Malachi. The simplistic view that 'all prophets spoke only what God instructed them to speak' demeans the individual and his personal vision, his *hazon* and insights, as well as diminishing the importance of what they spoke about.

Micah is said to have 'seen' the situation that obtained in the cities of Samaria and Jerusalem, the two centres of the divided Israelite kingdom. As an iconoclast, he was particularly critical of the civil and religious elite throughout Israelite society of the time for their abuse of power, their self-serving and unjust ways. Although Micah is not spoken of specifically as a *hôzeh*, a 'seer', unlike Isaiah, there is a nuance in the participle that suggests that 'seeing' was a state of being, an element integral to one's make-up as one who evaluated what he saw of communal life; it was not just a 'professional' tag. See below at 3.8.

The editor notes that this Micah was from Moresheth, in the Shephelah or foothills to the west of Judah's central mountains. It was a small town not far from the important city of Lachish. It was a strategic town as access to Jerusalem from the coast passed through the region. Good soils and rain-bearing winds from the Mediterranean meant that the area was Judah's main agricultural region as well. During the eighth century BCE there was a rapid expansion of villages and towns as the population in the region grew. So, Micah can be imagined as from a relatively developed location, in contrast to that of Amos, his contemporary, over on the edge of the wilderness to the east.

What kind of work Micah and/or his family were engaged in to support themselves and other personal information are unknown, but there are many references to agriculture and crops, along with grape and olive harvests, throughout these speeches, suggesting he had a broad exposure to this kind of rural economy. It would not be too far from reality to think of Micah as possibly a farmer of some kind; after all, he would need to have had a way of supporting himself, and perhaps a family, between his occasional speeches. This was the case with all those individuals, whether prophet or not, whose reflections and conclusions were shared with the community.

The historical period covered by the book of Micah is that recorded in 2 Kings 15–20, the Deuteronomic cohort's own version of the times as compiled from official sources known as the Books of the Annals of the Kings of Israel and Judah. In other words, what we have in the book of Micah is a mini-selection of one man's critical activities in Judah in the mid- to late-eighth century BCE, a very, very brief edited report of what was a seriously troubled time for the citizens of Israel and Judah.

Authorship

While Micah the man is credited with the overall content of the numerous speeches reported in the book, in the current written form one must acknowledge that the editor(s) has also played a vital role as author by way of the chiastic structure he has imposed—see below. Selecting the particular speeches from an unknown number that Micah might have made and that were passed down orally in the community, arranging the report and its presentation as Micah the book was ultimately the work of the editor(s). The text we now have represents a shared project between Micah and the editor, who may or may not have known each other.

Whether the editorial frame has imposed the editor's personal interpretation of Micah's messages or simply gathered and faithfully presented the disparate elements of Micah's message is uncertain, but what is obvious is that the frame celebrates a view of Yahweh as the incomparable 'God of the whole earth'. The editor's presentation of Micah's message has been absolutely crucial to highlighting Micah's underpinning theology rather than just assembling his pronouncements. That theology climaxes in the numerically central unit, 4.11-13, around which the book now revolves, with fifty-one verses preceding and fifty-one verses following that central unit.

Date

While it is obvious that the material content of the book of Micah relates to the latter half of the eighth century BCE, the date at which the oral material reached its earliest written form is uncertain. It would have been some time after Micah's mission, but just how long after is unknown. What can be said is that the book's incorporation into the Scroll of the Twelve was late, in view of its placement after the book of Joel, which is almost certainly postexilic. Adding Amos and Micah to the scroll after having recorded the text of Joel places the date of their now written forms some two hundred years after their actual missions took place. The incorporation of books in the scroll does not follow a chronological order. The date of Micah's mission in the eighth century BCE is not to be confused with the possible date of the written report, nor the date of its actual incorporation within the Scroll of the Twelve.

Structure of Micah the Book

The editor's report is a carefully crafted, chiastically arranged text organized around 4.11-13, the numerically central verses.

As an essentially poetic document, the traditional parallel bicolon is typical of most every verse, but there are other structures or patterns that are crucial and that mark this book's special literary and theological identity.

1. Using the calls to '*Hear*' and '*Listen*' in 1.2, followed by '*Now hear this …*' in 3.1, and '*Hear what the Lords says…*' in 6.1, this reader is adopting the three markers as indicators of a three-part division, 1.2–2.13; 3.1–5.14(15); 6.1–7.20. The first and third divisions begin with the call to 'Hear …!'; both then follow with a threat, 'Woe …!' (2.1-13 and 7.1-17), and each book-ends the middle section, 3.1–5.14(15), which has its own cleverly designed structure. That structure focuses on the numerically central 4.11-13, the book's core. These three central verses lie within the three '*Now …*' portions (4.9, 11, 14[5.1]) that themselves lie within the two '*And you …*' sections (4.8; 5.1[2]) that are enclosed within the wider '*In that day …*' frame (4.1, 6; 5.9[10]).

This careful chiastic structure (see diagram below) demonstrates how the many components of Micah's oral presentation(s) have been so arranged that 4.11-13 present the core message of his vision, namely his view of Yahweh his God. While many readers (e.g. Waltke) put the focus on and around the ethical statement in 6.8, important though that may be, the primary concern of Micah the book as now extant is revealed in the editor's carefully planned structure: Israel's God, Yahweh, is lord/master of the whole earth.

A. 1.2 'Hear ...' (*šim'û* ...)
    2.1 'Woe ...' (*hôy* ...)
B. 3.1, 9 'Hear ...' (*šim'û* ...)
    4.1, 6 'In days to come ...' (*wᵉhāyâ ... bayyāmîm* ...)
        4.8 'And you ...' *(wᵉ'attâ ...)*
            4.9 'Now ...' *('attâ ...)*
            4.11 'Now ...' *('attâ ...)*
            4.14 (5.1) 'Now ...' *('attâ ...)*
        5.2 'And you ...' *(wᵉ'attâ ...)*
    5.9 'In that day ...' (... *bayyôm hahû'* ...)
C. 6.1,2,9 'Hear ...' (*šim'û* ...)
    7.1 'Woe ...' (*'allay* ...)

2. In addition to its overall chiastic structure, one other special and closely integrated feature needs to be recognized. The name 'Micah' is literally *'who is like ...?'*, an abbreviation of Micaiah (Heb. *mîkāyāh[û]*) or *'Who is like (Yah)'?*—see Jer. 26.18. Yet *'Micah'* is more than just a personal name; *'mîcâ'* is a live and fundamental question, and as such it begins the editor's presentation, one that is deeply theological. The question *mîkāyāh[û]* is the initial component of the Inclusion that is completed in 7.18-20 with the rhetorical question *mî-'ēl kāmôkā*, 'Who is a God like you?'—it closes the book with what is actually a faith statement that there is no God like Yahweh! Not only does the personal name function as *inclusio* part A, the numerically central verses 4.11-13 specifically describe or define Micah's view as to who and what Yahweh is: Yahweh is the master of the whole earth. The *inclusio* finishes with its faith-claim that Israel's Yahweh is incomparable, unlike all other gods.

3. On a smaller scale, 5.6-7 offers another structure or pattern, perhaps it can be called an extended parallelism: v. 6a = v. 7a using virtually the same wording; v. 6b = v. 7b as both lines focus on similes; v. 6c = v. 7c each begin with a relative marker, v. 6c a clause using negative verbs, v. 7c verbs in positive mode. Two alternative visions are thus presented to the 'remnant of Jacob'.

Similarly, another structure lies in the repetition of parallel rhetorical patterns in 6.1-8; see the exegesis below for details.

Focusing on these structural elements gives the final edited work a strong sense of unity, despite the fact that it is composed of a wide range of discrete speeches. What it does clarify is that the book and its collected speeches find their primary function as setting forth Micah's theological view—*the incomparable Yahweh is master of the whole earth.* This is a clear faith statement, not a prediction.

Outline of Micah the Book

[A] *1.1   Editor's Superscript—Who is like Yah?*
    1.2–2.13   Yahweh's Complaint against Samaria and Jerusalem
        1.2-7   Yahweh Acts against Samaria and Jerusalem
        1.8-9   Lament over Israel's Incurable 'Wounds'
        1.10-16 Lament over Assyria's Threat to Judah
        2.1-5   'Woe' to Leaders Abusing Power
        2.6-11   Against the 'Preachers'
        2.12-13 A Promise of Restoration
    3.1–5.14   The Sins of the Rulers
        3.1-4   Rulers of Jacob and Israel Hate Justice
        3.5-8   Prophets Who Lead Astray
        3.9-12 Priests, Rulers and Injustice
            4.1-5   In Days to Come
            4.6-7   Gathering the Lame
            4.8   Daughter Zion
                4.9-10   'Now ...'
[B]   4.11-13   'Now ...' *Yahweh is lord of the whole earth!*
                4.14(5.1) 'Now ...'
        5.2-5(1-6) One to Rule Israel
        5.6-8(7-9) The Remnant of Jacob
    5.9-14(10-15) The Day of the Cut Off
    6.1–7.20   The Lord's Controversy
        6.1-5   O my People!
        6.6-8   What Does the Lord Require?
        6.9-16 Treasures of Wickedness
        7.1-7   Woe Is Me!
        7.8-13 The Lord's Vindication
[C]   7.14-20 *Who Is a God like You?*

Micah the book has been deliberately structured to answer the *mîkâ* question, with the editor having gathered a wide range of Micah's statements in support of the theme. Those statements form a series of very loosely connected pieces whose relationship and sequencing are often difficult to discern. They speak of concerns Micah expressed orally over a lengthy period of time, up to a possible forty years, directed at different issues and/or groups within the Israelite community as a whole, and now set within its chiastic frame.

How the three major divisions—chs. 1–2, 3–5, 6–7—are related to one another is tantalizingly vague. There is no discernible or clear inner plot development other than a general movement from the initial question *mîkâ* ...? to the core in 4.11-13 and final rhetorical question, 'Who is a God like you?' (7.18). No individual characters are identified apart from several past ancient ones in 6.4-5, and the language used throughout is so general that it is impossible to tie any one statement or oracle to a current or potential historical situation. The final sub-section, 7.14-20, however, is viewed as Micah's concluding faith statement about Yahweh.

There are scholars who prioritize two basic kinds of statement as characterizing the contents of Micah, one that condemns, and the other that offers hope, with the suggestion that these two elements balance one another in each of the three main segments of the book. One suggestion, for example, is that 1.2–2.11 speak of judgment, while 2.12-13 speak of hope; 3.1-12 of judgment, 4.1–5.14(15) of hope; 6.1–7.6 of judgment and 7.7-20 of hope (e.g. Fretheim). Others opt for the more traditional pattern of an indictment followed by judgment and promise.

Literary Features

Since Micah the book is a written document, the first step in our approach is to acknowledge that we are reading a report by a literate editor who has assembled materials from oral speeches of Micah the man that were circulating in Israel at a point in time. They were speeches that Micah no doubt repeated as occasion required given the lengthy regnal period over which he is said to have spoken (1.1). The editor's report covers a range of select topics and situations all placed within his chiastic structure.

Written form differs from oral speech in many ways: it is more formal; uses a wider vocabulary range: sentences are usually longer and can be more complex with relative clauses; and is normally well structured rather than casual, halting speech with its short memorable sayings. So, the assumption is that what one now reads does not reproduce the exact speech of Micah the man as delivered but offers an adapted version presented in poetic style, using the rhetorical forms appropriate to written reporting. We further assume, however, that what is written does accurately reflect the substance of what Micah had to say, if not his exact words.

The final written document opens with the standard superscript form in 1.1. While the form may vary slightly, as in the opening verses of Hosea, Joel, Amos and Jeremiah, it is essentially fixed: *'The word(s) of the Lord that were with PN, in the days of ... that he saw concerning ...'*. I shall be arguing in the exegesis that the Hebrew phrase *hāyâ 'el* refers to 'the presence of the word with ...' PN, rather than 'the word coming to PN'. The word shared by the one nominated, his own word, is not of a divine source in the traditional sense. The meaning and application of the single phrase 'word of the Lord' (Heb. *dᵉbār-yhwh*) found in this and so many texts will be examined in the broader context. See also the Postscript.

Given that this reader understands the text to be conveying what Micah's vision was in principle, references with a future cast are not read as 'prophetic' or predictive; the verbs that speak of a potential action are read as volitional, as threats or warnings expressing what God *would* or *could* do, or what Micah *hoped* God would do, by way of a response.

Mention has already been made of the generalized language throughout this book. Sweeping generalizations such as Micah used tell us a great deal about the individual and his personal outlook, and they present a challenge to readers who may wish to see more nuance. Furthermore, hoping to find a connection between a text and a particular historical or social situation is not possible within the scope of such language. The language used *defies* that possibility for the most part, though obviously it envisages Micah's local audiences in the divided Israel and Judah over an extended period in the later eighth century BCE. The book's purpose is not that of recording specific historical details about Micah, the precise wording he used, or of the period in which he operated; rather, it is a general survey of Micah's speeches surrounding his claim that 'Yahweh is the incomparable master of the whole earth'.

Directing generalized words to both Samaria and Jerusalem makes it impossible for readers to ascertain whether certain challenges reported relate only to the northern kingdom, or to the southern kingdom or to both communities together. Such generalized language, typical of the iconoclast, also implies that all citizens may be indicted by his outspoken and condemnatory oracles as the report portrays him as failing to make any distinction with regard to the audiences; all are embraced within his dismissive threats.

Intimately related to this generalized language is the need to determine the field of reference of the pronouns 'you', 'us' and 'they/them', as well as of certain noun suffixes and noun phrases such as 'this family' or 'this flock'. Numerous verses exhibit a mix of pronouns such that it is not possible to decide who is speaking or who is being addressed. The most challenging, however, are the first-person pronouns used in contexts where Yahweh is simultaneously referred to in the third-person—see 1.8, 15; 2.3, 12-13; 3.8. Without some clarity around pronoun use, it may not be possible in many places to grasp what exactly the text is saying, who is saying it or to whom it is directed.

Rhetorical questions that are a prominent feature of some other books such as Amos and Malachi are used sparingly in Micah—1.5; 2.7; 6.6-7,

10-11—but also used strategically, such as the initial *mîkâ* and the concluding *mî 'ēl kāmôkā,* central to the theme of Yahweh's incomparability.

As a general rule, many sections of text first refer to an issue or situation, then follow with a 'Therefore ...' clause representing the potential divine response that Micah hopes to see enacted—see, for example, 1.6, 14; 2.3, 5; 3.6 etc.—and justifying the action that might follow.

Woe-oracle forms are a feature of 2.1-7 and 7.1-7 as Micah pours harsh criticism on certain individuals whose evil behaviour he believes requires addressing.

The use of imperatives features perhaps more than in some other books in the collection, beginning with the initial call to 'Hear ...!' (1.2; 3.1, 9; 6.1, 2, 9). The impression is that Micah was apt to issue commands to his audiences, giving an authoritarian tone to a number of the speech units in the book—see 1.10-13, 16; 7.5, 8, 14.

On the repetition of phrases, see 5.5(4)b and 5.6(5)c, 6-7(7-8), 10-13; 6.14-15. These are reminiscent of oral presentations. In the case of 5.6-7(7-8) and 6.1-2 the extended repetition suggests that each may represent the one example created by Micah that later existed in two oral versions known to the editor who simply placed one alongside the other.

Thematic connections via the figure of 'the day' in 4.1, 6; 5.9; 7.11-12 play a significant role in the report's structure and carry the potentiality that marks Micah's speech.

Similes and metaphors are frequent—see 1.4, 8; 3.3, 12; 4.9-10; 5.6-7(7-8); 7.17—many using animal imagery. The metaphor of rulers tearing skin and flesh from people, then boiling the bones in a kettle, is particularly dramatic (3.1-3).

Being essentially poetic, parallel lines with synonymous or near-synonymous terms is an obvious feature, but there are often multiples of three terms used to illustrate a point, forming a tricolon in place of the normal bicolon—see 1.6 (Samaria, her stones, her foundations); 1.7 (her images, her wages, her idols); 3.11 (rulers, priests, prophets); and 3.12 (Zion, Jerusalem, the mountain of the house, i.e., Temple); or 6.14-15 (you shall eat, but not be satisfied; ... you shall put away, but not save; ...sow, but not reap; tread olives, but not anoint ...; tread grapes, but not drink ...); and 7.6 (son–father, daughter–mother, daughter-in-law–mother-in-law).

There is wide use of the connecting particle w^e in an adversative role to note contrasting options or situations—see 2.8; 3.4, 5, 8; 4.4, 5, 12; 5.2; 6.8; 7.7, 13.

The formula *'Thus says the Lord ...'* is a *pro forma* phrase used by editors in all so-called prophetic books in the Hebrew Bible. It is used to add authority to the speaker and his words. In Micah it appears sparingly, used only on four occasions (2.3; 3.5; 4.6; 5.10), with the closing *'says the Lord'* (4.6; 5.9[10]) suggesting that the editor's focus was on what Micah himself saw, thought and spoke about. Micah's editor thus focused on having the people hear what Micah himself had to say—1.2; 3.1; 6.1—as is fitting for a visionary.

In 6.1-8 we read that the Lord had a dispute to settle with his people with regard to the divine requirements of justice, kindness and humility. The 'lawsuit' form (Heb. *rîb*) is intimated, but its several formal elements are never used in the current text. However, the following sub-section, 6.9-16, might well relate to the trial scenario being raised in vv. 1-8.

The text of Mic. 4.1-4 reappears in Isa. 2.2-4, so there is a question of textual priority and of literary borrowing to consider; does one borrow from the other, or do both borrow from a third source, or, as happens in oral transmission, have reports 'migrated' between different players? See the exegesis below.

Micah 3.12 regarding the fate of Jerusalem is quoted in the later book of Jeremiah, in Jer. 26.18. While commentators note this literary connection, it can be assumed that the Micah text is prior. It is also of significance that Mic. 3.12 is the statistical middle verse of the entire Scroll of the Twelve, highlighting Judah's self-confidence and arrogance with respect of Yahweh's unconditional presence in their sacred space. The retention of this memory of Micah's words does speak to the importance being attributed to that insight by others who recalled it and transmitted it, apparently over a century and more.

Historical Setting

The superscript places Micah in the latter part of the eighth century BCE, the period in which a sequence of three southern kings—Jotham, Ahaz and Hezekiah—were on the throne in Jerusalem. The dates are: Jotham (743–729), Ahaz (743–727), Hezekiah (727–698), making Micah's mission perhaps an extensive one in terms of the historical period involved. On the other hand, it seems more likely, in view of the issues of uppermost concern in the book, that the primary focus of Micah's mission relates to developments in Judah during the reign of Ahaz, though some suggest it extended into the early years of Hezekiah (see Jer. 26.18-19).

Little is known about Jotham, who came under pressure from Israel's northern kingdom and from Aram/Syria, but he was soon replaced by Ahaz, whose reign, according to the DH 'purist' evaluation, was totally disastrous, for when pressured by Israel and Syria, Ahaz turned to Assyria for help, becoming a virtual servant to the Assyrians. Despite that subservient relationship, there were economic benefits for Judah: trading in wine and oil. Jerusalem grew wealthy on this trade, elevating it from a backward and isolated rump kingdom in relation to the larger and more prosperous north. Along with this, however, went a religious life that reflected an older period of Israelite religion in which worship of alien gods was made an integral part of the worship of Yahweh. Ahaz is reported in the DH to have been an apostate who even burned his own son sacrificially to local gods (2 Kgs 16.2-4). Once Samaria in the north fell to the Assyrians in 721 BCE, Jerusalem and its institutions assumed more importance, and with it the push toward 'Yahweh-alone' as defining orthodox religion over against the northern apostasy gave the Deuteronomic cohort considerable power and influence. Opposition to local shrines, often called 'high places' (Heb. *bāmôt*), developed in support of the view that the Jerusalem Temple, the claimed location where God had *'put his name'*, was the only place where religious activity was legitimate. The end of the eighth century saw the expansion of Jerusalem's boundary to cover the whole area of the western hill, the 'City of David', as well as a rapid growth in population.

Under Hezekiah there were reforms (see 2 Kgs 18.3-7) consistent with the ideology of the Deuteronomic cohort, that is, 'Yahweh-alone', with Jerusalem considered as the only valid religious centre for the nation. The Lachish stele, however, casts a little doubt on the true nature of Hezekiah's religious reforms; they seem not to have been as thorough as the DH report states! Part of Hezekiah's vision for Judah involved the hoped-for restoration of the Davidic legacy and the reunification of the nation; it failed. With the ascent of Sennacherib to the Assyrian throne in 704 BCE and his rampage through the region in 701, Judah faced an existential crisis. That Assyrian advance into the coastal region of Judah, including the Shephelah, Micah's home, devastated much of the countryside, though there is no certainty that Micah's mission extended to that late date. The Shephelah took a long time to recover from the Assyrian assault as the Assyrians then 'gave' large parts of the best agricultural land to the Philistines and many Judaeans were exiled to Assyria.

Micah's Relationship to Amos and Isaiah

The late eighth century BCE saw Micah, along with Amos and Isaiah, active in their respective missions as visionaries. Amos and Micah refuse the identification as *nābî'*, prophet; and Isaiah is referred to throughout as *ḥôzeh*, a visionary, never as a *nābî'* prophet, other than in the final chs. 36–39 of Isaiah part 1, which have been copied into the text from the DH (2 Kgs 18–20). Those chapters were not part of the initial report of Isaiah's mission, meaning that all three contemporary spokespersons were visionaries, not prophets. See further in Postscript.

It was the Syro-Ephraimite challenge and then the Assyrian threat that dominated their times and concerns, which led to the collapse of the independent northern kingdom in 721 BCE. While Amos predates Micah and Isaiah, the issues faced were similar—foreign aggression and its impact. Isaiah of Jerusalem was a slightly later contemporary of Micah, and both addressed the Assyrian challenge and its occupation of the Shephelah, in particular the threat to the city of Lachish. See Isaiah 7 for Isaiah's comforting words to Hezekiah, words that in fact proved impossible of realization in face of the Assyrian advance.

Micah's imagery in 4.1-4 of swords and weapons being retooled, swords into plowshares, spears into pruning hooks, is repeated in Isa. 2.2-4 as people from all nations were said to flow toward Jerusalem in search of divine instruction and peace. There is no certain explanation for this textual repetition: either one or the other invented the text and the other copied it, or both copied it from an independent source, though some have suggested that it was added to Micah much later in the postexilic period by an unknown hand. What one has to consider also is that in the oral period it was always possible for traditions to 'migrate' or to be attributed to more than one 'player', as exemplified in Genesis 12, 20 and 26. If that was the case with this particular text, then there is no way we can be certain which man originated the message.

A Reading Strategy

Approaching an ancient document such as the Hebrew Bible, seeking to learn and appreciate what it has to say, especially when reading it in translation, requires the reader to consider carefully that its origin or source is that of a culture, language and society that is alien, alien to the modern reader's context. One cannot simply assume that the words on the page always mean exactly what it might mean in, for example, modern English, and even there one has to recognize that individual meanings may change through the generations, as happens in all living languages. Cultural differences and linguistic turns of phrase in Biblical Hebrew have to be read in light of their ancient settings, not taken literally or read with a consciously imposed set of values and ideas deriving from the modern world, or from one's private theological commitment. Great care and sensitivity are required when working in a language other than one's mother tongue, no matter what the language! Even then, a modern reader is very likely to miss some of the subtleties, the connotations of the ancient text, its homonyms, homographs, idiomatic expressions and even jokes. Linguists know only too well that, even within the one language group, culturally determined expressions can carry markedly different senses.Consider the varieties of spoken English! While describing the technical elements of Biblical Hebrew is relatively easy, nuances and connotations are a different matter.

Applying a so-called Christian reading to the Hebrew Bible, for example, may impose a set of values and a reading projection that can distort an editor's 'original' purpose, one that did not centre around the life and times of Jesus of Nazareth. Micah in its true context holds the memory and worldview of another people and of a much earlier age. The reading offered in this commentary seeks to honour the text in that past context to the fullest extent possible, given the limitations that may apply.

That Micah the book now lies within the Scroll of the Twelve, the so-called Minor Prophets, suggests to so many readers that the book is 'prophetic', and that Micah himself was a 'prophet'. This assumption ignores the evidence now resident within the scroll and leads to a manner of reading that depends on one's prior concept of what a prophet is assumed to be and do. Whether one's assumptions about a prophetic role are valid or not can be determined only by referencing the text we now have. As noted already, Micah is nowhere identified in the text as a prophet, a *nābî'*, and more to the point was his desire to draw a clear distinction between himself and all *nābî'* prophets. See the discussion above.

A propos of the Hebrew verb *ḥazâ*, a key verb in this book, and the participial form *ḥôzeh*, 'seer' or 'visionary', this reader makes the point that context is what gives meaning, but meaning also depends on knowing whether a word is used with its basic or literal sense, or is being used figuratively. *Ḥazâ* can refer to real ocular sighting, to looking, to watching, as well as being used with a figurative sense, that is, to having insight, understanding, awareness, to comprehend. In this it differs from the earlier use of *rō'eh*, 'seer', referring to what later became known as the *nābî'*. Detailed exegesis of the editor's note in the superscript will follow, but here it is important to observe that in 1.1 there is no specific object of the verb *ḥazâ* provided, suggesting therefore that it refers to Micah's general insight into the nation's soul as could be witnessed in Samaria and Jerusalem. The understanding that this reader has, and from which he reads the text, is that whatever Micah 'saw' (*ḥazâ*) within Israel, it required evaluation in light of the covenantal relationship claimed between Israel and its God at the time.

The translation throughout is my own.

Micah's Theological Perspective

A. Micah's fundamental theological position as presented via the structure of the book is the incomparability of his God Yahweh—there is no God like Yahweh, master of the whole earth! His credo is basic and clearly stated (see 4.11-13; 7.18-20).

B. Given that Micah was a rural southerner, one can safely assume that his theological understanding was influenced by the southern or Jerusalem school, namely that its Temple was the only legitimate sacred location for all Israelite cultic activity. Like Amos, Micah predates the more hard-edged and increasingly narrow Deuteronomic perspective that developed in Judah, but that is clearly present here in early form.

C. The book opens with what was a thoroughly contemporary, but to modern readers perhaps a disturbing, view of Yahweh—God as a destructive and frightening power, a God who rocks the world in his anger at the nation's transgressions. It offers a picture of Yahweh as angry and vengeful (1.2-7) and continues in that vein, refusing to forgive (3.1-4), expressing anger and vengeance (5.10-15). In this regard, as noted above, Micah shows a similar view of God to that of Nahum. Clearly, within Israel's religious community at the time there was a very strong desire to emphasize Yahweh as an overwhelmingly awesome and destructive God, master of the whole earth. It was a view perhaps understandable given the external threats the nation was facing (see also Zeph. 1.2-6). Micah's personal view was not exceptional, though moderated.

D. Micah is viewed as deeply concerned with potential judgment, yet balanced against a measure of hope dependent on a community's change of heart. The balance offers hope to those who act in accordance with the covenant's requirements (2.12-13), for God's anger will not last for ever (7.7, 17-18); God will hear, respond and save—that was Micah's hope.

E. Israel is spoken of fondly as 'my people' (2.8; 6.2-5, 16), consistent with the claim that Israel was God's chosen one, a people with a special relationship with Yahweh borne out of the Exodus experience of national rescue. Yahweh was the God who played a vital role in the life of peoples and nations, but who, from Israel's point of view, had an even more special interest in Israel such that he called them 'my people'. He was thus believed to be 'their God' exclusively and above all (see Exod. 6.6-8). We do, however, need to identify more closely the subject pronoun 'I' in a number of cases where the phrase 'my people' appears, because often it is also Micah's manner of speaking about his own community (e.g. 3.1, 3).

F. The conditional nature of the Sinai covenant, meaning that there was an emphasis on mutual accountability in the perceived relationship, also helped shape Micah's reactions to national failures, whether they were those of priests, prophets or other community leaders. Because of the underlying covenant relationship (6.3-5), Micah's personal concern with

justice and faithfulness drove his criticism of those who arrogantly presumed that the relationship with Yahweh would remain in place despite those leaders' failures (see 3.9-12).
G. Micah also reflects a view that Yahweh is in control of the nations and of their fate, judging them for their policies and ruling the world from his 'seat' on Mount Zion. Yahweh is, after all, master of the whole earth!
H. Micah's perspective on the cult is an important feature of this book. While highly critical of the priestly failure, he does not dismiss the importance of religion and its enthusiastic cultic expression as did Amos. What he saw as even more important, however, were the inner qualities, the social ideals, by which one lived—justice, kindness, honesty and patience (walking humbly). No amount of ritual or cultic activity could replace the need for living faithfully with one's God (6.6-8).

EXEGESIS

Micah 1

1.1 Superscript

The word of the Lord that was present with Micah of Moresheth throughout the reigns of Jotham, Ahaz and Hezekiah, kings of Judah, (and) that he saw concerning Samaria and Jerusalem.

The initial phrase, *dᵉbār-yhwh*, usually rendered as '*the word of the Lord*', is used widely throughout the Hebrew Scriptures and, despite the ambiguity of the phrase or its broad semantic value, it has taken on a particular meaning for many modern readers, being generally understood to refer to words or speech sourced directly from Yahweh. Such a received message is then accepted as having divine authority, its specific words and intent then to be passed on to an audience. The phrase 'word of the Lord' is the typical rendering found in the Introductions to prophetic books in all English Bibles, for example. As a fixed linguistic form, however, an idiomatic expression, a codeword, its role is to mark a message as relating to matters concerning the divine, having that importance.

As an idiomatic expression, *dᵉbār-yhwh*, it would be helpful to 'unpack' its components. The '*word*' is singular, so it is generic for a matter, a message of some kind depending on the context; the Hebrew construction '*word of the Lord*' can refer grammatically both to its content as well as to its source or nature, that is, it contains information about or concerning Yahweh (objective genitive), and/or derives from Yahweh (subjective genitive). However, the Hebrew noun *dābār* also refers to abstracts, to things or matters, to a chronicle of events, to an issue or affair, a way of doing things, even a reason for something; that it should be confined to spoken words is obviously restrictive. As an important component of the Superscript for this book, it labels the work as a matter involving an individual human and his words about the divine Yahweh.

The full verbal phrase in 1.1 describes the *dābār* as *hāyâ 'el-mîkâ*. The phrase *hāyâ 'el* appears in many prophetic books in its introductory verse;

it is a fixed formal element always translated in English as *'(the word) ... came to ('el) PN'*. The preposition *'el* has a wide variety of applications, as do all Hebrew prepositions. It is generally understood to express movement toward, especially when the verb involved implies any kind of motion. However, *'el* in other settings also may mean 'concerning', 'for' (Mal 1.1), 'against', 'according to', as well as 'with' (static location). In the company of a verb like *hāyâ*, 'be/exist', where absolutely no movement is involved, the rendering that something 'came to' Micah from an external source is to be seriously questioned. A preconceived notion that messages were revealed by God to certain individuals as in the Deuteronomic definition usually predetermines how the idiom is read and translated. What one is really looking at, however, in the *hāyâ 'el* idiom is the 'word/matter' simply being present with Micah, or as something he possessed. I understand the phrase to mean that what Micah saw and spoke about was actually to be regarded as *his words relating to Yahweh*. Understanding it as a verbal message Micah received directly and in its entirety from Yahweh, from outside, following the Deuteronomic model in Deut. 18.15-22, is far too narrow a view—see further in Postscript.

On the name *Micah* see above. It is the first element in the inclusion that brackets this book and that sets its direction. The name *mîcâ* in 1.1 asks the question, *Who is like (Yah)?*, a question that in 7.18-20 is answered rhetorically—*mî-'ēl kāmôkā,* or, 'Who is a god like you?', meaning that Israel's God is incomparable. This is the underlying theme of the book and of Micah's words relating to Yahweh.

Micah is said to have perceived (Heb. *hazâ*) the word that is now here recorded. The verb and the descriptor derived from it, namely *hôzeh* or visionary, relate to having insight, a perception of something. What relationship there might have been between the *rō'eh* (seer) and the *hôzeh* is not very clear, though the *nābî'* is said to have originally been referred to as a *rō'eh*. I find it rather tiresome when so much commentary reduces the reading to one simple 'prophetic' paradigm, for each individual spokesperson had his own personality, experience and perspective.

Micah is described as 'of Moresheth', that is, domiciled in the small village by that name. This is the only personal information available about him. We have no idea what work he did, who his forebears were, his marriage status, his age, or anything that could paint a bigger picture of the man. There were in Israel's story several others with the same or similar names, but the name Micah or Micaiah, *'who is like (Yah)?',* does not provide information of real significance about the man.

Moresheth was a village in the Shephelah, the fertile slopes facing the Mediterranean west of the central mountain spine of Canaan. The town or village is referred to as Moresheth-Gath in 1.14, but this should not be taken to mean that it was a Philistine community. It was, in fact, just some short distance from the defensive city of Lachish, and 35 km southwest of Jerusalem. It was also on the important north–south road that ran along the base of the slopes, and the region generally supported a large proportion of the total population of the southern kingdom, Judah.

The period during which Micah was active is given as being the reigns of Jotham, Ahaz and Hezekiah, successive kings of Judah, that is, the latter half of the eighth century BCE. For a fuller review of the times see 2 Kings 15–20. Micah's mission, if that is the right term, was tied to Judah apparently, though it did involve an assessment of the northern kingdom, given that the troubles noted there were now 'infecting' the south (1.9). That situation was more typical of Ahaz's reign than that of the other two southern kings mentioned. Failure to include in the Superscript the regnal years of those ruling the northern kingdom at the time leaves the impression that Micah did not travel north, unlike Amos, but he clearly knew much about what went on there, presumably by hearsay. After all, Moresheth was on the road that gave access to and from the much more populous north.

A second clause relating to the phrase *dᵉbār-yhwh* states that what Micah saw had to do with *Samaria and Jerusalem,* the former name representing the central city of the large northern kingdom and the latter name being that of the tiny southern kingdom, Judah. What the issues were is not outlined in the Superscription, but it serves to indicate where Micah's concerns were placed, especially as life in the south under Ahaz in particular was, according to Micah, being eroded by ideas and practices imported from the north (1.9), as 'refugees' from the north escaped south in 721 BCE.

It is to be noted again that there is no mention or even a hint of Micah as a *nābî'* prophet—he was a visionary; he 'saw' things, then spoke out. This iconoclast did not hold back in his critique of the elite from every walk of life.

1.2–2.13 Yahweh's Complaint against Samaria and Jerusalem

1.2-7 *Yahweh Acts against Samaria and Jerusalem*
Hear, you people, all of you: pay attention, O land and all who are in it; may my lord Yahweh witness against you, my master from his sacred Temple.

For behold Yahweh is about to leave his place and descend to tread on the high places of the land.

And the mountains would melt beneath him and the valleys burst open, like wax melting before the fire, like water poured on the slopes.

All this is because of Jacob's sin and because of the transgression of the house of Israel.

What (literally 'who?') is Jacob's transgression? Is it not Samaria? And what (literally 'who?') are the high places of Judah? Is it not Jerusalem?

Now, I would make Samaria into a ruin in the field, into a planted vineyard; and I would throw her stones into the valley and uncover her foundations,

(All her images would be struck down, her wages burned with fire, and her idols be laid to waste, for she has garnered them as the wages of a prostitute, so as wages of a prostitute they would return.)

The opening call to '*Hear* …' is a familiar form—see 3.1, 9; 6.1, 2, 9, also Amos 3.1; 4.1; 5.1. The parallel line is also an imperative demanding that the land, that is, its people, tune in. It represents Micah's demand to '*all you people* …' that in the context can only mean the population of both north and south, which is to say that the noun *hā'āreṣ* has its more limited sense of the local land, not the whole earth. There are commentators, however, who read this as a universal call in view of the following cosmic imagery. This reader finds the cosmic imagery applies only to the following verses, not to the opening address.

A third imperative or jussive in v. 2 calls on Yahweh to be present in order to testify against the people. From the outset then, the editor makes the point that this message is Micah's; he is the one inviting Yahweh to join him in challenging the nation. From this perspective the first-person pronominal reference in vv. 6-7 becomes a fascinating expression of the 'unity' between Micah and his God; they are speaking as one!

The secondary clause '*my master from his sacred Temple*' relates back to and builds on the previous reference to '*my lord Yahweh*'. Yahweh, 'resident' in the Jerusalem Temple according to Deuteronomic theology, is about to set out, to sally forth—the participle is *yoṣē'*—to be a witness against what has been happening in the land.

In v. 3 there is a term *bāmôt*, which can have two potential meanings. The basic sense is of 'places that are of high elevation', and in this context parallels 'mountains' in v. 4. However, there is also a secondary religious sense as *bāmôt*, the 'high places', were where syncretistic or alien worship was said to occur. Recall the episode of Elijah and the prophets of Baal on the top of Mt. Carmel (1 Kgs 18; see also 2 Kgs 17; 18.4). So-called high places were religious centres to be banned under the reforms of kings such as Josiah (2 Kgs 23).

To encourage the people to attend to his words, Micah launches into an imaginary description of Yahweh's impending appearance as he emerges from his Temple, or from his heavenly abode—the language is ambiguous—to offer that witness. Micah chooses theophanic language and imagery to convey his sense of Yahweh's awesome impact, describing Yahweh as striding out; and wherever his feet touch the ground, the ground melts away—mountains shrivel like wax melting before the flame, the melted mountains then flow down the valleys, running like water poured out on the steep valley sides. This kind of language and use of similes is poetic, dramatic and culturally meaningful, not to be read literally as some are wont to do.

'*All this* …' refers back to the anticipated divine response to Jacob's transgressions, 'Jacob' being one name for the nation as a whole, and in this verse parallel to 'the house of Israel'. The 'transgressions' and 'sins' are not specified at this point, so the charge appears general.

The second half of v. 5 consists of two parallel rhetorical questions, generally rendered as impersonal—'*What is the …, is it not…?*'—that relate to the transgressions and sins of the divided nation. The Hebrew interrogatives that introduce v. 5a and v. 5b, however, both use *mî,* which is basically 'who …', so 'Who is the sin of …?' and 'Who are the high places …?' Both centres, Samaria and Jerusalem, are personified in this form, thus referring to all their inhabitants.

The response to the questions is concise—the transgression of Jacob is Samaria, and the sin of Israel is Jerusalem. Each capital city represents one component of the divided kingdom, thus alleging that the sinfulness of the entire kingdom is the reason for the divine 'descent' (1.3); neither part of the kingdom is exempt from the charge against it. But what is the nature of the transgression if it involves both north and south? Are both guilty of the same sin, or are they different? While the following vv. 6-7 focus only on the sins of Samaria, those same sins are now said to be infecting Jerusalem (vv. 8-9). What then becomes clear is that the fundamental problem as seen by Micah was a religious one, having to do with cultic worship that involved images and idols. In this Micah shows his Deuteronomic credentials as one for whom the reversion to syncretistic worship, together with the north's policy of an alternative to the Jerusalem Temple, was illegitimate. That was the original 'sin' of Jeroboam (1 Kgs 12.25-33), continued by his successors in the north. That syncretism was now being emulated in the south, especially during the reign of Ahaz.

The threatened response to the general situation in Samaria follows in vv. 6-7, introduced by the connecting particle *waw,* 'and/but,' rather than the more forceful *lākēn,* 'therefore'. The feminine pronouns refer to Samaria as a city, which, like nations, is grammatically feminine in Hebrew. The question raised by the use of the first-person singular verbs throughout is, 'Who is the speaker?' Is there a change from Micah, having referred to

Yahweh previously in the third-person? I have suggested above that there is no change in the actual speaker; it continues to be Micah himself. The grand scale of the destruction threatened in v. 6 certainly implies that Yahweh is the one who would actually achieve the destruction threatened in the passive verbs of the description, but there is no valid reason in the text to doubt that it continues as a speech by Micah himself. The verbs are to be considered volitional, Micah expressing what *could* or *should* happen, while only Yahweh could effect the result.

The rhetoric of the threat involves assonance, as Samaria is reduced to a heap (Heb. $š^e m\bar{a}m\hat{a}$). The city and its buildings would be demolished such that the land could look as though it had never been built up, soon to look as though prepared for the planting of vines. The stones of which the city was constructed would be cast into the valley, leaving only the foundations as evidence of what was once there—hyperbole or not? No human agent is identified.

In these two verses we note the rhetorical feature used often in Micah, namely the application of a tricolon rather than just a bicolon in the description of certain situations—Samaria, her stones, her foundations; 1.7 her images, her wages, her idols. See **Literary Features** in Introduction.

In 1.7 the cultic aspect of the potential outcome of Yahweh's appearance is clear with its general reference to 'images' and 'idols', all of which were to be destroyed. Israel's religious history was clearly complex and one that evolved through the centuries; there was never only one 'brand' as it were. Israel's religious experiences and ideas changed throughout the biblical period, but syncretism was always a feature, even making a place for Moses's bronze serpent. Micah was one who saw the use of images, idols, and other material representations of the gods, such as the *Asherah* pillars, as inconsistent with the worship of Yahweh, the unique tribal god.

It is the note about *'etnan zônâ*, 'wages of a prostitute', that is unusual, and there are any number of questions raised by the verse, whether of grammar or syntax, that make its meaning uncertain. The presence of prostitution, male and female, in Canaanite worship is well known, and far from uncommon in much popular Israelite worship, despite it being 'unacceptable' (see, e.g., 1 Kgs 22.38, 46; 2 Kgs 23.7). What exactly the 'wages' were if they could be burned is unclear. Was the burning an act of sacrifice or offering? The threat issued here appears to target the way in which Samaria, that is, its people, priests, and leaders, has sanctioned cultic prostitution in some money-making scheme, but how these 'wages' might return and for what purpose if burned is uncertain. This verse is an example of a text whose translation is largely possible but whose meaning is not just uncertain; it is virtually meaningless. Commentators may have a

138   *Micah*

lot to say about the problems in the text and how to resolve them, but readers are not necessarily thereby enlightened; it should be bracketed as a sign of our uncertainty.

1.8-9 Lament over Israel's Incurable 'Wounds'

> *For this I would make lamentation and wail; I would go barefooted and naked.*
>
> *I would lament like the jackal, and mourn like the ostrich.*
>
> *For her wounds cannot be cured; indeed, she/it has come to Judah, reaching the gate of my people, even as far as Jerusalem.*

The threat issued against Samaria in vv. 6-7 is followed by Micah's lamentation. The underlying problem for Micah is that the problems noted in Samaria have now begun to infect the southern kingdom—they have reached *'the gate of Jerusalem'*—vv. 9, 12.

Whether there are two separate 'laments' (vv. 8-9 and 10-16) or only one is an issue for some commentators, but this reading will deal with them as two separate but related reports of Micah's deep anguish, the justification being that the two sections are very different in character. While vv. 8-9 describe the past-present problem Micah faced, using poetic but relatively plain and intensely personalized language, vv. 10-16 are anticipatory, bemoaning what is impending. They offer a well-developed written text marked by imperatives addressed to a wide audience in the cities and towns of Judah, with the impending crisis attributed not so much to Samaritan issues as to the Lord (vv. 12b, 15a). The wailing and mourning in vv. 10-16 are not personal; they are communal. Also rhetorically, similes are lacking, but the more obvious difference is that the 'I' in vv. 8-9 cannot be the same 'I' in v. 15. Each 'lament' appears to this reader to have a very different origin and audience. For this reader, it is further evidence that the book as a whole consists of an editor's collection of independently sourced material relevant to the mission of Micah.

The opening Hebrew phrase *'al-zo't,* 'concerning this', in v. 8 refers back to what has just been noted in Samaria, taking in the sweep of destruction in vv. 4-7, rather than pointing forward as some would have it. Micah explains the situation in Samaria as the reason for his deep emotional response; he is prepared to strip naked (cf. Isa. 20.3) and howl like the jackal and moan (Heb. *'ābal,* 'mourn') like the ostrich to show how profoundly saddened he is at what he 'saw' had happened to Samaria, and even more so now that Judah is having to cope with the same difficulties. (See also Amos's response in Amos 5.16 using the same vocabulary.) The two similes, the jackal and the ostrich, are clearly 'of the location' and culturally derived to describe mourning situations, as Job 30.29 attests.

The three colons in v. 8 are marked by cohortative verbs with volitional focus, each paralleled with two complements. One should note here that the reference to the 'ostrich' is an uncertain identification as happens with many plants, animals and birds in the biblical text; it may well be a type of owl!

Verse 9 opens with an initial *kî* that could be the asseverative 'Indeed ...', or the explanatory 'For ...'. The text uses three adverbial phrases, each beginning with *'ad* to mark the extent of the infiltration of Samaritan practices into Judah—they have come 'as far as ...' the gate of *'my people'*. If these are really Micah's words, then the phrase does not carry a theological or covenant value, but simply Micah identifying his community, the folk of Jerusalem. The reference to the 'gate' or entrance to Jerusalem is a general comment about the closeness or immediacy of the threat to Judah rather than just a location.

The specific issues moving Micah to lament are described as *makkôteyhā* (NRSV 'her wounds') from the root meaning 'to strike', and they are said to be without a cure, irreversible. What then are they? The noun *makkâ* can refer to slaughter, a strike, a wound—clearly an attack by an external force. This suggests that the crisis over which Micah laments is the attack on Samaria by Assyrian forces from which the northern kingdom would never recover. While the attack on Samaria may have had a religious explanation from Micah's theological point of view, vv. 2-7, it nevertheless was a political move by Assyria that destroyed the city and spelled the end of the north's independent existence. Here then Micah is lamenting that loss and the now greater threat to Judah, a threat that has now come (Heb. *bā'āh*) as far as Judah's 'gate'. That the situation is incurable is lamentable; there is no prospect for Samaria's recovery, nor was there the possibility that Judah would not have to face the same danger.

1.10-16 Lament over Assyria's Threat to Judah

> *Declare not in Gath; do not weep at all; in Beth-l'Aphrah, sprinkle yourselves with dust.*
>
> *Pass on, you inhabitants of Shaphir, (in) nakedness and shame; the inhabitant of Ṣaanan did not go forth. There is wailing in Beth-ha'Ezel, he takes away from you support(?)*
>
> *For those who live in Maroth wait anxiously for good, but disaster has come down from the Lord to the gate of Jerusalem.*

> *Hitch the horse to the chariot, inhabitants of Lachish; she is the beginning of the daughter of Zion's sin, for in you were found the transgression of Israel.*
>
> *Therefore offer farewell gifts to Moresheth-Gath, the houses of Achzib as a deceiver to the kings of Israel.*
>
> *Again a conqueror I would bring to you, inhabitant of Mareshah; the glory of Israel may come to Adullam.*
>
> *Make yourself bald, and cut off your hair, for the children you delight in, make yourself bald like the eagle, for they have gone from you into exile.*

While it is clear that this poem has to do with lamentation there is much in the detail of its formulation that is unclear as Micah awaits the inevitable Assyrian assault. Imperative verbs are used frequently, calling to the population of a number of Judaean cities or villages—twelve are named, though some are not known. Micah calls them to communal action. There are several wordplays involving those locative names. The tone of the section differs markedly from that of vv. 8-9, as noted above, having moved away from Micah's personal lamentation to the wider Judaean population (Heb. *yôšebet* repeated in vv. 11, 12, 15) bemoaning the fact that they were facing a crisis that Micah attributes to divine intervention (1.12-15). This second 'lament' relates to a different set of circumstances from those in vv. 8-9. There is a rhetorical connection with the preceding verses via the phrase *'the gate of ... Jerusalem'*, suggesting the basis on which the two sections are placed adjacent to one another, but vv. 10-16 are clearly literarily independent. To what then do they refer?

It seems most likely that the background to this second speech lies in an Assyrian advance, or even an attack. Some commentators want to link this section specifically with the attack on Jerusalem by Sennacherib in 701 BCE. However, the fact that Samaria was captured in 721 and that large sections of the population were exiled makes it clear that throughout the closing years of the eighth century BCE the Assyrians were a constant threat to Judah as well as to the north; the lament could be dated anytime after Samaria fell. Reading these verses in light of an on-going Assyrian threat makes good sense, as Isaiah 10 demonstrates. Any enemy attack on Jerusalem, be it by Egypt or Assyria, was best made from the west, which meant from the Shephelah, Micah's home. Lachish was one of the more fortified cities in that area that would have to be conquered in order to gain access to Jerusalem, hence the towns mentioned in this section can all be assumed to be in that general region, even though some are now not identifiable.

At the literary level, these seven poetic verses are full of textual, grammatical and syntactical challenges that leave many commentators nonplussed about precise meanings. Interpretation is regrettably uncertain.

1.10 The phrase *'Tell not in Gath'* is a command not to talk about something in the Philistine city of Gath, but without the object supplied it is never clear as to what should not be spoken about. The words appear also in 2 Sam. 1.20 with respect to Israel's defeat by the Philistines. Obviously, what had happened to/in Gath was not to be discussed, 'Don't talk about what happened in Gath, don't weep over what happened'. The nuances of the imperative in this case are uncertain, but suffering a defeat in the past was not necessarily proof that it would happen again. Weeping over the past was not helpful in this case. Despite this, there is a parallel call, and it calls for mourning. There is a measure of uncertainty also as to whether 'at all' (Heb. *bākô*) is a place name and a pun on the verb 'weep'.

The following imperative is directed at a place called *Beth-l'Aphrah*, an uncertain location—if it is an actual location—but with a name like 'the dusty house' there is a clear wordplay on 'rolling(?) in the dust' (Heb. *'āpār*). One of the rituals associated with mourning involves throwing dust on one's head as one sat on the ground. It is assumed that the town is a Judaean town whose population was under threat. Whether this call is meant to evoke a literal or figurative response is unclear.

1.11 The inhabitants or residents of three more towns are addressed, Shaphir, Ṣaanan and Beth-ha'Eṣel. Of the three, only the last can be identified—a potential location, 16 km southwest of Hebron.

The inhabitants of Shaphir are called to pass by/on, *'naked and in shame'*. The latter phrase clearly implies going into exile, but the imperative carries the sense that this is preparatory, rather than as a result of having been overrun. The text is slightly contentious as the verse division marker comes after *'shame'*, indicating that the description applies to Shaphir, but some commentators link the 'naked and in shame' phrase with the inhabitants of Ṣaanan who *'did not go out'*. Beth-ha'Eṣel's wailing *'will remove its support'* is a statement whose meaning is also vague. The Hebrew term *'emdâ* is a *hapax*, and in such a brief clause the context offers no help in deciphering its import. Could it be that the whole verse is intended to convey a sense of impending chaos in which there is no mutual support, each community looking only to its own devices? To make matters even more cryptic, the identity of 'you' cannot be established without question, though that it refers to the inhabitants of Shaphir seems to be the most logical understanding.

1.12 The initial *kî* is probably the asseverative 'Indeed ...'.

This verse describes a town, rather than issuing it with an order; the people of Maroth, a town not now identifiable, are described as awaiting something good, whether it was good news or of some material help we have no way of knowing. Again, a wordplay perhaps, given that Hebrew *mar* means 'bitter', while they wait for something 'good' (*ṭôb*). However, what arrived (Heb. is *yārad*, 'came down') was *rā'*, often used to speak of 'evil' but here probably pointing to something unpleasant, even 'disaster'. More important is the note that it was disaster *'from Yahweh'*. Whatever the actual event or experience intended by this figure, the fact that it was sent by Yahweh seems to imply a kind of punishment for the people of Maroth, though that is not clear, nor is the reason for the absence of 'good' provided. The situation is now imminent, being already at the *'gate of Jerusalem'*, the phrase that links this 'lament' with the previous v. 9.

This reader has adopted the view that the general background of vv. 10-16 is that of an Assyrian advance on Judah following the fall of Samaria to the Assyrians in 721 BCE. Now that Samaria and its population had been overrun by Assyria, an event organized by Yahweh according to Isaiah 10, Micah reminds Maroth that they too must face divinely led 'disaster', for it is imminent.

1.13 The next command appears to call for the inhabitants of the fortified city of Lachish to harness their horses to their chariots, but the verb 'harness' is a *hapax* and so uncertain. The pronouns in the verse are also frustratingly unclear as to referent, and the specific meaning of the verse is far from obvious. Whether the call was to have the inhabitants of Lachish run away and escape or launch an attack on an enemy is unstated, though probably the former. It is, however, linked to a clause *'because the beginning of sin it (was) to the daughter of Zion ...'*. This is often taken to mean that as an important frontline defense Lachish was being blamed for bringing into Judah the *'transgressions of Israel'*, that is, the cult of the high places that would 'infect' Jerusalem. In v. 5 the charge against Jerusalem refers to *bāmôt*, the 'high places', and the sense is that it refers to the cult of a goddess that has been brought into Jerusalem from Samaria. The phrase 'daughter of Zion' (Heb. *bat-ṣiyyôn*) is a way of referring to the wider population of Jerusalem, with the noun *'daughter of ...'* meaning also the nearby area. In this case, Zion represents Jerusalem, though technically Zion was only a small but important development from the older city as it expanded. Despite all the above, however, there is genuine doubt about the meaning here given that much confusion is noted in pronouns, number and gender.

Lachish was one of the main fortified cities in the Shephelah, guarding access to Jerusalem and second only to Jerusalem in size. Unfortunately,

Lachish appears not to have been a chariot city as Judah was dependent on Egypt for chariotry. Furthermore, chariots could not be used other than on the plains, not in the more rugged and hilly environs of the Shephelah. The most famous sack of the city was in 701 BCE when Sennacherib attacked, built siegeworks and gained entry to the city; those ancient works are still visible following archaeological excavation. Sennacherib's attack probably took place some time after Micah's mission, though many commentators consider that attack to be what is in mind here. There is no absolute reason to accept that interpretation as the call and the language used here are generalized, making specific connections problematic, especially in a time when the Assyrians were pressuring the Judahites constantly.

1.14 The imperative tone continues here, but how it relates to the preceding verse is uncertain. What we have is another order from Micah that requires 'you' (singular) to offer gifts, but the *'al* preposition ('concerning/about') that follows does not seem to relate logically to anything else in the verse. It may mean that 'you' should offer gifts to the people in Moresheth-gath, but who is being addressed if it wasn't the inhabitants of Lachish is uncertain. Moresheth-gath the town may be Micah's hometown but it could also be a village between the two centres, Moresheth and Gath

Those gifts (Heb. *šillûḥîm*) are possibly farewell gifts to ones leaving, but this speculation is based only on the root *šlḥ*, which speaks of sending (away). It may mean 'dowry', as in 1 Kgs 9.16. Who is leaving, who is staying, where are the goers going and why, who is giving what to whom—all are questions that cannot be answered from the text. Could it mean that the folk of Moresheth-gath will have to leave their homes? There is no satisfactory answer.

Then the town of Achzib is mentioned, using perhaps another wordplay, for the name sounds like *'aḥzāb*, meaning something deceitful. In Jer. 15.18 the word is used of a stream that dries up in summer and thus disappoints the thirsty traveller; and this is the interpretation found in the JPS translation of the Jewish Bible of 1985. So, deceiving the northern kings expresses Micah's wish for them. On the other hand, if this section postdates the fall of Samaria, there would no longer be kings in the north; they were already exiled to Assyria. Even if they were not in exile, what point is served in their being deceived by the inhabitants of the town of Achzib? Little is clear about this verse.

1.15 The first-person pronoun again appears, so there is once more a question about the identity of the speaker—Micah or Yahweh? See the discussion in 1.6. Normally, one would assume that 'I' is God, the one who would bring an invader into Judah, but since the Lord is referred to in the third-person in 1.12, that possibility seems doubtful. The use of the adverb *'od*, 'again', implies that there was an earlier and successful enemy invasion of Mareshah, but if so, details are not available. The invader is described as 'the dispossessor' (Heb. *yorēš*), in this case one who would dispossess or drive out the inhabitants of Mareshah. The wordplay is evident here again as *yorēš* is a play on the towns' name. The town itself is known and is not to be confused with Moresheth.

Defining the 'glory of Israel' raises an issue as it is not clear whether it is the subject or object of the verb *yābô'*, 'come'. The abstract 'glory of Israel' may be a reference to the Israelite army, though usually it is an attribute of Yahweh. The phrase 'coming to Adullam' appears to recall its role as a place of hiding (see 1 Sam. 22.1), but who or what comes there? One translation (JPS) suggests the verb refers to Israel's 'glory' as 'setting', like the sun. Once again we are faced with a text the details of which are frustratingly obscure.

1.16 Imperative forms repeated in this verse can be interpreted not so much as orders but as invitations to action. That action was to 'make yourselves bald'. It is repeated in both halves of the verse, and strengthened by a similar verb, *gzz*, that usually is used of shearing sheep. The action, cutting one's hair or shaving the head, is related to a mourning ritual, so there is an indirect connection with the wailing and mourning of v. 5. Here it seems to be mourning for the loss of beloved children who have been taken into exile. There is no evidence to link this with Sennacherib's invasion of 701 BCE, and certainly no reason to link it to the Babylonian exile in 587.

This verse rounds out the survey of towns in the Shephelah that were under constant pressure from the Assyrians following the demise of Samaria in 721 BCE, with Lachish blamed for either actively or passively being the conduit for northern religious 'sins' finding their way into the southern kingdom. Micah's vision was of the impending 'infection' of the southern kingdom, so he calls on the people to mourn the potential loss, using children taken into exile as the metaphor.

The text of 1.10-16 consists of a bewildering array of textual, grammatical and syntactical challenges. It would be difficult to believe that any single rendering and interpretation of these verses is the 'correct' or sole intended one. What the original message from Micah might have been is not something that any modern reader can be confident in asserting, other than in a more general sense. Clearly, he is lamenting the situation that had come about in the northern kingdom and was appalled when he 'saw' the same issues infecting Judah and Jerusalem. This attitude seemingly suggests that up to that point Judah was not affected by the same 'sins' as the north, a rather unlikely scenario. What is evident is the tortuous path that the message has navigated on its way from Micah to the present written form.

Micah 2

The 'Woe ...!' oracle marks the closing portion of the initial section of the book, 1.2–2.13, and parallels the 'Woe ...!' section that closes the book's final division in 7.1-20.

The chapter can be divided into three sub-sections, 2.1-5, 6-11, 12-13, each of which is clearly demarcated with the primary focus being on Micah's assessment of the leadership within Judah: 2.1-5 is a Woe-oracle in which social justice issues are raised, particularly around the seizure of land by those with access to power; 2.6-11 are threatening words directed at a group usually called *preachers,* but here will be viewed as the priestly class; 2.12-13 are the closing verses, using a flock of sheep as analogy, offering a message of hope.

The chapter appears as a small collection of discrete speeches that Micah addressed to different components of the community at various times, whether both north and south is unclear, condemning their sinful practices—the selfish abuse of power by the privileged, of priests who offer false hope to those who pay them for service. Those who wait for 'good' could find that it is 'evil' that triumphs. Yet in the end, Micah in 2.12-13 holds out hope that God's goodness will overcome and protect.

The basic parallel colonic form continues, but there are within them textual issues that can be confusing, and the question of pronominal referents emerges again, especially in 2.1-5.

2.1-5 Leaders Abusing Power

> *Woe to those who, lying in bed, plan wickedness and evil! When morning breaks, they carry out those plans because it is in their power to do so.*
>
> *They covet fields and seize them; houses too, and take them, people along with their inheritance.*
>
> *Therefore, says the Lord, I am planning evil/disaster against this 'family/ clan' such that they will not be able to remove themselves from it, nor walk around arrogantly, for it will be a desperate time.*
>
> *On that day, one will raise a taunt against you, and wail with bitter lamentation, and say, 'We are utterly ruined; the Lord has changed the inheritance*

of my people. O how he removes it from me! He parcels out our fields among our captors!'

(Therefore, you no longer have anyone to cast the line by lot, in the Lord's assembly.)

The opening section of this chapter presents in Woe-oracle form a threat against the powerful who abuse that power and authority for their personal gain. It is another of the social issues that Micah 'saw' as prevalent in Israel (see also Amos 6.1, 4). The powerful devised ways and means to acquire property by pressuring the less fortunate; they strut about the town implementing their designs. The Woe-component or denunciation in vv. 1-2 is followed by a threatened judgment pronounced in vv. 3-5. In the latter, the participles denote actions that are imminent—they are not predictive; they announce that such persons may and should have to reckon with divine judgment when 'that day' comes, and come soon it will. The speaker is assumed to be Micah, but attention has to be given to the pronouns throughout in order to determine who is being identified; certainty on this front is not always possible beyond the general.

2.1-2 The picture presented is one in which the powerful in the community dream up schemes to defraud the less powerful of their real estate holdings, then carry out their plan. The verb form is imperfective, indicating frequency or habit. The constant scheming to that end is something they do *'on their beds'*, a figurative expression implying, on the one hand, their self-satisfied comfort, and, on the other, their obsession even when half asleep. They dream up plans that are malicious (Heb. *'āwen*), along with 'deeds of evil'; so not only do they plan what to do, they also work out how to achieve their planned acquisitions. Then, when the day dawns, they go about realizing their plan. This they can do *'because it is in their power to do so'*, literally 'it is *to the god of their hand'*. The use of *'ēl*, 'god', in this expression is idiomatic for 'power' (see Gen. 31.29; Prov. 3.27). Micah in these two brief verses presents the social inequality that is so typical of every society and laments its reality in Israel (see Amos 6.1-7; Isa. 5.8-10).

The structure or syntax of v. 1 is regarded by numerous scholars as unusual; hence there have been many suggestions for moving elements around, and for some textual emendation. For example, some have questioned the phrase *'doing evil on their beds'*, suggesting that it might refer to some pornographic entertainment, so they want to move the phrase *'on their beds'* elsewhere in the sentence. Surely any sensible reader can see that, even if the word order is a trifle ambiguous, it merely locates their evil plotting. This reader regards suggestions for most textual changes as deeply problematic, essentially because they are suggestions by those who are not native speakers of ancient Hebrew. Even native speakers of a language are (or should be) reluctant to 'fiddle with' another's writing style, to make it conform with one's own (limited) perception of another's language. The expression here as it exists is perfectly understandable to anyone other than literalists!

Verse 2 piles up clauses that show the outworking of their plans: *'they covet ..., they seize ..., ... they take, ...'* to acquire productive fields, houses and land from their fellow citizens. The powerful are presented as having both the opportunity and the means to deprive others of what is rightly theirs by taking advantage of their privileged access to power. The verb 'seize' (Heb. *gzl*) implies the use of force, applying pressure whether by way of abusing the legal system or by some other means (see also 3.2). The Hebrew noun *naḥᵃlâ*, 'land', is more than just a plot of dirt; it is the noun that describes the land as an inheritance from God, his gift of the land, making the sin even more egregious.

2.3 Micah threatens action about to be taken against the doers of evil—he announces Yahweh's attitude to this situation. The '(Therefore) *thus says the Lord'* is an example of the *pro forma* editorial insert that adds gravitas to Micah's judgment. This editorial formula, as noted above, is used very sparingly in Micah. The first-person pronominal use, however, raises again the issue of the relationship between Micah and Yahweh (see 1.8, 15). Micah's word is equated with the divine word because Yahweh's word *was present with* Micah (1.1). What this reader regards as the simplistic notion that Micah as 'prophet' (though the term is never affixed to him) speaks only words given him by God is a mistaken view that has to be reviewed; Micah's own insight into what was wrong within the community was 'inspired', but it came from his own observation and experiences, not from some external source.

Just as the powerful 'devise' (Heb. *ḥāšab*) plans to cheat the less powerful, so Yahweh 'devises' (*ḥāšab*) imminent action or judgment against those who exercise power. This is how Micah describes Yahweh's activity. And in a clever wordplay, what they plan 'on their beds', he says Yahweh plans 'on this family', that is, on that cabal of powerful ones. The Hebrew text here also involves sound play—*miškᵉbôt* and *mispāḥâ*. Likewise, the 'evil' (*rā'*) that they have devised, parallels the *rā'â* Yahweh is devising. The wordplay here is that the feminine *rā'â* mostly is used for 'disaster, trouble' rather than moral evil. That is confirmed by the relative clause that follows: *'from which you cannot remove your neck'*. The disaster brought by Yahweh will not be removed, or only removed by Yahweh, under the unspoken metaphor of a yoke of some kind.

Micah sees those subjected to Yahweh's 'disaster' as no longer able to swagger (Heb. *rômâ*) round town, because the time will be deeply painful for them (see also Amos 5.13). Whatever form the *rā'â* is to take, the powerful are threatened with feeling its full weight.

2.4 *'On that day ...'* takes us directly to the vague expression associated often with the prophets who speak of that imminent time in which God's plans or devices will be worked out. The problem here is in determining who the subject 'one/he' refers to, as well as the object pronoun 'you'. Is 'one/he' a reference to those who have been cheated, or a wider group? Does 'you' refer to those powerful ones responsible for the appropriation of houses and land? That seems to be the most reasonable solution. In that sense, then, the ones who lost their property would *'raise against'* the powerful ones a mashal. The mashal normally is a literary form associated with proverbial wisdom (see Prov. 1.1). Given that there is a related description of wailing and bitter lamentation, the mashal seems not to carry its wisdom connotation; it is more like a lament in which one complains, even to God, about injustice and unfairness. Here NRSV suggests 'taunt', while JPS suggests a less confrontational 'poem'. The associated phrase, *'against you'*, means that the cry of injustice is levelled 'against' the powerful 'you', a plea for God to act against them. So, the poor and disadvantaged plead with God to act against those with access to power, while mourning bitterly over their own loss, for to do so is their only recourse against those who hold the reins of power.

That this embodies a complaint directed against Yahweh is also clear in the quote attached, blaming Yahweh for what the poor see as deception, so not only are they oppressed by their community leaders, but Yahweh, they believe, has also failed them. At this point we can appreciate Micah as a spokesperson for those in the community who have been defrauded. The Hebrew text uses assonance, even if perhaps unusual; the phrase *nāhâ nᵉhî nihyâ* is built around the root *nhh*, which occurs only twice, here and Ezek 32.18. The reference is to wailing, but the syntax is disputed and the language cryptic.

There is then an accusation against Yahweh, claiming that Yahweh has 'exchanged', perhaps subverted, the *'inheritance of my people'*. The latter phrase involves the Hebrew term that speaks of the *naḥᵃlâ,* 'land', given to Israel as their 'inheritance', so this is a complaint that ancestral land has been taken away or lost. Has Yahweh reneged on his promise of the land? So, who then are 'my people'? Is it Micah complaining about a loss sustained by members of his community? If this a complaint addressed to Yahweh, then 'my people' cannot be a reference to God's covenant people but rather a plea from the community itself, specifically from those whose land has been taken.

The complaint continues with the exclamatory *'How ...!'* expressing disgust or deep disappointment because they are accusing Yahweh as the one responsible for taking away (Heb. *yāmîš*) the land. This charge against Yahweh is the people's perspective on the divine failure to bring the powerful to account. Yahweh's failure to intervene is seen as active support for the powerful! The following prepositional *lî*, 'to/for me', is problematic. The third-person singular verb *yāmîš* cannot refer to the evildoers, but to Yahweh. He it is who parcels out our land, our fields. So, yes!, Yahweh has reneged on his original gift of the land! The rare Hebrew participle *šôbēb*, 'captors'?, is another problematic form, the derivation and precise meaning of which are unclear.

2.5 Like v. 3, this v. 5 also begins with 'Therefore ...', suggesting a second result of the coveting of property on the part of the powerful. In this context it would appear as though the lamentation of v. 4 and the complaint that God has parceled out the inherited land to others left those deprived of their land empty-handed. The text is far from clear, however, and some regard the fact that it is prose, rather than poetry like the rest of the unit, means that it doesn't really belong here. This reader takes the view that whatever is now in the text as we have it must be assumed to belong, unless there is clear objective evidence that it belongs elsewhere. There are also other issues of consistency within the text, for example, the pronoun 'you' is singular, whereas the 'you' in v. 4 is plural. Difficulties for the modern reader simply indicate that the road from spoken presentation by Micah to the edited written copy now available has been tortuous and open to modification throughout.

Under Joshua (Judg. 20–21) the original division of Canaan among the tribes was determined by means of drawing lots (Heb. *mašlîk ḥebel*). The text here is related to that: the phrase is literally 'throwing the cord/rope', an idiom reflecting the process of drawing lots, establishing a line to determine where boundaries were located. Here there is said to be no current person like the original Joshua to act in that role *'in the assembly of the Lord'* (see Deut. 33). The 'assembly' (Heb. *qāhāl*) was a gathering of tribes with a religious purpose. How it relates to the situation envisaged here is difficult to determine. Perhaps all one can conclude is that the text has suffered greatly during its transmission both orally and in written form, and that there is little a modern reader can do to resolve the impasse. Some commentators determine that the text is 'unusable', and for that reason my translation above is set within brackets.

2.6-11

'Do not proclaim!' they proclaim. May they not proclaim such things; insults may not be removed.

Is it said, O house of Jacob?, 'Is the spirit of the Lord cut short?' Or these his deeds, are they not words that do good for the one whose walk is correct?

But you rose up to become an enemy to my people, you took off the cloak that covered his tunic from ones who passed by trustingly returning from war.

You drove away the women of my people from their delightful homes, from her infants you have taken my honour for ever,

Get up and leave, for this is not the resting place, because of defilement it will destroy and the destruction will be serious

If a person walks wind/spirit and deceptive lies, 'Let me proclaim to you for/ about wine and liquor', then let him be the preacher for this people.

While uncovering the general intention in this section is possible, namely attacks by certain individuals—identified as *preachers* (Heb. *maṭṭîp*) in some translations—the written form that we now have is so full of grammatical and syntactical problems and strange interconnections that translation and interpretation are exceedingly uncertain, indeed virtually impossible. First to note, however, is that despite many commentators' renderings, it is unjustified to assume that the so-called preachers are prophets, and although in this book the Hebrew noun *nābî'* is only ever used in a derogatory manner (3.5-6), that is not the noun used here; what we do have is the root *nṭp* whose basic sense is 'to drip', used at times figuratively of speech (see Prov. 5.3). This section has nothing to do with prophets, true or false, nor with prophecy. It stands as another independent section within the collection, only loosely related to the surrounding material.

The section begins with a quotation as Micah restates how a group of persons responded negatively to what he had said. The verb *nāṭap,* questionably rendered traditionally as 'preach', then serves as an inclusion for the section (2.6 and 11), and the assumption is that the speaker throughout is Micah himself.

So, who are these so-called *preachers* if, as I read it, they are not prophets? Clearly, from Micah's point of view, they are individuals prepared to say whatever people want to hear if they are paid in cash or kind to do so; they are corrupt officials of some order. In Amos 7.16 the root *nṭp* is used in parallel with the root *nbʾ*, and many assume therefore that both roots refer to the same or similar activities, that is, to 'prophecy'. That is a problematic assumption on which to approach the text of Micah. Both roots have to do with public speaking, that is true, but understanding the precise content of the root *nbʾ* is fraught such that the simplistic rendering 'prophesy' hardly begins to catch its full import. To then equate *nṭp* with *nbʾ* further detracts from the potential meaning of both. I would argue that here *nṭp* refers to instruction or advice offered to one in cases of serious personal conflict. The issue of justice in society was the province of priests administering *torah*, of sages instructing the young in traditional wisdom values, and of prophets. So, those in focus in v. 6 could well be the priests, and my reading will proceed on that assumption. For this reader, 'prophets' is not the group intended here. To suggest further that it refers to 'false prophets' is even more disingenuous. See the Postscript on the two root words *nbʾ* and *nṭp*.

2.6 Micah quotes the words of a certain cohort who appear to want him to cease 'preaching' (*ʾal-taṭṭipû*) whatever it is that they 'preach' (*yaṭṭipûn*). Clearly, by using this same verb in these two contexts some kind of parody is intended, as Micah's imperative accuses them of doing exactly what they order him not to do. By what right, or on what authority do they order Micah to keep quiet? What has he said that so upset them? When Amos was confronted by Amaziah the priest in Bethel, he was ordered not to *nṭp* against 'the house of Isaac' (Amos 7.16). Here then was a contemporary class conflict that provides the clue as to the identity of those who opposed Micah; the opposition was the priestly class who took exception to the visionary assessments and statements being made by Micah. They did not want Micah criticizing 'about these things' (Heb. *ʾēlleh*), namely the things Micah 'saw' happening in 'the house of Jacob'. Nationalistic priests were the ones offended by what Micah criticized, and moreover they rejected the threat that such 'shame' or reproach could ever come upon them (Heb. *loʾ yissag*). The verb here is problematic in every sense, but it does give the hint that the priests believed that whatever Micah had said would not become a serious issue for them.

2.7 The verse consists of four rhetorical questions put to the audience, the priests of the 'house of Jacob', the first of which has no subject, being the passive '*is/was it said*?' Without a subject and object the question is a little difficult to decipher. If Micah is the speaker, however, then these questions serve effectively as a denial of what is alleged. The second question is literally, 'Is it *short* the spirit of Yahweh?', in which some read 'spirit' (Heb.

rûᵃḥ) to mean patience, patience that has run out or is exhausted. The question form denies that as fact. The noun *rûᵃḥ*, as the quality or the essence of being divine, Yahweh's 'godness', is difficult to render or interpret other than to suggest a quality that a reader imagines is appropriate in the circumstance. Whether such an understanding is accurate or real is difficult to determine objectively.

The third question continues the second with *'im-'ēlleh*, asking about the divine deeds/workings (Heb. *maᵃlālâw*) and denying that the work of Yahweh is also 'shortened', that is, limited. We are not advised, however, as to what the actions were that are denied. The final question asks, 'Can my words not produce good with the one who walks uprightly?' In each case, Micah challenges those who demand he stop speaking to the issues. God's 'spirit' is not limited, nor are his 'deeds'; his words can produce good, that is, have beneficial effect, especially for the one who lives a righteous life.

The interpretation offered here is this reader's attempt to make some sense of a text that is incredibly problematic.

2.8-9 These two verses present Micah's more direct challenge to the priests who have told him essentially to 'Shut up!'. It begins with the adversative *waw*, here read as contrastive 'but', as in 3.8. The object of Micah's challenge is 'you', clearly meaning those who wish him to keep quiet, that is, the priests. Unfortunately, there are questions about most items in the text, and this reader accepts a very modest change to the opening words as it requires only a modified word division. See my translation above.

Micah contrasts his actions with that of the priests whom he regards as *enemies of my people*. Micah sees the priests as the ones who need to keep quiet, as they are opposed to *'my people'*, that is, the community that Micah represents. It is vital to be able to identify the speaker in order to know to whom he is speaking. Some commentators have Yahweh as the speaker on the basis that 'my people' is typical of covenant talk and that Micah is a prophet speaking God's message. However, that is not the conclusion being offered here. 'My people' is Micah's community, and Micah is the speaker.

A second charge against the priests is that they plunder the robe or strip the cloak from peaceful people, also described as those who pass by trustingly or innocently. The action noted is difficult to understand given the lack of context. Who are these people? Are they Micah's people, and, if so, what have they been doing? What is the significance of the 'returnees (from) war', and is it a figure of speech only? These are questions without an answer in view of the state of the text.

In v. 9 Micah accuses this 'enemy' with having driven women from their homes and cut their children off from Yahweh's *kābôd*, 'glory/honour', for ever. Such an accusation sounds serious, but what does it mean? Are they taken into exile, or is it more a matter of people being driven from their homes. The language is general, so it is not possible to be more specific about what has happened, nor why. If, as argued, the accusation is leveled against priests, then women and children being without access to divine 'glory' might even refer to their being denied access to any form of religious service.

2.10-11 Confusion or uncertainty remains an issue in these verses as the one who issued the two commands is unclear. On the assumption that this entire report is of Micah's oral presentations, the order *'Get up and leave'* is presumably addressed to the priests who are resistant to Micah's speeches. Others see in this a command by the 'enemies' of Micah, perhaps addressed to him, while others suggest it is Yahweh who speaks. This reader will persist with the view that Micah is speaking to priests, ordering them to leave a certain place, presumably a sacred space, for it is not a place for 'rest'. What kind of 'rest' is intended is uncertain; it can carry both positive and negative connotations. The noun $m^e n\hat{u}\d{h}\hat{a}$, 'rest', can refer to the land as promised, or simply a place to stop on a journey. This place has been made 'unclean' in some manner, however, and this is the reason (Heb. $ba^{'a}b\hat{u}r\ tom'\hat{a}$) they should get up and leave. Such a command would make good sense if the priests were those threatened by this kind of cultic contamination for such 'uncleanness' could destroy completely, threatening a grievous destruction (*hebel*). Mystery surrounds this text as it is not clear who was responsible for the contamination, nor what activity brought it about. The relationship to the preceding verse is also far from obvious.

Verse 11 does seem to offer a slightly better chance of a meaningful interpretation. It begins with a particle *lû*, which can introduce a conditional 'if ... then ...' clause. Here Micah is speaking down to the priests, castigating them for having such a materialistic view of their mission and for the lying words they utter for personal gain (see also Isa. 9.15). The text refers to one who goes about with a certain demeanour or perverse intention; that seems to be the function of the noun $r\hat{u}^a\d{h}$ serving as an adverb and portraying the intention to deceive. It refers to one who goes about saying: 'Let me tell you about (Heb. *'aṭṭip*) ...', a cohortative verb form. The condition envisaged is one where they speak about/in favour of, or for (receipt of) wine and liquour (Heb. *layyayin w^{e}laššēkār*). Whichever is the correct nuance, their self-serving words are empty lies. If one of those addressed happened to be such an individual, then, according to Micah, that one would qualify as an appropriate *preacher* (*maṭṭip*) for this people—not for 'my people', of course, but for 'this people'. There is a clear distinction within the community being made in this section's wording.

We note the inclusion *'aṭṭip, maṭṭip* from v. 6 that brackets the section, but precise details in terms of persons involved are lacking in the text.

2.12-13

I would gather together the entirety of Jacob, bring together the remnant of Israel, keep them together as a flock in Bozrah, like a herd in its pen; the people will make a lot of noise.

The one who breaks through has gone up ahead of them, and they have passed through the gate and departed.

And their king went before them, and Yahweh at their head.

This brief section is usually regarded as expressing the possibility of some hope following the more judgmental tone of the preceding sections; some readers find a more positive spin to the message here. The first-person pronoun 'I' obviously is intended to refer to Yahweh, using the analogy of a herder gathering his flock. There is, however, a disjuncture as the figure of breaching, of breaking through and of escape from the fold through the 'gate', clouds the issue by speaking of someone escaping from what appears to be confinement, when the pen or fold should represent a safe place.

The two verses are quite separate from the rest of the material in chs. 1–2 in terms of their general ethos, and they begin quite abruptly, though there are connections, via vocabulary use, with material in chs. 4–5 (see 4.7, 12; 5.7-8). Overall, the language is vague, and the theme of 'gathering' the people, even if only a 'remnant', appropriate to many different scenarios. Interpretation is not obvious as the nuance of the verbs is confusing, moving as they do from the imminent in v. 12 to 'past', that is, the present situation, in v. 13, while addressing 'you' in v. 12, but 'them' in v. 13. Clearly this passage has a more complicated history.

In view of this reader's understanding that Micah was a visionary, not a prophet, the imperfective verbs are being read as volitional, Micah challenging Israelites with what could or should happen, rather than predicting what will happen.

Commentators in the past have wondered whether these two verses reflect a much later situation than Israel was facing at the closing stages of the eighth century BCE, proposing that they relate to a time and situation following the Babylonian exile. This would mean that the two verses are read as a much later scribal addition from the sixth century BCE and not part of Micah's original vision. While that is not an impossibility, the vague and problematic nature of the text we have offers no assurance regarding that proposed reading. We could also note that this same uncertainty exists in

156   *Micah*

the LXX text. In the reading being offered here, however, Israel's pre-721 situation is assumed to be that to which Micah is alluding.

2.12 The editor's report begins with an announcement from 'I' that can only be meant to refer to Yahweh, though we have met already the problem of distinguishing between Micah and Yahweh as first-person speaker (e.g. 1.8-9). The verb phrases *'āsop 'e'ᵉsop* and *qabbēṣ 'ᵃqabbēṣ* are emphatic, underscoring Yahweh's determination to 'gather' people together. The emphasis on Yahweh 'gathering' implies that the 'you' in question have either themselves scattered or been scattered by others, with the text offering no explanation for the scattering. What is now about to be 'gathered' is described as the *šᵉ'ērît* of Israel, often rendered as 'the remnant ...', which in postexilic contexts meant those who returned from Babylonian exile. In other contexts, it simply means a portion, 'the rest', something other than the total number. Here it is impossible to identify them any more precisely. The in-gathering of the flock for safety is the analogy used, so they are being gathered to the 'fold', normally a figure for rest and protection.

In the analogy used here, what might the 'fold' signify? First to note is that the Hebrew text refers to *boṣrâ*, literally '*into an enclosure*', but also a place name, a city in Edom. The root letters can also indicate the action of cutting off. Parallel to this is the phrase that sees the herd (*'ēder*) in its pasture (Heb. *dōber*). Both images suggest a peaceful and tranquil situation. So, in this context, is it the land of Israel, or at least the Shephelah, to which these people are to be gathered, implying that they currently are in exile, or at least in a dangerous location? Is it merely a metaphor with no specific location in mind? Or is it a hope of Micah's that if exile were to occur, as is suggested in 2.10, then they could be gathered (by whom?) and made safe? Whatever the case, the text suggests it will involve a noisy gathering, presumably in celebration, though the final phrase *mē'ādām*, 'from man'—perhaps even 'from Edom'—is a mystery.

2.13 Once in the fold, 'the scatterer' (*happorēṣ*) is said to '*go up before them*'. The participle *happorēṣ* is active, not passive, so it alludes to a third party having scattered the community, of which a portion may now be brought back. Who?, why?, when? where? are questions one wants to ask, but there is nothing in the text that offers answers.

The remaining two verbs in this line are plural, suggesting numerous individuals 'breaking through' perhaps a wall(?) and 'going out', or leaving by a 'gate' (Heb. *ša'ar*), normally meaning a city gate (1.12). The phrase 'before them' presumably refers to the ones brought into the fold, but 'their king' leading them is not an identifiable royal persona. It is further complicated by the next phrase, which places Yahweh at their head ($b^e ro'\check{s}\bar{a}m$). Is Yahweh personified as king, or are these two distinct identities?

Overall, there does seem to be a slightly more positive tone to these two verses, but the issues that the text throws up are such that a reasonably confident translation and interpretation are elusive. The one thing that is clear is that the text's transmission from an oral form to this finally fixed written form has been a very discombobulating one. A modern reader will never find an answer here to all the questions asked of it.

Micah 3

3.1–5.14 The Sins of the Rulers

In the Introduction to Micah the question of the book's structure was raised, noting a division of opinion as to whether the first section of Micah consisted of chs. 1–2 or 1–3. The choice this reader has made was that chs. 1–2 formed the initial unit, followed by chs. 3–5 as a second section, with the main criterion being the introductory 'Hear …' or 'Listen up …!' forms at 1.2 and 3.1, 9, and the third division beginning at 6.1. See the discussion in Introduction.

This third chapter thus begins the second major division of the book, with its opening call to *'Hear …!'* addressed to various classes or groups within the community who are most at fault. They are then faced with the threat of judgment in the fourth and fifth chapters, which are concerned with the present—*'now …'* (4.9, 11, 14)—set against the context of future judgment *'in days to come'* (4.1, 6; 5.9, 13). Within this overall plan the material is diverse, suggesting that the editor is the one who has brought together Micah's disparate oral speeches, providing a measure of order via the chiastic structure that circles around 4.11-13. See the Introduction.

Chapter 3 consists of three easily noted sub-sections: vv. 1-4, 5-8, 9-12, the first and third beginning with the imperative 'hear!' with its accusatory force, and the intermediate or second sub-section, vv. 5-8, having a distinctive thematic unity around prophets from whom Micah expressly distinguishes himself. Within each sub-section there are other markers such as 'therefore …' in vv. 5 and 12 that respond to the problems, outlining the deserved punishments. Much of the focus in this chapter is upon those who are 'leaders' in Israel, the *'rulers of Jacob'*.

3.1-4 Rulers of Jacob and Israel Hate Justice

> *And I said: 'Listen (to me) heads of Jacob and rulers of the house of Israel! Does not knowledge of justice belong with you?*
>
> *You who hate the good and love evil; who tear the skin from off them and the flesh from off their bones,*

And who devour the flesh of my people, the skin you strip off, the flesh from their bones, and who have broken their bones to pieces. You have cut it up as in a pot and as meat in a cauldron.'

Then/If when they cry to Yahweh may he not answer them, but hide his face from them at that time according to the evil they have committed.

As noted, this section returns to the theme of the problems Micah perceived within the Israelite leadership. It opens with a call for people to '*Listen/ Hear*' (Heb. *šim'û*), the audience identified as the *heads of Jacob* (Heb. *rā'šê ya'qob*) and the parallel form (*q^eṣînê bêt yiśrā'ēl*), those who rule in Israel. The terms themselves are generic so it is not possible to single out any one class or civic role, including royalty. The speaker is obviously Micah as the first word of text indicates, even though it is unusual to begin such a form with *wā'omar*, which is presumably an editor's contribution.

All those addressed by Micah the iconoclast are equally condemned as hating good and loving evil, and, using the analogy of an animal being butchered, he applies that description to the manner in which these leaders metaphorically 'strip the flesh from the peoples' bones' (3.2-3). The subsection ends in 3.4 with the threat of divine silence should the leaders call to the Lord, but for what purpose they might call is left unspoken.

3.1-3 These verses establish both the audiences addressed by Micah and the charges laid against them.

The call to an audience to 'Listen ...!' or 'Hear ...!' introduces a formal literary type found often in the texts relating to those who speak with authority, such as prophets and teachers (see Joel 1.2; Amos 3.1, 13; 5.1; 8.4 etc.). The form is used here by Micah's editor, probably because Micah himself spoke thus.

There follows a rhetorical question by which Micah affirms the responsibility of the leadership to hold and promote the knowledge or awareness of justice (Heb. *mišpāṭ*), together with its administration, throughout the kingdom. This perhaps narrows the definition of 'leader' somewhat as it carries more of a legal or *torah*-based notion; on the other hand, *torah* touched many aspects of life, including the economic and agrarian. The opening verses of ch. 2 listed already some of the evil and unjust practices that were carried out by those with power and influence.

Micah's targeted audience is then described by means of participles to indicate what was an on-going problem he wanted to address. Simply put in v. 2a, they were those who were *haters of (what was) good and lovers of (what was) evil* (see also Amos 5.15). This black-and-white characterization was typical of the Deuteronomic categories of thought that were in early development at this time in Judah. The 'good' can refer to moral values they themselves should be pursuing, as well as the manner of living that law-abiding citizens preserved. What was 'evil' related to their actions that were against the principles of justice and fairness, as in 2.1. The root *gzl*, 'tear, seize, rob', appears in both contexts to focus on the violence with which the leaders acted against the less powerful.

From this basic accusation, v. 3 turns to an analogy, characterizing the leaders' evil behaviour as like that of a hunter attacking then butchering an animal before cooking and eating it. It develops the analogy by making repeated use of parallel terms, 'skin' and 'flesh', adding in references to 'bones', all to be cut up and thrown into the pot to be cooked. The imagery portrays the leaders' selfish disregard for the community and the violence and injustice with which they rule. As is the case often in these texts, the language is general rather than specific, so that when speaking of a class or group, all are included. Whether every leader in Israel was as corrupt as is implied is a real question; it is another example of Micah's use of hyperbole to emphasize his point.

3.4 The language used in this verse changes from a more poetic cast to something closer to narrative. It begins with '*āz*, 'Then ...', a particle that can have two functions—that of a temporal marker for the next event, or to introduce the apodosis of a conditional clause. Here the conditional sense seems the correct interpretation of its function; it envisages a time to come when the leaders will seek divine help, though help for what is not spoken about. As a visionary, Micah saw that the leadership's failure to ensure 'justice' should have consequences. If, in time to come, the leaders were to call out to Yahweh for whatever it is they might require, Micah assures them that Yahweh would not respond; there would be no answer. Yahweh would 'hide his face' from them, that is, not look on them kindly. Micah's warning was that Yahweh the Just could not respond to their prayer because of the evil they have committed (v. 2).

The verbs 'call out' and 'answer' used in this verse suggest a liturgical or cultic context, so the leaders involved in this case could well be more those of the priestly class. This would support reading 2.6-11 as directed primarily against the priests rather than, as many prefer, against the prophets.

3.5-8. Prophets Who Lead Astray

> *Thus says Yahweh with regard to the prophets who lead my people astray, who announce 'Peace' when they have something to chew on, but declare war on any who refuse to feed them.*

'Therefore, may it be as night to you without a vision, and as darkness to you without any revelation,

May the sun set on your prophets, the day become dark for them'.

The seers are ashamed, and diviners in disgrace; all cover their lips because there is no response from God.

But for me, I am filled with power by the spirit of Yahweh and with justice and might

to declare to Jacob its transgression and to Israel its sin.

There is little question in this section that Micah, like Amos before him, denied being a *nābî'* prophet; he clearly makes the point that he is different from those who identify as prophets. Micah's statement in 3.8 constitutes justification for his speaking out, significant because he was not called to be a *nābî'*.

For Micah and/or Yahweh, the particular prophets noted in this section are portrayed as deceivers. Of course, this blanket dismissal of all prophets is another case of hyperbole, but it shows Micah's determination to claim his independence of them. Isaiah of Jerusalem made the same point (Isa. 9.15; 28.7). Whether one is justified in regarding these prophets as false prophets, as some are wont to assume, is another question, since the adjective 'false' should only be applied to a false message, one that is demonstrably inconsistent with the divine will. Such a message is almost impossible to prove. But these *nābî'* prophets spoken of by Micah were deceptive, greedy for personal gain and self-serving, rather than 'false'. Prophets occasionally had differing or competing visions and messages, and there were no specific criteria for a quick test to prove one's message to be true or false—see Jer. 28.5-9. Micah's generalized language lumps all *nᵉbî'îm* together as deceivers, allowing no exceptions. It is no wonder that he exempts himself from that class! See the Postscript.

The section has three component parts: 3.5 issues the indictment; 3.6-7 states the consequences of the prophets' failures; 3.8 presents Micah's rather self-righteous but no doubt exemplary mission. To express the concern Micah had with regard to the prophetic ministry as he saw it, one notes the use of contrasting imagery, 'day and night, light and darkness', applying the negative imagery to them. See Amos 5.18-20 for this pattern in respect of the 'day of the Lord'.

3.5 Unusually, Micah's message is introduced by the *pro forma,* 'Thus says Yahweh...'. It is one of very few references to any divine interpolation found in this book (2.3; 4.6; 5.10; 6.1) though there are two indirect references in 4.4 and 6.9. Even here the use of the phrase 'Thus says Yahweh …' is indirect, as it expresses Yahweh's assumed attitude to prophets who mislead what Micah calls 'my people', that is, his community, not God's people.

The language used is again general—'Peace', or better *šālôm,* is shorthand for a situation free of trouble, a time and place of rest, not simply an absence of war. This the prophets promise when they *'have something to chew'* (JPS). This sounds like a derogatory and somewhat crude expression for receiving metaphorical 'food' as a reward for giving a comforting message, but it is actually idiomatic. 'Bread/food' (Heb. *leḥem*) had become a codeword for corrupt gain; it was the local slang. It relates directly to Amaziah's sarcastic comment in Amos 7.12 that he should go back to Judah and 'earn his bread' there. The report then continues with Micah's further denunciation; these so-called prophets *'declare war'* on any who fail to 'feed' them, who refuse to give them 'bread'. This picture of the prophets is deeply offensive, but it is presented as universal, typical of all prophets in Israel at the time, and in light of Amos's and Isaiah's similar reaction, indicates a genuine crisis in the world of Israelite prophets and prophecy (see the Postscript). The editor has ensured that readers are made aware of Micah's desire not to be associated with them and their corrupt practices.

3.6-7 As a consequence of the scenario outlined in v. 5, 'Therefore …', *lākēn*, threatens an appropriate punishment. These two verses outline a negative outcome that seems to presume a connection with 3.4 via the verb *'ānâ*, 'answer', that speaks of a time when, despite seeking divine response or guidance, no answer would be forthcoming.

First to note is the fact that the opening phrase in v. 6 has no verb; both halves of the line are nominal—*'night to you without vision, and darkness to you without divination'*. The sense is that the prophets are metaphorically blind; the vision and the divination powers required of, or afforded, prophets are not available to them. Is that the present situation, or is it a threatened possibility? Most translations regard it as a future prediction, but it simply states a timeless fact, and it is a fact that contrasts with the situation in which Micah sees himself (3.8). Micah's vision (1.1), what he was able to see, was not something available to the prophets.

A second line contains two statements, but whether the verbs (Heb. *bā'â* and *qāder*) speak of the present or the future is to be determined. If the verbs are read as imperfective equivalents, then one has to ask whether they are predictive or expressive of a desired or potential outcome. For this reader the verbs are to be read as volitional. Micah longs to see the prophets and their work come to an end. It is clear that he looks for the crisis he saw in the prophetic movement to be resolved. See my translation above.

Verse 7 continues Micah's negative depiction of the prophets, using the alternative terms 'seer' and 'diviner'. The double expression is more than a simple case of poetic parallelism; it is doubled for emphasis. It makes the point that the prophets are already in that embarrassed state because whatever they expected to hear from God has not earned a response, so they have nothing significant to say—*'ên ma'ᵃnēh 'ᵉlohîm*. That is not a future 'promise' but a present reality. The idiomatic phrase 'cover the lips' suggests their power or readiness to speak is thwarted; they have nothing of value to say and their words are deceptive, offered only on the basis of them receiving payment. We note also that the language has changed in this verse from second- to third-person forms, but the grammatical shift appears not to detract from the overall content and message.

3.8 The adversative 'But ...' introduces Micah's testimony regarding his own status. It reads as a smug self-serving apologia that intentionally puts a vast distance between himself and the prophets he condemns: *'they are ..., but I am ...'*. It is expressed as a strong assertion, *wᵉ'ûlām 'ānokî mālē'tî ...*, 'As for me, I ...!', using the pronoun 'I' plus the first-person verb form.

In contrast to the corrupt prophets, Micah claims to be *'filled with power, with the spirit of Yahweh, (the spirit) of justice and might'*. This is quite a confronting and ego-driven claim, but it certainly indicates what kind of personality we are looking at in this man. Micah asserts that he is totally different from those whom he has charged with deception and with pandering to their more base instincts (3.5-6). He does not equate this 'filling' with any call to be a prophet, but makes much of his relationship with the 'spirit' of Yahweh (Heb. *rûᵃḥ-yhwh*) that has 'filled' him, giving him 'power'. The noun *rûᵃḥ* refers to that invisible yet experiential sense that can have an impact on one's being, whether it originates in nature or music, be heard or seen. It is a term that in this context may well refer to his own stubborn, unrelenting desire to press forward with his opposition to those who hold all the political power; it is, he claims, what drives him. He attributes the source of such energy to Yahweh his God, and asserts that it makes him 'better' than all those he condemns; it energizes his mission with a sense of justice. This man is no shrinking violet! That is how he now has the courage and temerity to denounce Jacob/Israel for its broad range of transgressions and sin, the gall to condemn the failure of its leaders, including prophets, and the desire to act in the interests of the whole community.

3.9-12 Priests, Rulers and Injustice

> Hear this, heads of the house of Jacob and leaders of the house of Israel!
> you who detest justice, and all who make crooked the straight.

Who build Zion with bloodshed and Jerusalem with wrongdoing;

Her heads dispense justice by bribes, her priests for a fee make their rulings, and her prophets for money issue divinations, but they depend on Yahweh and say: 'Is Yahweh not in our midst? Disaster will not overcome us!'

Therefore, because of you, May Zion become a plowed field and Jerusalem a heap of rubble, and the mountain of the House become a forested high place!

This third sub-section attacks all three classes of leadership within the divided kingdom, the civil leaders in particular, but also the priests and prophets. All are condemned for failing in their duties as defined by their specific roles. Injustice is the problem identified as rife within civil leadership; corrupt priests demand a fee for their rulings, and prophets similarly require some personal reward, 'bread', for their prognostications. These latter two are the more egregious errors because they, it seems, claim a special relationship with Yahweh, selling the message that everything is fine and positive because they believe Yahweh is present in the midst of his people. For Micah, nothing could be further from the truth, so a threatened divine judgment can but fall on both kingdoms, and upon Zion in particular.

Micah's language is similar to that used in Woe-oracles, when speakers lament a situation that has developed: it uses participles to identify the ones at fault (vv. 9-10) and verbs to spell out their failings. The imperfective verbs in v. 12 then are volitional as Micah expresses his thoughts and feelings as to what should happen next—'*Therefore* ...'. The problem, for most readers, is that the punishment Micah believed could or should follow is directed not specifically at the perpetrators, the national leaders, but indirectly at two central and representative religious locations. Furthermore, the wording in v. 12 seems to suggest that Judah could suffer more than the north.

3.9 Micah's call addresses the leaders, the rulers and chiefs of the whole nation—'Jacob' and 'Israel' as synonymous terms. These secular leaders are denounced as *haters of justice*, meaning that they actively pervert the course of justice in the courts to the advantage of those with power and influence whether by false witnesses or by simply denying just and fair treatment to the average citizen. The parallel charge speaks of them as those who 'make crooked what is straight'. While 'straight' normally refers to a pathway, it is also an appropriate adjective for describing a manner of correct living, adhering to the rules, not 'bending' them to personal advantage.

3.10 The reference to those who 'build Zion' must be metaphorical since Zion and Jerusalem were already well-established sites; some have suggested that the description of it being built on 'blood(shed)' and 'wrongdoing' links to humans being sacrificed when the foundations were set as per the charge against Ahaz (2 Kgs 16). However, the imagery is more general and refers to the forced labour and its hardships endured by those who were engaged in the building or expansion of Jerusalem. The two verses provide examples of the leaders' problems as seen and described by Micah and defined as in-built injustice.

3.11 The trilogy of established groups—heads, priests and prophets—are each targeted with Micah's charges, a crisis that has its origin in the leadership's corrupt practices. Each is performing a service, but its focus is on the financial reward that is sought for so doing, implying that without the 'reward', a bribe, they would not do what is required of them, be it administer justice, instruct in *torah*, or intercede with Yahweh. Again, the charge is general and universal. On the rhetorical feature of a tricolon, here and in the following verse, see **Literary Features** in the Introduction

Each of the groups claims to be reliant on Yahweh; the verb *šāʻan*, 'lean on', has both positive and negative connotations, dependent on the context. Here quite obviously it is a sarcastic comment about what they say when deliberately flouting the rules by which they should be operating. The form of their claim, '*Is Yahweh not among us*?', is their claim of legitimacy, but as a rhetorical question, Micah is dismissing that, along with the conclusion that the leaders draw from their claim. Since Yahweh is present, they say, nothing disastrous can happen to us! They see themselves as above the law and claim the covenantal promise as assurance despite their evil ways (see a similar claim in Amos 9.10).

3.12 The section closes with Micah's judgment: '*Therefore, because of you* (pl.) …', or 'because of what you do …'. This introduces Micah's longing as expressed in the tricolon of volitional verbs that follow—a trilogy of failed leaders and a trilogy of hoped-for results for Zion/Jerusalem, that is, Judah, to match the demise of Samaria in 1.5-7. Micah states what could or should happen to Judah as represented by its capital and Temple. Unlike unfulfilled prophecies, Micah's words express what this visionary saw as the appropriate end for Judah, using traditional imagery (see 1.5-6). Jerusalem should be punished, turned into a heap of ruins, plowed over like a field, and allowed to return to being nothing more than an elevated hill with a few trees for cover. It speaks of demolition and a return to nature. Zion becoming a plowed field is obviously hyperbole; the rocky outcrop that was Zion is hardly an area that could be literally 'plowed', so the imagery is purely traditional; Jerusalem was to become a heap of rubble, suggesting that all buildings be demolished; and the 'mountain of the house', the Temple mount, become 'high places' (Heb. *bāmôt*), a wordplay given the significance of 'high places' as sacred spaces associated with foreign worship (see 1.5).

Jeremiah 26.18 quotes Mic. 3.12 almost verbatim, drawing attention to Micah's vision in the context of Hezekiah's reforms following his father's failed regime. It demonstrates that the vision of Micah was kept very much alive in the discussion of the nation's situation, and while his vision for Samaria was realised, his vision of what should also happen to Jerusalem was not. If Yahweh was the one to bring judgment on Samaria via his Assyrian agent, why was that same judgment not meted out on Jerusalem? This was not a case of failed 'prophecy'. Quite to the contrary, it was a failure of what should have been divine judgment—God was to blame! No wonder that the Jerusalem establishment could feel confident that despite Micah's so negative critique, they felt safe from all harm!

Micah 4

This chapter begins a collection of materials that relate to some threatened future judgment with the introductory verb form *wᵉhāyâ,* (4.1; 5.4, 6, 7, 9) marking that possibility. Micah 4 is read as outlining what he hoped to see happen; it was the potential that he 'saw', and so the verbs in our reading are considered volitional, imperfective equivalent forms, not 'prophetic perfects'.

It is clear that some careful thought has been given by the editor as to how best to present the material at his disposal; he has chosen a chiastic form (see below). The broader or outer frame uses the *wᵉhāyâ* in 4.1, 6 and 5.9(10) as a future time marker and relates to 'the day(s)', that vague moment that is to be anticipated. The next frame level is marked by the pronoun *wᵉ'attâ,* 'and you ...' (4.8; 5.1[2]), which identifies two addressees, Jerusalem (4.8) and Bethlehem (5.1[2]). These then enclose material relating to the present, the more immediate *'attâ,* 'now' (4.9, 11, 14), and it is in this triad of notices that the editor has located the book's primary focus, with 4.11-13 serving as the book's numerical centre: there are fifty-one verses preceding it and fifty-one verses following. The structure highlights these three central verses that must be seen as forming the crux of Micah's message, as understood by the editor.

> 4.1, 6 *wehāyâ* ... (In the <u>days</u> to come ...)
>   4.8 <u>But you</u> *wᵉ'attâ* ... (re Jerusalem)
>   4.9 Now *('attâ ...)*
>   **4.11-13 Now *('attâ ...)***
>   4.14(5.1) Now *('attâ ...)*
>   5.1(2) <u>But you</u> *wᵉ'attâ* ... (re Bethlehem)
> 5.9(10) *wehāyâ* ... (In that <u>day</u> ...)

4.1-5 *In Days to Come ...*

> *Then in later times let the mountain of Yahweh's house be established on the top of the mountains, and may it be raised above the hills and the people flow upon them.*

> *And may many nations go, and say, 'Come, let us go up to Yahweh's mountain, to the house of the God of Jacob, and may he teach us of his ways and let us follow in his paths because torah goes out from Zion, the word of Yahweh from Jerusalem'.*
>
> *And let him judge between the many peoples and let him adjudicate for the stronger distant nations; may they beat their swords into plowshares and their spears into pruning tools. Let not one nation raise its sword against another, and let not them practice for war any more.*
>
> *Let every person sit under his vine and under his fig tree and (let there be) no one to disturb him. Truly the mouth of Yahweh of Hosts has spoken.*
>
> *Even if all the peoples walk each in the name of his gods, let us go in the name of Yahweh our God for ever and ever.*

The editor has employed a standard phrase, '*at the end of the days* ...', introduced by the time marker $w^eh\bar{a}y\hat{a}$, indicative of some future moment, whether imminent and pending or later. At least it is anticipatory, not to be confused with a modern concept of forecasting. As a visionary, Micah was not prophesying, but expressing his hope for an impending action when Yahweh's mountain would become established and 'elevated'—not physically, but in reputation/importance—over the mountains to which peoples might come. They would come to Mt. Zion to learn, seeking instruction that would emanate from there; instead of injustice, people would walk in Yahweh's straight paths, eventually enjoying his *šālôm* with no more war. That was Micah's vision, his longing, the ideal in eternal security.

The vocabulary with which 3.12 concluded—'*the mountain of the house*' (of Yahweh) and '*heads*' (leaders/tops)—provides a link with the beginning of this collection (4.1–5.15[16]). Zion/Jerusalem is again the geographical focus.

4.1-2 Micah saw a potential future for Judah despite the destruction that he believed could bring to an end the injustices and wrongdoings that marked its current or 'now' situation (4.9–5.9[10]). That future, whenever it might arise, could see torah rolled out from the Temple and be a period in which people would flock to Jerusalem to learn. When might that be? It could come *at the end of the days,* that is, after some unspecified delay. What could transpire? It would establish (Heb. *nākôn*) Jerusalem at the 'head' (*ro'š*) or top of the mountain range that was Judah's backbone. There is some slight ambiguity in the wording of Micah's vision, in that the noun 'head of ...' or 'the highest of' the mountains may refer to physical height as well as importance, that is, its importance as a centre of *torah* instruction, while there is clear reference to the physical mountain-top location of Jerusalem and its Temple.

Micah saw 'peoples', a noun often suggestive of foreign nations (NRSV), making their way to Zion in significant numbers; the verb used suggests they came 'flowing like a river'. Obviously, there is in this vision a hope that northerners would flock to Jerusalem, as the Deuteronomists hoped, but it could also involve foreigners as well. These unnamed peoples are seen to decide together that they must '*go up to* Yahweh's mountain', the Zion of Israel's God. The verb 'go up' implies intention, namely to worship (see the Psalms of Ascents; Pss. 120-134). Here the purpose also speaks of 'learning' what is required in order to 'walk' in God's ways/paths, for that is ultimately of what true worship consists (see 6.8). They would also recognize that the Temple was the source from which Yahweh's *torah*, his instruction, emanated. There lies within this the claim that only in Jerusalem could truth be found, never in the northern breakaway centres of Bethel and Samaria.

4.3 Micah anticipates that a third-person 'he' would decide (*šāpaṭ*) or judge between 'many peoples' (Heb. *'ammîm rabbîm*). The notion of 'judging' is far more than simply making a determination based on some divine principle, or settling disputes and resolving issues between litigants (see the book of Judges). It has to do with punishment as well. Here the litigants are defined so broadly that it is difficult to determine who or which 'people' will be found to be the ones 'in the right'. At the theoretical or theological level, the idea that Yahweh was God of the universe would suggest that Micah is talking about Yahweh as global judge, deciding matters in relation to these 'many peoples', far and near, based on the standards of *torah*. This 'peoples' phrase reappears as *goyîm rabbîm* in 4.11 and as *'ammîm rabbîm* again in 4.13. What specific issues are to be adjudged cannot be identified, given the general nature of the language, but it must involve open conflict between various groups of people, presumably Israel and its enemies, unless the following note about 'war' is completely figurative.

The potential result of Yahweh's 'judging' is then expressed as people deciding to turn military weapons into agricultural implements, thus signifying an end to hostilities between the many peoples or between factions within the one people. The hope was that they would cease to '*lift up the sword*' or bear arms, nor '*learn* war', meaning preparation by regular training of the military in ways to fight 'better'(?). This latter phrase of 'learning' war is idiomatic (see 1 Chron. 5.18). Zion should rather be the place of learning, learning how to walk in justice and peace, not of 'learning war'.

170   *Micah*

The '*swords into plowshares*' example is a motif that celebrates the outbreak of peace, one that is found later reversed in Joel 4.10. Even though there is some small question about the exact identification of the tools mentioned, the point is blindingly obvious that whatever weapon they had could be turned into a useful agricultural tool. The imagery used suggests that we are in touch here with a common cultural expression.

4.4 In contrast to conflict, all should be able to live in peace 'without fear' (Heb. *maḥᵃrîd*). The vision of peace is then spoken of in terms of the idealized rural idyll: everyone sitting contentedly '*under his own grape vine and/or fig tree*', all basic needs met, and with no worries, an expression that the DH used to describe the nation under Solomon (1 Kgs 4.25 [Eng.]). This ideal of local and international harmony was fundamental to Micah's vision. There would be nothing to fear, because such a resolution was grounded in a divine promise, the words had come from the very 'mouth of Yahweh of Hosts' (see Lev. 26.3-6). Here Micah refers back to the *torah* tradition, leaving the impression that his vision was a nationalistic one, that foreigners would no longer be a threat to Judah. That was his wish or longing for his people; unfortunately, it was not to be realized.

4.5 The relationship between this v. 4.5 and 4.1-4 has been widely discussed since the almost identical text is found in Isa. 2.2-5 but lacking our v. 5. The place of 4.5 is further questioned given its content that seems to fly in the face of all that was emerging in Israelite monotheism; it appears to promote the worship of alien gods by foreign entities. A key question in resolving this issue may lie in determining the meaning and function of the initial particle *kî*: is it explanatory, 'for/because', or is it conditional, 'if'? This reader suggests that the particle here marks a conditional situation, namely 'Even if all the peoples walk each in the name of his god …'; see, for example, 2 Kgs 4.29, where the particle establishes a potential case while the *waw* connector in v. 5b has an adversative function, leading to a contrast. The nations may continue to 'walk' their own way, BUT let us walk in the name of our God …! Just as 'each' may *sit* calmly at peace under his vine etc., the nations may walk 'in the name(s)' of their foreign gods, *but* let Israel walk 'in the name' of Yahweh. Who is included in this 'we' is unclear. Is Micah speaking on behalf of one small Deuteronomic group or on behalf of the nation? The verb *hālak*, 'go, walk', means a manner of living, a religious regime, and is a rhetorical feature of this sub-section (see v. 2 used three times, and twice in this v. 5). The imagery may invoke the idea of 'walking' under the flag or banner of one's leader whose name or identification mark adorns the banner. There are commentators who raise the possibility of Micah being broadminded as to religious attachment, but surely the sense is more in the nature of recognizing that foreigners may have their gods BUT WE have Yahweh, expressing a sense of superiority. Attributing religious broadmindedness to Micah is not intended.

The final phrase *for ever and ever* closes this component of the vision, but whether it applies to both elements of v. 5 or only to Israel is not clear. In any event, the phrase should not be interpreted as saying anything more than 'for a long, long time' as *'ôlām*, often thought of by modern readers as 'eternity', was not the view of the Israelites at the time; their thinking was much more confined to the present world order.

As noted, this sub-section in Micah appears in virtually the same form in Isa. 2.2-5. Commentators have spent much time and paper comparing the two pieces and seeking to determine which might be the earlier, who borrowed from the other, or whether both editors knew of the text and included it independently. All attempts essentially reach the same conclusion, that there is no convincing evidence that any borrowing has taken place. The simple fact is that we have two almost identical texts, and their journeys to the fixed forms now available cannot be determined absolutely.

4.6-7 *Gathering the Lame*

> *In that day, says Yahweh, let me gather the lame and those driven away, let me assemble together my afflicted ones.*
>
> *For I would make the lame for a remnant and the cast off to become a strong nation.*
>
> *And may Yahweh rule over them on Mt Zion from now to the end.*

These two verses are considered together here as a single sub-section rather than including v. 8, as do many commentators. The structure identified above provides the basis for this decision.

The unit begins and ends with temporal phrases that isolate it from the context, and the content itself adds to that sense of separateness, though the general and figurative language makes it difficult to be certain as to its specific field of reference. The JPS translation adds [sheep] after 'lame' in the opening line, directing readers' thoughts in a specific direction!

4.6-7 The initial '*In that day* ...' places these two verses and what follows in the wider context of Micah's vision as bound by 4.1 and 5.9(10). The phrase '*In that day* ...' is essentially confined to literature relating to the eighth century BCE (19 of 25 occurrences). Here it is accompanied by the *proforma* 'says the Lord' (Heb. *nᵉ'um yhwh*), mostly found as the closing component of the bracketing formula that usually opens with 'Thus says the Lord ...', both phrases being editorial additions to give emphasis and gravitas to the words of the text.

Continuing with the view that the imperfective verbs used by our visionary are volitional, we see that Micah expresses the wish that Yahweh gather together four groups of people, the lame, those driven away, those whom he has afflicted (Heb. $h^a r\bar{e}\,'\bar{o}t\hat{\imath}$) and those cast off. The question then is how to identify these groups more closely, but apart from 'the lame', assuming it is meant literally, the general language denies that possibility. The other feature of the call is the clear implication that Yahweh is the one who has caused the affliction and presumably also is the actor behind the passive forms '(those) driven away' and '(those) cast off'. Yahweh is the one who has acted against these certain people, but no reason for that action is offered in the text, so commentators have, for various reasons, assumed these people's sufferings have been applied as divine punishment, whether direct or indirect. Is that assumption justifiable? Some commentators then argue that the basic message of these two verses is that Yahweh is about to gather or bring back those whom he has previously punished for their evil ways. Neither explanation can be applied to 'the lame', who are obviously not to be blamed for their physical condition, thus casting doubt on the motive for such an explanation. To claim, as some have done, that such an ingathering as this points to a late, even postexilic, date for this sub-section is baseless.

In v. 7 the goal of this ingathering is seen to be twofold: to establish the lame as 'a remnant' (Heb. $\check{s}e\,'\bar{e}r\hat{\imath}t$) and the 'cast off ones' as a strong nation (Heb. $g\hat{o}y\,'\bar{a}\d{s}\hat{u}m$). The meaning of the noun 'remnant' normally relates to the remaining portion of a larger group, but in 2.12 it refers to the whole of Israel; so does it carry the same meaning here? If the parallelism of the half verse has a function, then both the weak and the cast off together are to become a strong community. Without that result, Micah's words have little value.

The ultimate purpose of the gathering is that Yahweh might 'rule over them' on Mt. Zion. Yahweh as king over a reconstituted community is the vision Micah has, and as noted in 4.5, that community and that relationship will be permanent (Heb. $'ad\,'\hat{o}l\bar{a}m$). Moreover, it is a kingship that begins in the 'now', to be followed in vv. 9, 11, 14(5.1) with explicit information about that 'now' time.

4.8 This verse also seems disconnected from its surroundings, while the connections within the verse are complex. It does, however, refer to a number of place names, all of which relate to Jerusalem, giving some sense of unity. Here it will be treated as an isolated saying.

> *And you Migdal-'Eder Ophel of Daughter-Zion, let it come to you, and may the former rule come, the kingdom for the Daughter of Jerusalem.*

A significant marker, *wᵉ'attâ*, 'and you ...', begins the verse, with the same form at 5.1. Micah's address is to his contemporary leaders in Jerusalem, and balances with the next 'And you ...' with its focus on Bethlehem. These two references wrap around the three 'now ...' sub-sections in 4.9-14(5.1).

The first name is *Migdal-'Eder*, which translates to 'Tower of the Flock', an unusual and essentially unknown architectural feature. 'Ophel' is the name of the site of the Temple; 'Daughter of Zion' uses the noun 'daughter' as a reference to a location closely associated with the main name, Zion. Similarly, 'Daughter of Jerusalem' refers to the towns and villages around Jerusalem. This much is clear.

There are two notions associated with movement toward, a coming or moving into, Jerusalem. The first is *memšālâ* and the second *mamlākâ*. Both relate to ruling or having dominion. They are abstract terms, but obviously some individual is represented, presumably Yahweh, though some commentators suggest it might be another David or David-like figure since the phrase *hāri'šonâ* linked with 'rule' seems to hint at Judah's primary royal person. Overall, the verse then can be seen as Micah's hope for the restoration of ideal kingship to Jerusalem on a permanent basis.

Does Micah's vision actually imply that the kingdoms have been destroyed, the people exiled, requiring Yahweh's action in bringing people back? Does this text require a postexilic reading for it to be appropriate? Many commentators accept that approach. There is no specific evidence demanding that interpretation, however. Rather, what Micah envisaged was a restoration of ideal royal rule, something lost during the period of Ahaz's devastating religious policy, which saw a return to foreign and syncretistic practices detested by the Deuteronomic cohort. Micah's strident critique of the priests and prophets of his day indicate the need for a revolution, a fresh start to bring justice and faithfulness back to kingdom life. This section reflects his longing for that to be realized.

4.9-14(5.1)

> **Now,** *why do you cry out (in pain)? Do you not have a king, or are your advisors destroyed?*
>> *Indeed, writhing (in pain) has seized you like a woman giving birth.*

> *Writhe and groan O daughter of Zion like a woman giving birth, for now, leave the city and dwell in the field.*
>
>> *And come to Babylon, there may you be rescued, there may Yahweh redeem you from the hand of your enemy.*
>
> *And **now** assembled against you are many nations who say, 'Let her be profaned! May our eyes gaze on Zion!'*
>
> *But they do not know Yahweh's thoughts, nor do they comprehend his counsel, for he has gathered them like sheaves to the threshing floor.*
>
> *Arise and thresh them, Daughter of Zion, for I will make you into an iron horn, and your hoofs bronze so that you can crush many peoples and dedicate their riches to Yahweh and their wealth to the master of all the earth.*
>
> ***Now** gather together your troops, O Daughter of G'dud (the troops??) He has placed a siege against us,*
>
>> *With a rod they struck on the face the judge of Israel.*

In contrast to 'the days to come ...' in 4.1-7, this sub-section turns to the present. It is marked by the adverb '*Now* ...', which initiates three brief units in 4.9, 11, 14(5.1). It also forms the core of the whole section 3.1–5.14(15). Furthermore, the second of these three units, 4.11-13, constitutes the numerically central verses of the book, as noted. This tripartite core lies within the next level of the frame, where the phrase '*And you* ...' identifies the addressees, namely Jerusalem and Bethlehem, both important centres in Judah. See the diagram above (p. 167).

4.9-10 Micah has addressed Jerusalem/Zion, that is, its population, asking, Why is it constantly(?) crying out, and although the verb often has association with a war cry, the similarity of Hebrew 'cry' ($rē^a‘$) and 'disaster' ($rā‘â$) suggests that the city is distressed and is calling out 'like a woman in the anguish of childbirth' does. The point of the simile is to heighten the intensity of the cry, though some suggest it may be to assure that there would be a happy outcome from the painful experience. The latter suggestion may be taking the simile a little too far. Presumably the anguished cry is for some kind of rescue or assistance. The 'why?' question in v. 9 may not be asking for a response, but rather is rhetorical, demanding that 'you' be quiet. That would fit with the following rhetorical question that answers itself, meaning 'you have a king and you have advisors, so be strong like a woman in childbirth must'. Some see this to mean that she is screaming out because her king is absent, along with his advisors, but it could just as well be a call to Jerusalem/Zion to simply appeal to their king and advisors who are present to do something in face of the danger that threatens. Certainty as to the intent of the analogy is not possible when interpreting the two questions in this verse, but this reader prefers to read them as critical of 'you' who fail to rely on king and sage to advise them. Stop whingeing!

Verse 10 encourages the people, the daughter of Zion, meaning the city and its environs, repeating the call to *'writhe like a woman in childbirth'*, but why they would or should do so is not made clear. What is the nature of the current distress that it can be likened to childbirth? The analogy with the woman giving birth may suggest that there will be a happy outcome. Is this a message that offers some hope once the distress is over? Why does Micah's vision speak only of the process, not of the outcome?

The two imperatives call for the people to now depart the city and live in the open field. Does the open field represent safety more than does the city? Does everyone have to leave? What is the point of the commands? Then, *'come/go as far as Babylon'*, for from there you may be rescued. There are two issues (at least) here: Is *bābel* a literal reference to Babylon when no contextual support for the name is obvious, or is it a metaphor, even a play on words for 'the gate of 'El', meaning Zion? For there 'you will be delivered', with the possible meaning that the 'wailing in childbirth' analogy will see the child delivered, in other words, be rescued from whatever the crisis is. The text in its present form is unable to answer our fundamental questions.

The climax to this journey comes when Yahweh redeems Zion's people from the hands of its 'enemies', though they are not specified. Micah, in our reading, is a visionary who longs to see certain actions taken by the Judaeans who are facing a disaster. The verbs in this verse are thus read as volitional, though it is not possible to discover what the nature of the disaster is that threatens nor the reason for travel, if that is what the text implies. Commentators struggle to make good sense of this section; but, while translation is not difficult, there is little consensus as to its meaning and significance. One possibility that some commentators prefer is that the reference to Babylon implies that the text is a much later addition. That may be so, but it cannot be proved. Some see a contrast between v. 9 as a people doomed and v. 10 as their salvation. Clearly, the precise contribution of the two verses is difficult to discern.

4.11-13 The position of these three verses at the numerical centre of the book means that they function as the book's core message, a guide to the primary concern in the editor's report. It immediately reveals that the disaster noted in 4.9-10 has to do with enemies who have gathered together for an attack on Zion/Jerusalem. Micah's vision, however, sees their designs on the city founded on their ignorance of Yahweh's grand scheme, for Yahweh as *lord of the whole earth* has a plan to defeat them. Micah saw disaster about to fall, not on Zion, but on the enemies who would be smashed and their wealth paid into Zion's treasury. Micah again uses hyperbole to convey his hopes for his community.

In the Introduction to this commentary, I drew attention to the name 'Micah' as the question form *'Who is like (Yah)?',* and to the concluding text in 7.18-20 in which the question is raised again as *'Who is a God like you?',* which is to say that these two questions form the *inclusio* for the report. Central to this report of Micah's vision are the three verses in 4.11-13 in which Yahweh is declared to be the 'master' (Heb. *'ᵃdôn*) of the whole earth! In other words, the name Micah itself denotes his claim that Yahweh is the incomparable lord and master of the universe, for there is none like Israel's God, the God who from of old has been faithful and loyal.

'Many nations' have assembled against Judah. None are named, as is consistent with generalized language throughout the report, so there is no point in attempting to tie the vision to any historical situation or event. The nations' intention was to humiliate Zion, its Temple, its citizenry, and its royalty. The joint call by the enemy to *'Let her be profaned!'* or 'Let's humiliate her!' by staring at her vulnerability is in direct contrast with the earlier international call for all to gather and go up to Zion to worship (4.2-4).

Originally the Zion Temple site was a threshing floor (2 Sam. 24.18-25), the place where the sheaves were brought to dry and where the seed could be separated from the stalk. Threshing was also an analogy for battle, and, in this case, for the defeat of the threatening nations. This was Yahweh's plan according to Micah; the nations would be defeated, so to that extent this sub-section expresses Micah's message of hope for Israel/Judah. That Yahweh had a plan and purpose to execute was a basic notion that Micah shared with others of the time (see Isa. 5.19; 14.24 etc.). It was this very aspect of Yahweh of which the nations and 'many peoples' were ignorant—yet another element of Yahweh's incomparability.

Thus it was that Micah, reversing the 'swords into plowshares' imagery of 4.3, called the people of Judah to *'Arise and thresh'* the enemy (4.13). Here the 'horn' and the 'hooves' of the animals used to tread out the grain are metaphorically turned into iron and bronze devices for smashing the enemy. The verb used for this action is *śîm*, 'place/put', as also in v. 14. Along with the complete annihilation of the enemy, their riches and treasures, no matter how derived, are to be donated to Zion. Temple treasures were usually taken as war booty but also as a sign of the power of the gods of the winning side over the gods of the defeated. This verse appears to suggest that at some point in the past, treasures from the Jerusalem Temple had been taken or captured; Micah saw them now being returned as the nations holding them were defeated. The treasures would be consecrated (Heb. *ḥrm*) as an offering to Yahweh.

The climax of this central statement and thus of the book as a whole lies in the statement that Yahweh is the 'lord/master of the whole earth' *('ªdôn kol-hā'āreṣ*).

4.14 (Eng 5.1) The editor has placed this one verse here to complete the 'Now ...' section of the structure he has provided for the book. Apart from its function, however, there is not a great deal one can confidently say about its content, despite commentators having spent a lot of ink trying to solve the problems it raises. One of the obvious issues is the pronominal use that moves between 'you', 'he', 'they', 'us' and their referents. While the initial 'you' is clearly a reference to Zion and its population, the other pronouns lack clarity. The town has been 'walled around'—the Hebrew root here, *gdd*, seems to have a range of meanings—cut, penetrate (JPS preference); the form *gᵉdûd*, a marauding band, furrow—so there is a challenge in identifying the phrase *bat-gᵉdûd*, 'Daughter of G'dud', apparently a place name.

Then the general statement that 'they' strike the 'judge of Israel' does not identify the strikers nor does it clarify the identity of the 'judge'. Perhaps he represents a community, even of Zion itself, though some believe it is the king. Being struck on the cheek generally has to do with being humiliated, rather than the kind of savage personal attack that could be life-threatening. What is clear is that this object or city has been put under siege (Heb. *māṣôr*). So, what can one make of this single verse when so many uncertainties lie within? This reader's conclusion is that the oral text has suffered greatly in the complex transmission to this final written form so it is unlikely that its significance, if any, can now be resurrected.

Micah 5

5.1-9 (Eng 5.2-10)

And you Bethlehem Ephrathah, small though you are among the clans of Judah, from you for me will one depart to become the ruler in Israel, one whose departures are from the past, from days of old.

Therefore, may he give them until that time when she who is giving birth gives birth, and the rest of his brothers return to the sons of Israel,

And may he stand and be a shepherd in Yahweh's strength in the pride/glory of the name of YHWH his God,

And they will sit/dwell because now he is great to the ends of the earth.

(And may there be peace should Assyria come into our land and if he should walk on our strongholds, then may we establish against it/him seven shepherds and eight princes of Adam,

And may they shepherd the land of Assyria with the sword and the land of Nimrod with its openings, and may he deliver from Assyria if he were to come within our borders and trample upon our land.)

Then may the remnant of Jacob among the many peoples be like the dew from Yahweh, like showers upon the grass, (a remnant) not dependent on people and not placing hope in any mortal.

May the remnant of Jacob among the gentiles, in the midst of many peoples, be like a lion among the beasts of the forest, like a young lion among the flocks of sheep, which tramples and tears everywhere, with none to rescue.

May your hand be raised against your adversaries and all your enemies be cut down.

Moving out from the 'Now ...' sections at the book's centre, the scene returns to the 'And you ...' level of the frame, as in 4.8, and moves from Zion to the small town of Bethlehem south of Jerusalem.

Micah sees the town of Bethlehem-Ephrathah as ṣā'îr among the 'alpê of Judah, perhaps meaning that it was the least important of the family groups in Judah, though this is uncertain—at least one can say that here the emphasis is on its relative unimportance. So why choose this town? What was it about the town that called for such a comment? Readers would really like to know why Micah has seen it to be significant given its minority status!

The phrase 'from you for me comes/goes out', using the verb *yāṣa'*, appears to identify some person who has arisen in Bethlehem, the birthplace of David, and who is at the time or had become in the past a 'ruler' (Heb. *môšēl*) in Judah. The line then refers to 'his comings out', *môṣā'ôtāyw*, a *hapax*, so its precise meaning is far from certain. Some see in the noun a reference to a lineage, as 'that which proceeds from ...', and then they suggest that it refers to the Davidic line. Despite the general nature of the text, it would seem as though arguing that possible connection is reasonable, but in the end there is not sufficient concrete evidence for readers to determine the import of the text.

The other element that follows in this verse is a locative phrase *miqqedem*, which could refer to a direction, *from the east*, or, if previous time is in view, *from the past*. This latter seems more likely given the time phrase, '*from the days of 'ôlām*, that follows. To whom or to what this might refer is another issue resulting from the vague language employed, but many commentators see in this an echo of the Davidic promise as expressed in 2 Samuel 7. While *'ôlām* is integral to the language surrounding the Davidic promise, it looks forward rather than back, whereas here the *'olam* speaks of the past.

5.2(3) The verse opens with '*Therefore* ...', but its connection with the preceding verse is unclear as is the very content of the verse. Presumably it sets out a result or consequence of the preceding 'coming forth'. This suggests that the 'he' referred to is the one who is the *môšēl*, 'ruler', and that 'he would give them until the time ...'. Neither giver nor receiver are further identified; the verb 'give' may mean something like 'make a donation' or 'to hand over' since there is no clear subject and no direct object, only an indirect 'them' undefined. Whatever the action, it is then linked with a phrase that relates it with a woman giving birth. Again, whether this refers to a specific woman known to those addressed, or simply is a reference to a nine-month period of pregnancy, or the last moments of the birthing process, it is totally lacking in detail. Depending on the reader's preconceptions one may be tempted to make assumptions about this reference, but to do so leads to an arbitrary conclusion that has no textual justification.

The verse continues with further challenges. The statement that reads, literally, '*let the rest of his brothers return upon the sons of Israel*' is likewise a mysterious one, with no clear evidence with which the interpreter might work. Each concept here is uncertain. From where might they be 'returning', or is the verb the homograph 'sit/dwell'? Who constitutes 'the rest'? And from whom are they to be separated? Who are 'his brothers', if literally understood, or his community, if taken as representative? Added to this is the particular emphasis of the preposition *'al,* whether it suggests 'against', 'for', or 'about'. In other words, there is no way that one can be confident about fixing the meaning of this verse. It lacks contextual details, but if Judah is under threat from the Assyrians or some other enemy, perhaps each element would have been understood within that context.

5.3(4) The challenge continues here as the subject 'he' now *stands* (= stand firm?) in order to *feed (his flock) in the strength of Yahweh'.* How the two notions belong together is something to ponder, especially when the reliance on *Yahweh's strength* is reaffirmed in a parallel statement as dependent also upon *the majesty of the divine name.* The two notions hardly are appropriate to a pastoral context of guarding sheep. So, what exactly has Micah seen that led to such a speech? Or has a complete misunderstanding arisen and been transmitted thus to the final editor? It is difficult to imagine what is being spoken of here, so this reader is forced to simply recognise a problem and move on.

The second half of the verse draws a contrast between 'standing', in part (a), and 'sitting', in part (b); that much is clear, but what does it imply for this one from Bethlehem? Security and greatness are asserted, and they are to extend 'to the ends of the earth' (Heb. *'apsê-'ereṣ*). This hyperbolic expression claims universal rule and power for the one from Bethlehem, though this idiom should not be given a modern global application; it would have simply meant the world as then known. Is Micah offering a vision of some wonderful future for the southern kingdom while the north is about to yield to the Assyrian power? How is his hyperbole to be understood? How might it have been understood then? Was there such an individual in Judah at the time in question? If so, why was he(?) not named?

Commentators have sought connections between this verse and the Davidic dynasty. While there may be echoes of the Davidic era in some of the vocabulary used, there is nothing concrete from which to draw any conclusions. It is a good reminder that readers need to be cautious when confronted by a vague text such as this, as the temptation 'to make it fit' somewhere identifiable is at times overwhelming.

5.4(5) It is unclear whether the opening words *'And it shall be this peace ...'* refer back to the preceding description of Bethlehem or forward to the conditional situation of Assyrian invasion; the demonstrative 'this' is ambiguous. As a result, commentators differ in their interpretation.

This reader has argued for the imperfective verbs in Micah to be seen as volitional or jussive, not as predictive. Thus, the reading proposed here sees Micah expressing his hope that an emerging situation will bring peace. That possibility is then expounded in line 2, which anticipates an Assyrian invasion and suggests how Israel might respond, the two *kî*-phrases being conditional: 'If Assyria were to come ... and if they were to trample ...', *'then we may establish against it/him seven shepherds and eight princes of Adam'*. The temporal relationship between the first and second lines that seems incongruous can be read as line 1 suggesting that peace will come, but only after victory over the Assyrian advance (line 2). The verb used is first-person plural, but the 'we' is not further elaborated, though it is also possible that the Hebrew form is actually 'he may raise up for us ...', which fits the context better.

The victory hoped for is presented in terms of the establishment of *'seven shepherds and eight princes'*, a most unusual description of a leadership team. The significance of this numerical saying is unknown, even if there is some proverbial form lying behind it. It is further complicated as shepherds and princes are hardly the leaders who could confront the Assyrian invaders with swords and expect to overthrow them. The text, however, provides no clues whatsoever as to possible meanings, so readers are left none the wiser. Perhaps there is some idiomatic significance in the expression that is now lost. To suggest that the saying indicates numerous or proliferating leaders is really clutching at straws.

5.5(6) The function of the 'seven shepherds and eight princes' is minimally spelled out. The shepherds will 'shepherd', that is, lead or rule, Assyrian territory, not with a shepherd's implements but with the sword. If that is what the text is saying, then there are serious questions to be raised as to its integrity. The second expression, 'and (shepherd) Nimrod in its entrances', is even less clear. Nimrod was a mythical hunter and soldier, a great-grandson of Noah according to the genealogy in Gen. 10.8-12. His name is associated with a region of Assyria.

It would appear that Micah then 'saw' those taken away returned at some point as 'they' (undefined) might rescue 'us' (undefined) from Assyrian control, a virtual impossibility surely. The noun 'entrances' does not match the word 'sword' as a parallel, so commentators often seek to emend the text to achieve a better relationship. There was no possibility that these insights could be realised, so Micah's point here is completely unclear, though many commentators have sought ingenious ways to explain this away as a 'failed prophecy'. This reader accepts that the text as we now have it is so confused and corrupted that it now unfortunately is meaningless, hence the brackets in my translation above.

5.6-8(7-9) *The Remnant of Jacob*

This intriguing sub-section refers to a 'remnant', a term first encountered in 2.12 where it had reference to a group specially gathered, a group marked out for special treatment, so it does not carry a pejorative tone as the English term can suggest, that is, left-overs! That positivity is clearly expressed in the opening v. 6b where the group is compared to dew and rain showers, and followed by the same positive tone in v. 8. In v. 7, however, the tone changes markedly—the 'remnant' tears its prey as do lions. These two perspectives on the 'remnant' and its activities make it difficult to decipher.

Both vv. 6 and 7 are parallel in design. There is in each verse an opening statement that clearly locates the remnant in the context of 'many nations' (*b^{e}qereb 'ammîm rabbîm*), that is, Jacob's current situation. The two verses then continue with similes that are each followed by a relative clause, in v. 6 set in the negative and in v. 7 in positive format; the one balances the other as an alternative. In its present location among the nations, the remnant or representative Israelites could be as 'dew' and 'showers on the grass', so Micah in v. 6 is clearly speaking of them as making a positive contribution, though of what kind is not further elaborated. In v. 7, however, their role is more aggressive—they hunt, capture and kill. So, what was Micah's vision of the role for this 'remnant'?

Though not specifically named, the reference to 'many peoples' would include Assyria and perhaps Egypt, but other locations or communities are less certain. The future dimension that the initial *w^{e}hāyâ* suggests, refers to the role Jacob could play, not that Jacob was going to be dispersed among those foreign parts, as some commentators envisage. Jacob might play a positive role or strike out against the enemy. Reading this section as prophecy leads to misunderstanding, for the text simply makes a present existential statement—Jacob is one among many nations.

The Hebrew text in v. 6c that I have rendered as *'(a remnant) not dependent upon people and not placing hope in any mortal'* is difficult, as a cursory look at various translations will show. The sense is far from obvious. I have understood the verb *lo' y^{e}qawweh l^e'îš*—literally 'not wait for a person'—to refer to dew and rain as not dependent on human intervention. The accompanying clause also speaks of not waiting on or being dependent on a human action. Whatever that means is nevertheless unclear—on what then are they dependent? Some commentators suggest that all dependence is on God who will reverse their state of helplessness, but that reading also depends on mistakenly regarding the text as 'prophetic'.

In the case of v. 7, the remnant of Jacob is likened to attacking lions, a frequently used image for a violent attack, with the lions seeking prey, be it in woodland or open fields. On the surface there appears to be a conflict between the two pictures of the remnant's function in these verses. So, what is Micah saying? This reader's understanding is that Micah's vision offers two potential alternatives to Jacob/Israel in its present situation, the one expressed in negative format (v. 6) and the other in positive form (v. 7).

Verse 8 moves to second-person address, a more direct form in which Micah encourages Israel, in view of the alternatives presented in vv. 6-7, to choose the latter and prepare to attack, to 'raise its hand against' its adversaries and to cut them down. The verbs are volitional, so Micah was giving priority to the possibility outlined in v. 7 that, like the lion, Jacob would stand against whatever attack came from its neighbours. Whether this vision was realistic or not is another question. The verb 'cut off' is frequently used to refer to action that destroys or brings something to an end as punishment (see Amos 1.5, 8; 2.3; 3.14; Nah. 1.12, 14, 15; 2.13 etc.). In the sub-section that follows, the entire unit is dependent on this verb.

5.9-14(10-15) *The Day of the Cut Off*

And on that day, says Yahweh, I would cut off your horses from your midst and destroy your chariots,

I would cut off the cities of your land and destroy your fortresses,

I would cut off the sorceries from your hands and no longer would there be soothsayers for you.

I would cut off your idols and your sacred pillars from your midst, and you no longer would worship what your hands have made.

I would tear down your Asherah from your midst and destroy your cities.

I would exact vengeance with anger and fury on the nations who do not listen/obey me.

With this sub-section we step back one level in the overall framework and take up again the 'day' theme as in 4.1-5. As noted, this unit focuses on the verb 'cut off/down' with which the previous sub-section concluded. The verb appears four times in the causative mode, *hikrattî* (vv. 9b, 10, 11, 12), in verb-initial position as a volitional that expresses what Micah would long to see happen 'in that day'. The verb sets the tone for the sub-section, namely judgment upon 'you' (sg.). The singular suffix 'you' appears then to identify

Jacob/Israel as the target, in view of its use in vv. 6-8(7-9), and that may be the correct interpretation. There are, however, no other specific grounds for that view, especially when the sub-section has a separate introduction and concludes with the threat directed at every nation that was 'disobedient'. That would include Jacob/Israel as well as the foreign unnamed nations.

So, we begin with the question of the relationship between this subsection and the preceding vv. 6-8(7-9). Given that there is a major challenge when reading Micah in determining the relationship between individual units of speech within the overall frame, it appears that this unit is placed here by the editor because of the shared use of the verb 'cut off'. There are no other grounds for thinking that the two units are directly linked or consecutive, for they speak of different situations, meaning that the pronominal suffix 'you' (sg.) has a different referent here; the singular 'you' is collective, not restricted to either Jacob/Israel or the nations, for no matter which entity is involved, it will face the divine 'cut off' if disobedient (5.13[14]).

The formal introduction to the unit has an attached *ne'ûm-yhwh*, 'says Yahweh', normally a *pro forma* closing marker, and the only example used in this book; on both counts it is an irregular addition. While it reports in third person what Yahweh is supposed to have said, its function is to underline the significance of the words. The unexpected appearance of the 'closing' marker here strengthens the argument that the unit 5.9-14(10-15) is an independent editorial attachment based on the shared verb 'cut', not as a logical consequence of the preceding verses.

Micah, on behalf of Yahweh and using first-person speech, lists ten items that he would want to see 'cut off' or destroyed universally: horses and chariots (v. 9), cities and strongholds (v. 10), magic and magicians (v. 11), idols and sacred pillars (v. 12), asherim and cities (v. 13). The list is rather comprehensive—war, buildings, religion and cult—and concludes with a warning to the nations who fail to obey that the divine anger and vengeance will be poured out upon them (see also Nah. 1.2-3).

In the preceding verses the remnant of Jacob was located *bᵉqereb*, 'amidst', the many nations. Here in this sub-section that adverbial phrase, *miqqirbekā*, identifies where the 'cutting off' would happen, so it becomes plain that those addressed, or better, threatened, in this speech-act are the nations, the *goyîm* among whom Jacob dwells, as well as Israel. Notice also that the language used is general, so no nation or city is singled out or identified. And the 'cutting off' is widespread: it includes both attacking and defensive elements, religious advisers and objects, and all (?) cities throughout the region.

5.9(10) We note that the opening phrase *wᵉhāyâ bayyôm hahû'* is a marker in the wider framework of the book, and it is the context in which Micah sees a potential divine action.

The first item on the list to be 'cut off' are the horses that the nations use. The possibility is that this refers to Egypt, given their reputation for breeding and using horses, but the note here cannot be confined to one nation. This is paralleled by the accompanying 'chariots'—I will destroy (Heb. *ha'ᵃbadtî*) them. This combination of horse and chariot indicates that the context was one of warfare, for the horse and the chariot were primarily used when waging war. The 'I' pronoun implies Yahweh as speaker and agent.

5.10(11) The next group focuses on the *cities of that land*—they would be 'cut off' along with 'your fortresses' or strongholds that would be torn down (Heb. *hārastî*). We might ask for further information about the cities envisaged here, and the extent of the land (Heb. *'ereṣ*) in question, but to no avail. Nor do we have information about how many of its cities might be involved—perhaps all? The vision of comprehensive destruction of cities and all occupied land is so generalized that seeking to identify details more closely is pointless.

5.11(12) Micah's thoughts then move to religious practices and practitioners proscribed by Israel's religious regime. *Kᵉšāpîm* are magic arts or sorceries, and *mᵉ'ônᵉnîm* are the ones who practice divination. The sorceries would be cut off 'from your hand', suggesting some practical activity being prevented while the practitioners are described as 'they will not be for/to you', perhaps the sense of them being of no assistance or not being available. Are these the particular 'evil' influences impinging on Jerusalem from the north (1.9), or are they part of Judah's world as well? Certainly, under Ahaz such religious practices were encouraged and thrived. The language used, however, prevents reading the threat as being directed to only one side rather than another, and whether it envisages foreigners as well as Israelites can not be determined.

5.12(13) Your 'idols/images' (Heb. *pesîlîm*) would be cut off or cut down. These could have been made of metal or stone; wooden ones were usually burned. The other element in the pair is your *maṣṣēbôt*, which refers to sacred pillars, another religious object considered illegitimate in the eyes of Israel's religious establishment, but widely used nonetheless.

The verse then goes on to ban any further worship of these objects on the grounds that they are the products of human design and workmanship, so the focus here is a ban on all human-made religious paraphernalia.

5.13(14) Micah threatens to uproot the Asherah that are found in the land. 'Asherah' was the name of an important Canaanite goddess, and of the sacred wooden poles erected in her honour; the belief was that the goddess was 'resident' in the pole. Initially an *asherah* may have been a tree viewed as sacred, later modified to a tall pole, and worshipped at local shrines (see Deut. 7.5; 1 Kgs 14.23; 2 Kgs 17.10). Israelite religion has its own history, evolving from an early form of El-religion through to Yahwistic religion, while throughout influenced by Canaanite practices. It was never monolithic, and under Deuteronomic influence became more sectarian, dividing north from south (see Josh. 24.14-15).

What needs to be acknowledged is that whatever threat is extended in this sub-section, it applied to both Israel and the nations as the language is too generalized to allow a more specific definition of the pronoun 'you' (sg.).

The editor closes this second section of Micah's collected sayings with his vision of Yahweh as one who acts in 'anger, wrath and vengeance' against all and any who offend, in a vein similar to that of the anti-Assyrian Nahum (see Nah. 1.2-3).

Micah 6

6.1–7.20 The Lord's Controversy

Based on the threefold division of Micah that this reader has adopted, 6.1–7.20 represents the third and final section of the book (see **Structure** in the Introduction). It opens with duplicate calls to '*Hear* ...' (6.1-2), followed by a '*Woe*' oracle (7.1-7), as does the first section (1.2–2.13), and ends with the closing element of the *inclusio*, '*Who is a God like you?*', in 7.18-20. There is no development of a plot within the section, however, and the connection between its constituent parts is not always obvious, as is true throughout the entire document.

Chapter 6 has its own structure beginning with the calls to 'Hear ...', which then convey Yahweh's 'controversy' (Heb. *rîb*) with his people, a case to which mountains and hills are summoned as witnesses (6.1-2). It rehearses the divine requirements for Israel within the historical covenant relationship, especially the demand to 'love *ḥesed*', kindness or goodness (6.3-8), and accuses the nation of failure at all levels with regard to what is called the 'treasures of wickedness'—an oxymoron—they have accumulated by evil means (6.9-16).

In addition, another structural element is to be noted, namely the use of parallel rhetorical forms in 6.1-2, 3-5, with a climactic 6.8:

6.1 Hear ... (*šim'û* ...)
6.2 Hear ... (*šim'û* ...)
6.3 O my people ... (*'ammî* ...), ...what (*mâ* ...?), *and what* (*ûmâ* ...?)
6.5 O my people ... (*'ammî* ...), ...what (*mâ* ...?), *and what* (*ûmâ* ...?)
6.8 He has told you *'ādām* ..., what (*mâ* ...?), *and what* (*ûmâ* ...?)

The chapter is marked initially by imperative forms in 6.1-2a, then by question forms beginning with Yahweh's—or is it Micah's?—question in 6.3 as it asks for an explanation as to how the current situation with the people has come about. The text asks what had gone wrong with the relationship despite all that Yahweh had done for them in the past. Rhetorical questions dominate vv. 6-8.

In the concluding sub-section, 6.9-16, Yahweh charges the community to 'Listen up …!' once again, and threatens to punish.

6.1-5 O my People!

> *Hear now what Yahweh has to say: 'Arise and plead the case with/before the mountains and let the hills hear your voice!'*
>
> *Listen up, you mountains (to) the controversy Yahweh has, and (listen) you eternal foundations of the earth, because Yahweh has a case against his people, and against Israel he would argue.*
>
> ***O my people**, <u>what</u> have I done to you? <u>What</u> affliction have I imposed on you? Tell me!*
>
> *For I brought you up out of the land of Egypt, from the house of servitude I rescued you; I sent Moses, Aaron and Miriam to go ahead of you.*
>
> ***O my people**, recall now <u>what</u> Balak king of Moab had planned, <u>what</u> Balaam son of Beor responded, and <u>what</u> happened from Shittim all the way to Gilgal in order that you should know/experience the righteous deeds of Yahweh!'*

Calls to 'Hear …' or 'Listen up …!' often preface speeches that relate back to Israel's historical narrative (see especially Deut. 5.1; 6.3, 4; 9.1 etc.). The point of such was to remind Israel of its obligations under their claimed covenantal arrangements, so they were frequently set in the context of Yahweh's criticism, his disappointment, and even anger at the nation's rebellious ways despite the privileges claimed and assumed. Here the editor has reported a call by Micah referencing Yahweh's concern regarding 'his people'. Yahweh is spoken of using the third person in 6.1-2; then there is a switch to first-person reference in vv. 3-5. It is this pronominal confusion that makes precise identification of 'my people' in vv. 3 and 4 impossible, unless one assumes some kind of *literary* unity of Micah and Yahweh, that what Micah says is regarded as identical to what Yahweh might say. This pronominal issue is critical throughout the book.

Using the *rîb* formula, sometimes called the lawsuit form, Micah demands that Israel face Yahweh's judgment. The hills and mountains were called as witnesses to Israel's failings. Micah's tone here reflects what he believed to be Yahweh's bitter disappointment that once again 'his people Israel' (v. 2b) had failed to live by the demands of the covenant mediated through Moses, one based on a historic divine rescue. However, there is no specific problem cited as the basis for the complaint. As for the literary form itself, the elements typical of the form are not used beyond the initial reference to a *rîb* in vv. 1-2, though there is the probability that vv. 9-16 do perform something approximate to that role.

Micah 6 189

Micah speaks of God in the third-person as the one who is 'bringing a case against' (Heb. *rîb*), or is in dispute with, Israel, yet the one who is troubled by the situation is Yahweh, not the people. There is a deeply plaintive note in the case—*What have I done? Tell me, please!*—as though Yahweh is non-plussed as to why this dispute has arisen, and that somehow it is all God's fault (see vv. 3-5). That plaintive note derives from the editor or from Micah himself.

6.1-2 Micah calls his audiences twice to 'Listen up ...!' to what it is that Yahweh has 'said', though there is no specific content mentioned, only that Yahweh has a dispute with Israel.

The repeated call and a number of minor repetitions in these two verses are suggestive of them being two differing versions of the call. The first audience addressed is very general, presumably directed at all Israel; and the second audience is the hills and mountains, the witnesses. Four times in these two verses the root *rîb*, 'controversy', appears, making it very clear that Yahweh has a serious issue to raise with his people Israel. The command to 'stand up, and dispute' (v. 2) addresses Israel, calling on the people and/or their leaders to present their case to the hills and mountains, the 'foundations of the earth', that presumably would 'hear' any evidence in the case before Yahweh the judge. The initial command to 'stand up' (Heb. *qûm*) is usually a non-literal order that marks the beginning of an action, and often a call for God to act (e.g. Ps. 7.6[7]).

This scenario exemplifies a significant poetic tradition in Israel in which cosmic elements and 'everlasting hills' are said to serve as witness to the relationship between Yahweh and his people (Gen. 49.26; Deut. 4.26; Hab. 3.6). This poetic imagery should be read with the imagination. Since the mountains, hills and cosmic elements 'say' nothing in these scenarios, their role is that of the eternal bystander, the unchanging Nature, the divine handiwork. Nor is there any specific word directed to the hills and mountains; they are simply present as silent witnesses.

6.3-5 The *rîb* or complaint that Yahweh has with Israel is not detailed, while the question form in v. 3—*'what have I done to/for you?'*—seems to imply that Israel has challenged Yahweh, by action if not by word, rather than the other way around. It is Israel who has a complaint against Yahweh for causing them to be 'weary'. Again, specific actions are not identified in this general complaint, so it is not possible to identify who is complaining about whom, nor why.

Just as 6.1-2 consisted of two similar and parallel statements, so also in vv. 3 and 5. The statements begin with the same address—*'O my peo-*

ple …', adding to the possibility that here we have further evidence of statements repeated in two differing versions now set alongside each other. While Micah clearly is the spokesperson in v. 1, here that is not certain, so the first-person address, '*my people*', appears to be Yahweh's speech. That Yahweh literally speaks is a problematic issue throughout this book for it eludes clarification given the virtual absence of speech markers and the utter confusion surrounding the referent of most first-person pronouns. In these few verses the pronoun may apply to either Micah or Yahweh, and while in vv. 3-4 it appears to be Yahweh speaking, in v. 5 that is far from certain as Yahweh is referred to in the third person.

Referencing the exodus rescue and leadership, the conquest and settlement traditions, makes for an unusual speech. This interpretation by Israel in vv. 3-4 of its tribal story is essential to understanding its sense of self, along with the claim that Yahweh's righteous actions (Heb. *ṣidqôt-yhwh*) were actually proof of Yahweh's initiative in the nation's founding. This 'historical review' or memory seeks to remind Israel of the constancy of Yahweh, and that Yahweh therefore has every reason to take up this dispute with the nation.

Referring to Moses, Aaron and Miriam, the three siblings, is unique in the tradition, though the specific role of this 'trinity' as a leadership team is not further expounded. What it does do, however, is to rehearse the tribal story as beginning with the exodus rather than with the call of Abraham and the fathers, the latter being a tradition that was promoted by the Deuteronomic cohort (Deut. 26.5-9).

The *rîb*-dispute itself is structured rhetorically by way of 'what?' questions (Heb. *mah* …, *ûmâ* …?) consisting of two pairs: (a) what have I done? …, in what way have I wearied …?; and (b) 'what Balak devised …', 'what Balaam answered …'. The pattern is repeated in vv. 6-8.

Balak was said to be the 'king' of Moab whom the Israelites encountered during the exodus journey and Balaam a 'prophet' whom he consulted (see Num. 22–24). The verb *'ānâ*, 'answer', also carries the sense of being an oracle reader, so perhaps Balaam's mission was related to 'magic' in some manner. The significance of this tradition to the narrative of the journey is not elaborated; rather, the audience is assumed to recall what Balaam said to Balak and what was its outcome. It is possible that this call to remembrance is from Micah rather than Yahweh.

Two locations are mentioned—Shittim and Gilgal. Israel's encounter with Balaam is reported to have taken place at Shittim on the Moabite or eastern side of the Jordan (Num. 25.1), and it was from there that the Israelites traveled and crossed the river to establish their first base at Gilgal on the western side (Josh. 4.19). What happened 'from Shittim to Gilgal'

6.6-8 *What Does the Lord Require?*

> *With what should I come before Yahweh and bow down to God of the heights? Should I come before him with burnt offerings, with year-old calves?*
>
> *Would Yahweh be pleased with (a gift of) thousands of rams, with thousands of rivers of oil? Should I offer my firstborn for my sins, the fruit of my body for the transgressions of my life-spirit?*
>
> *He has advised you, O mortal. What is good, and what does Yahweh seek from you?*
>
> *It is, to do justice, and to love kindness, and to walk humbly with your God.*

As noted above, the structure of these three verses follows the same pattern noted in vv. 3-5, namely the interrogatives *what* (*mah...?*), *and what* (*... ûmâ ...?*) in v. 6a, 8a, 8b within the series of rhetorical questions that begin vv. 6b, 7a, 7b. The climax of the unit lies in v. 8b and its threefold elements of an ideal life that can be related to the wisdom question, 'What is good ...?' (see also Qoh. 6.12 and the following 7.1-13 for a definition of the 'good').

The sub-section is significant for its cultic language and its use of hyperbole. It also moves from a personal self-reflective question in v. 6a, to five rhetorical questions about appropriate offerings, to a broad or universal requirement in which 'you' (sg.) represents the generic *'ādām*. From the point of view of language used, this sub-section co-ordinates linguistic elegance with theological practicality.

With 6.6 there is no question that the first-person pronoun is representing Micah and his own reflection on what is an appropriate cultic response to his God. The verb *'ªqaddēm*, 'to meet, confront', is generic and not exclusive to cultic activity. The cultic context is given by the parallel verb *kpp*, 'to bow down'. Referring to Yahweh as 'God of the height' (*'ªlohê mārôm*) is idiomatic based on the notion that God is in the heavens.

Four options are proposed as potential offerings that could be considered adequate: burnt offerings involving year-old calves; thousands of rams; ten thousands of rivers of olive oil; and his firstborn son, the 'fruit of his body'. The options are exaggerated versions of recognized sacrifices for personal sin (Heb. *pš'* and *ht'*), though the final option was normally associated with the non-Israelite cult. Hyperbole is used deliberately in these descriptions of what would be normal cultic practice, and each option implies a negative response; God does not require these demonstrations of repentance, so suggesting such enthusiastic excess before God sounds very much like *mockery* of the cultic system.

In contrast to the preceding, 6.8 is terse and climactic, but somewhat impersonal. 'He' is probably a reference to Yahweh in light of the contrasting '*O mortal*', or perhaps to the priestly community as the ones to teach torah and its demands. All personal references in the verse are singular with possible collective value. 'He' has announced (see the verb *ngd* in 3.8) three requirements for the community under the notion of it being representative of humanity (*'ādām*): to do justice, to love kindness, to walk humbly together with God. The demands of the covenant sound simple, but they were the most difficult to keep for they require a God-like life—see Micah's criticism of these elements missing in Israel's leaders (3.2). The qualities required of *'ādām* are those that are the essence of Yahweh's very being, here summarized as *mâ-ṭôb*, 'whatever is good?' Defining what was 'good' was a pursuit of the sages, as in the more general 'Better-is-this-than-that' proverbial form found exemplified particularly in Qoheleth and Proverbs.

The two qualities of justice (Heb. *mišpāṭ*) and kindness (Heb. *ḥesed*) are not abstract ideas but practical actions; both have to do with interpersonal relationships, with *ḥesed* referring to that special covenantal trait of faithfulness or mutual accountability. Using the verb 'love' in connection with *ḥesed* refers to the close intimate interpersonal dimension. The verb 'walk' used to describe the relationship with God is also closely connected because it speaks of a mode of constant daily living. It is the attached *haṣnē*ᵃ' that is slightly difficult because as a *hapax* its precise value is determined only by its context—perhaps 'carefully', or 'with fullest attention to …'. Its wisdom association has also been recognized.

Although the section began with a *rîb*, a dispute that Yahweh was expected to take up with Israel, there is little in 6.1-8 that refers to the dispute's formal elements. The interrogation and threats that follow in 6.9-16, however, certainly relate to issues one would expect to encounter in the context of a dispute.

6.9-16 *Treasures of Wickedness*

> *The voice of Yahweh: to the city he calls (and wisdom may it fear your name!)*
> > *Listen, you tribe and/for who appointed her yet again?*
>
> *Are there in the house of evil, treasures of evil? And a false detested ephah?*
>
> *Should I regard as pure the wicked scales, (together with) the bag of inaccurate weights?*

(the city) Which her rich men have filled with violence, whose inhabitants have made false agreements and whose tongue speaks falsehoods.

And I also caused injury when I struck you, I destroyed (you?) because of your sins.

May you eat, but not be satisfied, (and emptiness be in your belly; may you be in labour, but not bring anything to life; what you rescue I would put to the sword).

You may sow but not reap, you may tread the olives but not be rubbed with its oil, and grapes but not have wine to drink.

Thus he kept the statutes of Omri, along with all the actions of Ahab's house, walking in their policies, that (therefore?) I would cause devastation upon you, and her residents I would give over to hissing. So may you bear the reproach of my people.

Of all the confusing material in this book, these verses are perhaps the most frustrating, largely because of pronominal 'chaos', varied verb forms, and disconnected phrases, but also because of textual aberrations that testify to a complex transmission process both from oral to written and within the written tradition itself. The LXX version indicates that the problems that surface for modern readers go back at least to its own attempt to make sense of these verses. There is no plot development or detectable structure in this sub-section, for it appears as a collection of separate issues, all of which ring with negativity.

Despite the very practical problems, however, it is clear that cheating and deceiving were identifiable evils in the society addressed, and the speaker warns of negative results from people's labours. The final verse is perhaps the most problematic in terms of language, but it does appear to offer a summary of conditions, presumably in the northern kingdom represented by Samaria if the references to 'the city' in v. 9, and to Omri and Ahab in v. 16 are the real targets of Micah's attack. There is very little 'good news' from Micah in this sub-section.

Much of the scholarly discussion of this sub-section rages around the complex linguistic and syntactic elements of the Hebrew text. That is as it should be for the specialist, yet it is a reminder that, when dealing with an ancient document, not all problems can be resolved, and non-native speakers should be extremely cautious about emending such a text if they are to avoid arbitrary changes to suit an imported agenda.

This commentary will aim to keep the discussion of the passage a little less technical and more general while recognizing that many questions will nevertheless remain without an answer.

6.9-11 These verses open with what is said to be a call from Yahweh to 'the city', which, unfortunately, is not identified—we presume it is Samaria; nor is the speaker identified, since the text refers to Yahweh in the third person. Its function seems to be that of an editorial heading. It then continues with what is a conundrum in terms of syntax, but may be a call to either 'see' wisdom or to 'fear' it—the verb *yir'eh* is ambiguous and the noun an oddity—perhaps 'success' or 'wisdom'. If the verb is read as volitional it might mean, 'May it (the city) fear your name!' In this case the city represents those who live within it, or if the city represents the kingdom as in 1.5, then it could refer to the nation as a whole. The line is often seen as a scribal comment that has found its way into the text somehow, and some decide it should be removed! This reader prefers to retain it, but brackets what can only be a guess at its sense.

The call to 'Hear ...' follows, but what appears as its addressee is a noun, *maṭṭeh,* which could be a 'sword' or 'sceptre' (JPS), or 'tribe', so there is little enlightenment there.

The final two words in v. 9 and the initial two in v. 10 are so problematic that there is no sense to be made of them. Verses 10-11, however, do introduce readers to *'a house of evil'* and *'storehouses of evil'*. Clearly these are figurative and describe the city/nation as full of activities that are corrupt. The questions that vv. 10-11 ask are obviously rhetorical, for under normal circumstances there could only be one response, a negative one. The speaker, presumably Micah, points to the injustice and corruption that relates to merchandizing, with the *ephah,* a measure used for dry materials such as grains, the scales for weighing goods for sale, and the weights themselves all fraudulent. The question form—'should I regard as just/correct (Heb. *zkh*) the scales of evil, that is, the fraudulent scales, along with the non-standard stone weights being used?'—is Micah's response to the situation he saw, in which the attitude common among the merchants was that this corrupt activity can or should be overlooked. Micah determines to expose their corruption.

6.12 The verse begins with the relative marker that refers back to the 'city' mentioned in v. 9, now further described as full of violence (Heb. *ḥāmās*) as a result of the corrupt activities of those who were wealthy (see also 3.9-13). Though the wealthy are the real target of this accusation, it continues more generally with 'the inhabitants'—presumably not all of them—who are said to be liars who speak only to deceive. The idiom of 'the tongue in the mouth' is expressive of duplicity.

6.13 The text of this verse begins with the words *'And/But I also ...'*, which would point to a context that relates to a situation already stated, but such is missing, so from the outset we have difficulty evaluating its significance. One would have to assume the first-person speaker to be Yahweh rather than Micah. If so, then Yahweh has beaten someone for sins committed, but the specific referent is unknown. There seems not to be any connection to the preceding verses unless one assumes further that all the corrupt merchants are those who have been punished in some manner, but such an assumption is beyond any proof. The statement appears to just hang without any obvious connection to its present context.

6.14-15 These two verses clearly form a small unit using imperfective verb forms that carry either the threat of dashed expectations or describe a past or on-going situation; the actions noted fail to have the desired outcomes, so the second half of each colon begins with the negative particle *lo'*, though several of the verbs have no specific objects. The pattern is as follows: you eat, but are not satisfied; you conceive, but do not give birth; you sow, but do not reap; you press the olive, but do not have oil; you crush grapes, but do not have wine. All these basic requirements in life are present, but there is no result or expected benefit from any of the activities mentioned. Is this failure to enjoy outcomes the 'punishment' that may be implied in v. 13? If so, it does not match the seriousness of their corrupt practices. Each of the outcomes that are denied go against what would be expected in a Deuteronomic context where obedience guarantees such material benefits.

In v. 14b, the first phrase, involving a *hapax*, is problematic. Then the phrase relating to the verb *plṭ*, 'make safe, survive', is negated, perhaps meaning that there is nothing safe, but it continues with an even greater threat that whatever could have been enjoyed is to be put to the sword, a military expression. The confusion in this second half of the verse means that it is impossible to ascertain its meaning and significance, so one can only put brackets around it and admit defeat. Positing potential meanings in a case like this is far too speculative, arbitrary and, in the end, pointless.

Verse 15, on the other hand, is remarkably clear apart from the time implied in the imperfective verb forms. The three agricultural examples involving corn, oil and wine typify crops in the area; here they exemplify a failing harvest. Such failure is, in the Deuteronomic worldview, to be expected if one fails to live by torah, so one can make a link between this verse and v. 13 in which the community would be or has been 'struck' because of its sin. The moral problem of course is that it is the community as a whole that would suffer thus, when the culprits causing this divine reaction are the wealthy who are liars and cheats.

6.16 The final verse in this chapter seems entirely unrelated to the preceding material, first, for its mention of two northern kings, Omri and Ahab, and, second, because the threatened destruction is directed not at the nation more generally, but at an unspecified segment, 'you', who are distinct from 'my people'. In any event, the *rîb*, 'dispute' with Israel, his people, in 6.2 seems to be the more appropriate setting for this final verse and is its justification.

The laws of Omri and the actions/policies of Ahab are those that the DH accuses the northern kings of pursuing, after the example of Manasseh, the great 'sinner' (2 Kgs 21.1-9). It is for this reason that they and their city are despised and threatened with humiliation. The notion of 'devastation' or complete ruin is Micah's expected punishment for Israel (6.13, 16; 7.13), though the specific object remains uncertain because of the apparent distinction between 'you' as the addressees of v. 15 and 'my people' in v. 16. The possibility is that the 'you' in this sub-section refers to Samaria and the northerners, and 'my people' refers to those in the southern kingdom, with Micah the speaker.

Micah 7

This final chapter in the collection consists of three main parts: 7.1-7, 8-13 and 14-20, with the final sub-section being further divisible as vv. 14-17 and vv. 18-20, the latter closing off the *inclusio* begun in 1.1. It is a very personal section with first-person references clearly relating to Micah himself, while other pronominal referents are only marginally identifiable.

The text of vv. 1-7 is deeply challenging in view of many grammatical and syntactical issues, made more complex by the brevity of many phrases, especially in vv. 5-6, and the generalized language employed. Who exactly is being targeted? Is it everyone, or are those mentioned merely representative of some 'bad apples'? As a result, any translation offered cannot be absolute. The translation below has expanded some of the expressions in order to seek improved readability.

7.1-7 *Woe Is Me!*

> 'Woe am I!' because I am like one who after summer harvest and after gleanings of the vines has no bunch (of grapes) to eat, no ripe fig such as I desire.
>
> The righteous have disappeared from the land, and no upright person among men; they all await the chance to shed blood, each traps his brothers in a net.
>
> Both hands are proficient at evil, the official requests (a payment?), and the judge a reward, the great one speaks, his mind is treachery, and they have woven it.
>
> The best of them are like a thornbush, the upright worse than a briar hedge, on the day you were anticipating your visitation (doom) has come; now their confusion is present.
>
> Do not rely on your friend. Do not trust a lover, from her who lies in your bosom guard the doors of your mouth,
>
> Because the son treats the father as a fool, the daughter rises against her mother, daughter-in-law against mother-in-law, and one's enemies are those of his own family.
>
> But I shall look to Yahweh, I shall wait upon God my saviour. My God will respond to me!

The chapter begins with an interjection, using another lament form (Heb. *'al^elay*) similar to *hôy*, 'Woe ...!', which expresses personal distress at a current situation rather than introducing an oracle directed at another agent as in 2.1. Micah pictures a situation where, at the end of the harvest season, the fruit having been picked, there remains nothing for the gleaner. The farmer in the analogy has stripped the vines and trees of all their grapes and figs that Micah longed to enjoy. Micah uses this harvest analogy to express how bereft he feels since he sees none in the community who are faithful or trustworthy—another of his generalizations. So his despair is for the state of the nation in which he believes injustice and social breakdown are endemic. Despite the anguish felt in vv. 1-6, v. 7 begins with the contrastive *wa'^anî* to mark his surprising confidence that Yahweh will hear and respond (Heb. *šāma'*) to his plea.

7.1 Micah pours out his distress, likening his situation to that of a poor gleaner who finds that the farmer has so stripped his trees and vines that there is nothing left for him, nothing to satisfy his longing for its fruit. Farmers were required by torah to intentionally leave some of their crop, no matter its type, for the poor, the orphaned, and the widowed (see Exod. 19.9-10; Deut. 24.21). Micah's plaintive description introduces his analogy with the wider social situation in Israel.

The introductory '*Alas* ...' is an interjection rarely found in the Hebrew text—elsewhere only in Job 10.15. Is it too much to suggest that Micah compares his deep, deep sorrow over Israel's condition to that of the ancient Job's personal sufferings?

Using the illustration of *qāyiṣ*, the summer fruit, as in Amos's vision (Amos 8.1), offers an intriguing linguistic connection with his contemporary.

7.2-4 The gleaning analogy is now explained. Using rather extreme language, Micah describes the situation in the land as desperate—there is not one person who can be called a *ḥāsîd*, a pious or godly individual, nor anyone who is 'upright' in their manner of living. From this general and sweeping judgment, Micah then offers examples of official corruption, of 'bent' judges, of the powerful and wealthy who misuse their influence. The extent of their evil is caught in the idiomatic expression 'two hands', which portrays full commitment to their evil doings.

The image of people waiting to 'shed blood' is probably meant figuratively, but could also be taken literally, painting a picture of physical violence. The metaphor of people being caught 'in nets' is yet another dramatic statement implying that humans are regarded as little more than insects, small animals or fish, anything but human. It can be taken literally or figuratively to portray the uncertainty of life and lack of public safety.

In v. 3 the participle 'ask/request' (Heb. *sho'ēl*) lacks an object, but in combination with the charge against the judge it joins both officer and judge as guilty of corrupt practices. The verb ending the verse is perhaps meant to accuse both of working together, conspiring to cheat the public, but the subject 'they' and the object 'it' are typically vague.

Verse 4 uses a comparison: even the best among this community of corrupt persons is no better than briars, the upright like thornbushes. The briars/thornbush similes represent a range of painful experiences and interference or barriers, as well as implying uselessness, for even when burned no heat is generated (Qoh. 7.4). Here is a totally negative picture of Israelite society at the time. There were none that Micah saw as worthy, and most were well below even a minimal standard of decency. All would be judged in the imminent 'day' to which they were looking forward, but it would be a time of 'visitation', of threatened doom.

7.5-6 These two verses begin with the negative commands *'Don't rely on ..., do not trust ...!'* with the objects identified as one's neighbours and friends. A third warning relates to *'she who lies at your bosom'*, an even more intimate relationship. Micah's concerns here move from the wider society and its evils to the more intimate.

The family relationships are presented using the triplicate form found elsewhere in Micah—see **Literary Features** in the Introduction.

Micah's point in these two verses is that no relationship can be trusted, so one should not speak, or only speak in a guarded manner—literally 'Keep the doors of your mouth closed!' What specifically is not to be talked about is left to the imagination, though promise keeping or trust is the more likely object. The grounds for these generalized warnings are that all close and family relationships are, or can be, a source of deep disappointment and antagonism—the younger generation against the older, with the younger regarding the older as foolish and lacking in understanding. There is an all-inclusive warning: every relationship is a potential source of danger, and the closer the relationship the more the level of danger increases. If this is Micah's genuine experience of community life at the time, that one's enemies are one's own family, it is no wonder that he pours out his frustrations with the opening 'Alas for me!' Micah does often use hyperbole to make his point, but it is clear here that he is thoroughly distraught about the lack of harmony and mutual trust within the most intimate relationships in the community.

7.7 The adversative *waw* begins the contrasting statement in which the separate pronoun 'I' *('ᵃnî)* adds emphasis to the verb by which Micah expresses his personal attitude despite the present conditions (see also 3.8). *But I shall look to Yahweh,* he says, a God who he then describes as the one who would save, but save from what? Does he expect God to effect some change in the community to bring about more harmony? Does Micah wish to be removed from this situation? Are his thoughts only of and for himself? The text certainly gives that impression, though it is possible that the lament in these verses should be read as a prayer offered on behalf of the community at large rather than just of his personal pain. Micah expresses his great confidence that Yahweh who 'saves' will respond positively, leaving readers with a meagre sense of hope that the situation might be turned around. Unfortunately, Micah does not define what the divine response he anticipates might be, yet his confidence is emphasized by the deeply personal expressions, 'the God of my salvation' and 'my God', with which the section closes.

7.8-13 The Lord's Vindication

Do not rejoice, my enemy, over me! Whenever I fell, I got up; whenever I was dwelling in darkness, Yahweh was my light!

I bear the anger of Yahweh—if I have sinned against him—while he completes his complaint against me and carries out his justice toward me. May he bring me out into the light that I might see his righteousness.

And may my enemy see (it) and may shame cover her who says to me, 'Where is Yahweh your God?' May my eyes witness her (...). Now may she become a trampling place like the mud outside!

(A day for building your walls, that day may it be a distant day.

May that day when it reaches you from Assyria and the cities of Egypt, and from Egypt to the River and sea from sea, and mountain of the mountain.)

And may the land become a desolation for her inhabitants as the result of her deeds.

Apart from the overall sense that Micah—assuming he is the speaker—is confident of Yahweh's righteous judgment on himself and on the enemy, there are no clues in the text as to who is being specifically addressed by these words. The enemy is not identified, though many commentators seek to date the text in the exilic period of the sixth century BCE, meaning the enemy would be the Babylonians rather than the Assyrians, and the plea not that of Micah but of some much later person(s). Given the generalized language that we find throughout Micah, this reader sees little positive value in trying to fix a time and location for a text such as this. It is clear that the editor has attached this material to what he knew was circulating orally about Micah, and modern readers have no plausible grounds to dispute that, disappointing as that may be to some. So, as 'speaker', and using first-person address in vv. 8-10, Micah represents God's people Israel; he speaks here on their behalf.

There are a number of questions generated by the grammar and broken syntax of the unit that create real difficulties for the modern reader, but this reader has made two decisions: the imperfective verbs are to be read as volitional in accordance with Micah's visionary role, and the *kî*-particles are read as introducing temporal clauses, as testimony to past experience rather than as result or explanatory clauses.

7.8 Micah scoffs at the enemy who has celebrated Israel's 'fall', perhaps meaning a military defeat but one never explained—why not the fall of the northern kingdom in 721? Micah then testifies that *whenever* Israel 'fell', it rose up again; the perfect verbs speak of past experience. Then, *whenever* matters 'grew dark', Yahweh was its light. In this second example, the imperfect *'ēšēb,* 'sit/dwell', points to a frequent or on-going general situation. If the second half of the verse is read as a true conditional, then it may be read as, 'If I was to be left in the dark, then Yahweh would be my light', the second part being the apodosis. The brevity of the expression here opens itself to both possible interpretations. The message to the enemy is nonetheless clear, that no matter what the past or current state of God's people, Micah is confident that Yahweh would be on hand to rescue.

The 'enemy' referred to is cast as feminine, suggesting that it is a 'city' that is in mind, but which one is debated. Is it here merely a generic term? Or is it Samaria? Or even Jerusalem? Ultimately we cannot more closely define the feminized addressee.

7.9 Micah now states that divine anger (Heb. *za'ap*) is something that has to be accepted and borne. How this connects with the previous verse is unclear, but it does repeat the metaphor of 'the light' as something positive, his vindication.

The verb *'eśśā',* 'I bear …', as imperfective can refer to frequent past acts, but here probably links to the following phrase *'until he resolves the dispute (rîb) with me'*, suggesting that the dispute mentioned in 6.1-2 remains current.

Micah anticipates that once Yahweh's dispute with his people is settled, he will have witnessed divine justice exercised against him for deeds done—the form *mišpāṭî* meaning 'judgments against me' rather than 'my judgments' (subjective). Once settled, Micah hopes that he can be brought out into the light, that is, that he would wish to see divine vindication, or 'his righteousness (toward me)' (Heb. *ṣidqātô*) applied.

7.10 Micah now longs for the enemy to be able to witness this divine rescue and consequently for them to be covered in shame for having taunted Israel with the question as to Yahweh's reality. '*Where is Yahweh your God?*', as a rhetorical question, is the enemy's denial of Yahweh's presence. What an affront to Yahweh, lord and master of the whole earth (4.13)! Micah's hope for God's rescue is followed by another confident prayer—*May my eyes witness …!'*, meaning, 'I long to see (it so happen!)'. Whether this last expression refers to his seeing the foreigners' shame, or to Yahweh's rescue itself, is unclear, but both outcomes are inextricably linked.

The adverb 'now' in this context followed by an imperfective verb carries the sense of 'shortly', so it expresses that hope on Micah's part. Using another analogy, Micah longs for the enemy to be defeated, to become a trampling ground (Heb. *mirmās*), just like the muddy ground outside on the road. The metaphor suggests a defeated enemy trampled into the ground with the additional ignominy of it being in a muddy field.

7.11-12 The Hebrew text is severely problematic, so translation and interpretation are equally difficult. For that reason, the offered translation above is bracketed to mark its uncertainty.

While the general direction is clear from the repeated use of the noun 'day', little of its significance can be determined. The time to build or rebuild walls is linked with a time relating perhaps to an expansion of the bounds (of a city?). Normally, the 'day' implies some vague moment that is imminent, but in the present context there is little meaningful context for it.

Verse 12 continues the 'day' theme and involves both Egypt and Assyria in some manner, its impact extending as far as the Euphrates (the River). The verb phrase 'they may come to you' is used here but no indication of its subject 'they' is provided unless one reads *'ādeykā* as 'your witnesses' (JPS suggests 'tramplers'). Other commentators suggest emending *'ādeykā* to 'your cities' (*'ārēkā*) as in the following half of the colon. Clearly, the original text is uncertain other than to note that some kind of movement is envisaged, but 'who, what and where' remain unnamed.

A final rhetorical quirk is the unusual reversal of a 'from …, to …' pattern—*'(to) sea from sea, and mountain from the mountain'*, both nouns in the singular and impossible to identify, so the phrases are simply making a vague general comment about the widest possible extent, or pointing 'everywhere'.

7.13 If the adverb 'now' in the previous verse implies something about to happen, then this verse suggests what Micah hopes will transpire, namely that the land will be made desolate, perhaps meaning the land of the enemy. That desolation, as in 6.13, will come about as the *'fruit/result of their deeds'*. The metaphor of 'fruit', which normally has a positive connotation, is here reversed. Again, readers are left in the dark when pronouns are not more closely defined than 'her inhabitants'. Who are those doing the deeds? What deeds have been done? What has not been done? Readers cannot find any certainty in the text.

The feminine endings used presumably relate to the land and its inhabitants, whether a specific national territory or more generally 'the earth'.

7.14-20 Who Is a God Like You?

> *Use your staff to shepherd your people, flock of your inheritance, who dwell alone (in a) forest in the midst of Carmel. Let Bashan and Gilead shepherd as in days of yore.*
>
> *As in the days when you came out from the land of Egypt, show us wonders.*
>
> *Let the nations see and be ashamed, despite all their might; may they cover their mouths with their hands and their ears be deaf.*
>
> *May they lick the dust like a serpent, and the earth like the things that crawl on the ground. Let them tremble (and leave) their fortresses, to Yahweh our God may they be in dread, and be afraid before him.*
>
> *Who is a God like you, removing iniquity, and passing over sin? for the remainder of his people. May he not retain his anger for ever, for his covenant-love (ḥesed) is his delight.*
>
> *Let mercy return to us and cover up our iniquities, and may you dispatch our sins into the sea's depths.*
>
> *May you keep faith with Jacob, covenant-love to Abraham, as you swore to our fathers from days of old.*

This final sub-section brings the reader to Micah's faith statement of the incomparability of his God Yahweh. The *inclusio* that began in 1.1 with the name 'Micah' and that focused on the declaration in 4.13 that Yahweh was the 'master (Heb. *ʾᵃdôn*) of the whole earth' closes here with the affirmation in 7.18 that there is no God like Yahweh.

The sub-section is bracketed by time references that look back to the distant past—'from days of yore' in v. 14, and 'from days of old' in v. 20—and the relationship with Yahweh claimed since the nation's founding. In between these markers, Micah, using volitional verbs, expresses his longing for the enemies to be humiliated and Israel to be restored in its relationship with its ever-faithful and compassionate God.

7.14 Micah addresses Yahweh on behalf of his people, using the metaphor of a shepherd with his shepherd's staff in hand. The people are referred to as 'your people' and the flock that 'belongs to you', that is, your inheritance, highlighting Micah's acceptance of the claimed relationship between Yahweh and Israel. The second-person pronoun appears to exclude Micah himself. The verb 'to shepherd' (Heb. *r'h*) occurs twice in this verse by way of emphasizing the paternal relationship of the idealized past that the parties have enjoyed.

The further metaphorical description of the people as 'living alone in a forest' and 'in a garden land/Carmel' is imprecise but appears to refer to Canaan as described in traditional and highly idealized terms. Presumably, the phrase that Israel 'lives alone' is a reference to their claim to sole possession of Canaan, in disregard of other tribes' presence. The 'garden' may then be referring to the fertility of at least some select regions of the land such as Bashan and Gilead, unless Mt. Carmel itself is intended; this latter description certainly did not apply to the southern sector and the lower Jordan region. Micah hopes that, as in the past, Yahweh will continue to be the 'shepherd' with the implied values of care, of leading and providing, as in the exodus.

7.15 Strangely perhaps, the text refers to Yahweh—'you' singular—as the one who alone 'came out' of Egypt, rather than including the people. On the other hand, since Micah is most interested in elevating Yahweh as *master of the whole earth*, it should not surprise that the focus is primarily on Yahweh who alone 'led' the community from Egypt. The verb in the second half of the line is problematic as it suggests a change of speaker from Micah to Yahweh—literally 'I showed him …' (Heb. *'ar'ennû*)—that can be understood as Yahweh showing Pharaoh his overwhelming power, as in Exod. 3.20. The 'wonders/marvelous deeds' (Heb. *niplā'ôt*) referred to, if not confined to what was shown to Pharaoh, then may be assumed to embrace the entire story of the nation's escape, the Reed Sea crossing, the provision of food and water, and the overall protection said to have been given during the journey from Egypt into Canaan.

Nevertheless, the change in speaker from Micah to Yahweh remains an issue. Inevitably commentators have sought to 'solve' this problem with suggested emendations, and many English versions adopt the suggestion that it should read as a plea—'Show us …!' rather than 'I showed him …',—to make it consistent with the text as a prayer.

7.16-17 Micah now expresses his longing that the nations would 'see' (who Yahweh is and what he has done) and feel humiliated, as in 7.10. The following phrase, *mikkol g^ebûrātām*, is dependent on the initial *mem* for interpretation. Is it 'more than all …'? or 'because of all …'?, perhaps 'in relation to all …', the enemy's might (see 3.8). I have chosen to render it as *'despite all their might …'* to convey the reality of the foreigner's power, which is to turn to shame when they realize that Yahweh at whom they scoffed (v. 10) is the *'master of the whole earth'*. That expected embarrassment is further expressed as them putting their hand over their mouth, and their ears becoming deaf, signs of their human limitations or relative weakness. Then using two similes, a snake 'licking' the dust and insects crawling over the ground, Micah further denigrates the enemy.

In v. 17b Micah visualizes the enemy trembling in fear, emerging from places they thought were safe havens, followed by the phrase *yirg^ezû 'ēl-yhwh,* 'turn to Yahweh our God'. Does it mean that this is his wish that the enemy might come trembling to Yahweh? Opinion is divided because the text is abbreviated, but that seems to be the possible sense if vv. 14-17 are understood as Micah's prayer.

The final clause is also volitional, as Micah longs to see his God 'deal with/visit upon' (Heb. *pāḥad*) the enemy what he considers to be its justly deserved fate.

7.18 We have now reached the final sub-section of the book, which carries Micah's theology to its conclusion. Having begun in 1.1 with the question as to *'Who is like (Yah)?'* the *inclusio* closes with the question, *'Who is a God like you?'*, a rhetorical form in which Micah affirms his belief in Yahweh's incomparability. It also cleverly mimics the questions posed in the ancient Song of Moses in Exod. 15.11, a text that, given its significance, would have deep resonance in the Jerusalem community. The rest of the sub-section changes to third person as it becomes descriptive of Micah's God rather than speaking of his own hope; it expands on the fundamental elements of Yahweh's character; using participles, Micah defines God as one who *forgives iniquity* and *passes over transgressions*, who *does not retain his anger* but *delights in ḥesed*. To experience again these four basic qualities (see also 2.12; 6.3) is Micah's hope for those described as 'the remnant of his inheritance' (see 5.6, 7).

7.19 Micah's prayer continues, expressing the longing that divine compassion will again be shown 'us', the people of Jacob, and that their sins would be metaphorically trampled underfoot. He also calls for all (their?) sinful acts to be thrown into the deepest parts of the sea, Yam/Sea, and be lost.

The changes in pronoun in this verse are, in one sense, problematic, but the overall direction of the prayer is obvious. The editor appears to have assembled material circulating in the oral community in its various versions and simply reported it without any attempt to make every component consistent.

7.20 The final verse calls for Yahweh to uphold the promised gift of truth/trust (Heb. *'emet*) to Jacob and of covenant love (Heb. *hesed*) originally offered to Abraham. Both of these fundamental qualities are here said to have been promised, 'sworn to our forefathers', since 'the days of the past'. This latter is a vague expression but affirms Israel's belief that from the very outset Yahweh was the nation's God. The statement itself reflects the Deuteronomic view of the tribal story that read Yahweh back into the mists of time, not just beginning from Moses's encounter with the desert God of his father-in-law (Exod. 3.1-6).

Verses 18-20 are a fitting conclusion to the Micah collection for his prayer delivers a deep theological statement of Micah's conception of his God Yahweh.

Postscript

Micah, Amos, Isaiah and a Prophetic Crisis.

The conservative *Jerusalem News* splashed across its headlines one morning in 735 BCE in bold type the words 'CORRUPT PROPHETS', only to be met by a barrage of tweets and posts on social media that it was an oxymoron. 'Prophets' were God's spokespersons, passing on God's Word!! How could they be corrupt? The *News*'s three investigative journalists, Amos Smith, Micah Jones and Isaiah Doe, however, claimed that the old prophetic mission was now so inextricably mired in Judah's modern capitalist economy that one had to expect that a measure of corruption would follow. The three whistleblowers were then targeted by readers with the charge that they must be part of the corruption conspiracy themselves.

The definition of a 'prophet', a *nābî'*, as one who spoke only and whatever God commanded the person to speak, as presented in Deut. 18.15-22, represents the concept of 'prophet' only within that Deuteronomic tradition. As such, it is a sectarian definition that seems to have become generalized as the sole understanding of such spokespersons and of their mission. Amos, Micah and Isaiah challenge that definition by their disclaimers.

Both Amos and Micah denied being a *nābî'*, and each sought to ensure that he was not mistaken for one, pointedly emphasizing that they had nothing to do with the *nābî'* cause. While Amos's motive for denying any prophetic connection is not absolutely clear, that of Micah certainly is, as he charges all *n^{e}bî'îm* with corruption and self-serving greed. Obviously, Micah wanted to ensure he was not regarded as one such. Isaiah of Jerusalem likewise regarded the *n^{e}bî'îm* as drunken liars (Isa. 9.15; 28.7), and so his record identifies him differently; he is never identified in the core part of Isaiah book 1, chs. 1–35, as a *nābî'*, nor are those speakers who are represented in the later exilic portions of the book. Isaiah is referred to throughout as a visionary, a *ḥôzeh*. Only in the Deuteronomic material inserted from 2 Kings 18–20, that is, chs. 36–39, is there a third-person reference to Isaiah as a *nābî'* (Isa. 37.2; 38.1).

The three contemporary individuals, Amos, Micah and Isaiah, clearly had a negative view of *n^{e}bî'îm* and their activity. For them, to identify as a *nābî'* was something shameful, and they saw the movement as contaminated. Micah, in his iconoclastic and hyperbolic manner, dismissed all *nᵉbî'îm,* claiming rather arrogantly that none had 'the spirit of the Lord' as he did (Mic. 3.8)! From the perspective of these several gentlemen, the *nābî'* movement itself at this moment in the mid- to late-eighth century BCE was in deep crisis; it had lost its way and the moral high ground belonged to other spokespersons, the visionaries. Despite this textual evidence, it is amazing that so many readers continue to speak of these three men as 'prophets'; they were not.

Concluding from this textual evidence that the *nābî'* tag had become such a disgraced epithet has serious implications for translators and commentators alike; it means that a more refined definition and description is required; the Deuteronomic definition is obviously inadequate.

On the Verbs *nb'* and *ntp,* and 'Prophecy'

Two of the Hebrew verbs that seemingly relate to forms of public address are (1) *nb',* frequently rendered as 'prophesy', and (2) *ntp,* which may be used in parallel, and usually therefore rendered in Enblish versions as 'preach'. While the origin of the root *nb'* is uncertain, though linked commonly with Akkadian *nabu,* to name (something), the English rendering as 'prophet' derives from the Greek *prophēteuein,* 'to declare beforehand'. What the Hebrew root actually entails is the actions of one known as a *nābî',* that is, it is a denominative verb. As a tautology, that description is not particularly informative.

In Amos 7.16 Amaziah's reported speech uses the two verbs *nb'* and *ntp* as seemingly synonymous, that is, that *lo' tinnābē'* is assumed to mean 'Do not prophesy!' and the parallel *lo' taṭṭip* then taken as similar, a reprimand, 'Do not preach!' Those interpretations are based on dictionary definitions only and are thus problematic.

Amos's denial that he was ever a *nābî'* and his affirmation that he had never had any connection with the movement meant that despite his claim to being called to *hinnābê'* in 7.15, he certainly did not regard that as a call to 'prophesy'. How he understood that *hinnābê'* command is to be defined only by the content of his speeches as reported by his editor, not by the dictionary, nor by popular assumptions about the function of a *nābî'* derived from elsewhere. As Amos 1.1 makes clear, he 'saw' things; he was a visionary who spoke out about matters, and the editor clearly has refused to name him a *nābî'* throughout. His words were mostly threats as to what might, could or should happen to those he warned; they were not 'prophetic' predictions (see my commentary on Amos).

Many commentators, perhaps following the example in Amos 7.15, assume that when the verb *nāṭap* is used in Mic. 2.6 it means 'preach', inviting readers from an English-speaking background to conclude that (a) it is a presentation or address within a religious context, or (b) was being used derogatively, implying hypocritical advice. Micah was in fact simply ordering certain individuals to 'Shut up!', for they were telling people what they wanted to hear while looking to be paid for doing so (Mic. 2.10-11).

The definition of a 'prophet' as one who spoke only and whatever God commanded the person to speak, as in Deut. 18.15-22, represents a sectarian definition of the 'prophet' only within that Deuteronomic tradition. Unfortunately, it seems to have become the generalized understanding of such a person and mission. Evidence from other books in the scroll such as Micah, Amos, Habakkuk, Nahum and Isaiah, for example, indicates that they were spokespersons reporting from their own reflection and conclusions regarding the state of society. They were *hôzeh,* visionaries, individuals who thought long and hard about matters, and took critical aim at those who held power and misused it, whether king, priest, *nābî'*, business person, lawyer or government official. Reports relating to what these visionaries said cannot and should not be simply lumped together as 'prophetic' based on a broad application of the Deuteronomic definition of a *nābî'*. To do so is demeaning of the genuine concerned observer who must speak about and warn the community as to what he sees (*hazâ*) to be negative or dangerous.

On Translating the Phrase *dᵉbār-yhwh hāyâ 'el PN*

The verb phrase that editors of biblical books have introduced to give gravitas to the collected sayings of those in the 'prophetic' collection is *dᵉbār-yhwh hāyâ 'el PN*. It has become standard practice in most languages to render it as 'the word of the Lord came to PN', though the verb *hāyâ* simply is the existential verb 'be'. The traditional rendering is influenced by the Deuteronomic definition of a prophet in Deuteronomy 18 and is assumed to be idiomatic. The source of the *'word of the Lord'* is, in this definition, external to the individual, hence the word 'coming to' a person seems a correct understanding; it implies that the person receiving the word is simply the channel by which YHWH communicates that word to the community, and that the speaker, a prophet, is the divinely chosen mouthpiece. It is a view, however, that does not fit with the ethos of this book.

Other assumptions about the 'word' may follow from the Deuteronomic definition, but the point to be made here is that we are dealing with a stock linguistic phrase applied by editors to several books in the Hebrew Bible that are listed within the later $n^eb\hat{\imath}$'$\hat{\imath}m$ category. As a broad category it does not determine how the individual texts themselves are to be read, as is demonstrated by important exceptions to this DH definition in the collection—Amos, Isaiah, Obadiah, Nahum and Habakkuk, none of which is identified as relating to a divine source in their superscriptions. These exceptions, each carrying its unique personalized superscript, demand a complete revision of the *hāyâ 'el* phrase found in most standard Bible translations.

From the point of view of Hebrew syntax, the *hāyâ 'el* phrase speaks of a state not an action. Which element in the phrase has priority—the verb or the preposition? Notoriously flexible Hebrew prepositions such as *'el*, when appended to a verb, force the reader to consider what its contextual function might be. In this case, is the *'el* preposition suggestive of movement to/toward, or of location, 'along with/by/with', or some other such as 'for/concerning', 'against', 'relating to ...', all of which are possible? Given the locative sense of the verb *hāyâ*, it would be more correct surely to think of the preposition in this phrase to mean that the 'word of the Lord' *was present with* the person named, or similar. This nuance moves the emphasis away from a 'word' extraneous to the person and affirms the authenticity and authority of the word or vision present with the person named, without defining how that came about; that process is contained within the verb 'saw' that is frequently attached. The 'word of the Lord' phrase itself then is an objective genitive, a word spoken with reference to or about YHWH, not a word provided by or sourced from YHWH. It is how Micah perceived Yahweh to be.

Furthermore, the *pro forma* phrases *'Thus says the Lord'* and *'says the Lord'*, which editors have provided in their reports for emphasis and gravitas, are literary complements. They are to be understood within that literary context, not read literally. Since the phrase appears in so many introductory statements to books in the Scroll of the Twelve, it is clearly a formal editorial phrase. One question that has to be asked is, From where did the phrase and its implications arise? How could one be sure, beyond a simple belief, that the words put together by the editor(s) did have that claimed divine authority? The Deuteronomic tradition in Deut. 18.21-22 offers its response, but as such it is problematic since, if 'fulfilment' was the only condition guaranteeing the 'word', it was one that was often, perhaps mostly, never realized.

As for the word coming from God, one only has to read Habakkuk to see that that point of origin is misleading. An individual like Habakkuk, for example, though identified by his editor as a *nābî'*, addressed a bitter complaint to God about God's failure to answer his most basic questions surrounding the violence and injustice he saw in his Israelite community. Habakkuk simply poured out his frustrations to a God who had nothing to say to him; God was his problem, never his source of enlightenment! Despite this reality, most readers disregard it and persist in applying to him the Deuteronomic definition of a prophet!

Prophets there were, obviously, but they were not the only spokespersons contributing to the social and religious life of ancient Israel, nor were they themselves exempt from some of the human failings they sought to uncover. Visionaries also had much to say to those who would listen, and even a book like Jonah, a parable created by a highly imaginative writer, could and did convey a message of the later Assyrian period addressing a profound theological issue of God's overwhelming grace and mercy beyond Israel (see the concluding rhetorical question in Jon. 4.11). A range of spokespersons and writers throughout the biblical period provided the community with warnings, threats, challenges reflecting their daily experience. Assuming and calling them all 'prophets' as per the Deuteronomic definition of *nābî'*, and confusing the *nābî'* and *ḥoseh*, fail to do justice to those who really were prophetic as well as to those who, for good reason, refused to be so identified.

'Bread' as a Codeword

Amos's words regarding his identity are set in the context of Amaziah's contemptuous challenge to him to 'go back to Judah and earn your bread (*leḥem*) there' (Amos 7.12). The 'bread' phrase may well be idiomatic for earning a living, but the critique of *nᵉbî'îm* launched by Micah in 3.5 also indirectly mentions food as the incentive for them issuing a comforting message for their audiences. Similarly, in a scenario in 1 Sam. 9.7 there is a report of Saul searching for his father's donkeys that had wandered off and become lost. Saul was about to abandon the search when his young companion suggested that they find the local 'man of God' and seek his help in locating the donkeys. Saul responded that they had no 'bread' remaining to give such a person, hinting that this was the local custom. In other words, 'bread', whether actual or metaphorical, was the way of referring to the payment required by the *man of God* for advice given. 'Bread' became the codeword for the corrupt payment system that had debased the so-called prophetic movement of the time.

Coincidentally, in 1 Sam. 9.7 there appears another written form *nābî'*, a rare example of a hiphil imperfect first-person plural of the root *bw'*, 'come', meaning 'we should bring ...'. While there is no linguistic connection between these two *nābî'* forms—they are merely homographs—it is intriguing that the *mah-nābî'* form relates to paying a man of God for advice.

Selected Bibliography

Andersen, F.I., and D.N. Freedman, *Amos: A New Translation with Introduction and Commentary* (AYB, 24A; New York: Doubleday, 1989). Beware of information overload!

Finkelstein, I., and N.A. Silberman, *The Bible Unearthed: Archaeology's New Vision of Ancient Israel and the Origin of its Sacred Texts* (New York: Simon & Schuster, 2001).

Fretheim, T.E., *Reading Hosea–Micah: A Literary and Theological Commentary* (Macon, GA: Smyth & Helwys, 2013).

Mason, R., *Micah, Nahum, Obadiah* (T. & T. Clark Study Guides; Sheffield: Sheffield Academic Press, 1991).

Smith, R.L., *Micah–Malachi* (WBC, 32; Dallas, TX: Word Books, 1984).

Stuart, D.K., *Hosea–Jonah* (WBC, 31; Waco, TX: Word Books, 1987).

Waltke, B.K., *A Commentary on Micah* (Grand Rapids, MI: Eerdmans, 2007).

—, and M. O'Connor, *An Introduction to Biblical Hebrew Syntax* (Winona Lake, IN: Eisenbrauns, 1990).

Wessels, W.J., 'Reflections on Micah, the Prophet of the Book Micah', *Pharos Journal of Theology* 100 (2019), online publication.

www.ingramcontent.com/pod-product-compliance
Lightning Source LLC
Chambersburg PA
CBHW051057230426
43667CB00013B/2339